Aligning for Learning

Aligning for Learning

Strategies for Teaching Effectiveness

Donald H. Wulff
University of Washington

EDITOR

Wayne H. Jacobson
Karen Freisem
Deborah H. Hatch
Margaret Lawrence
Lana Rae Lenz
University of Washington

ASSOCIATE EDITORS

ANKER PUBLISHING COMPANY, INC.
Bolton, Massachusetts

Aligning for Learning
Strategies for Teaching Effectiveness

ISBN 1-882982-82-7

Composition by Lyn Rodger, Deerfoot Studios
Cover design by Dutton and Sherman Design

Anker Publishing Company, Inc.
563 Main Street
P.O. Box 249
Bolton, MA 01740-0249 USA

www.ankerpub.com

Library of Congress Cataloging-in-Publication Data

Aligning for learning : strategies for teaching effectiveness / Donald H. Wulff, editor ; Wayne H. Jacobson ... [et al.], associate editors.
    p. cm.
Includes bibliographical references and index.
  ISBN 1-882982-82-7 (hard)
  1. Effective teaching. 2. Communication in education.
  I. Wulff, Donald H. II. Jacobson, Wayne H.

  LB1775.A419 2005
  371.102—dc22

                                                    2004031033

About the Authors

The Editors

The editor and five associate editors bring to this volume nearly 175 years of combined professional experience as teachers, administrators, and instructional consultants, with 94 of those years spent working directly with faculty and campus leaders to address issues in teaching and learning. The editors represent a range of disciplines and varied experiences in publishing and presenting on their campus, at conferences, and at other institutions nationally and internationally.

Donald H. Wulff is director of the Center for Instructional Development and Research, associate dean in the Graduate School, and affiliate graduate faculty in the Department of Communication at the University of Washington. For more than 25 years, Don has taught, consulted, and published widely about issues of teaching and learning in higher education. His most recent publication is *Paths to the Professoriate: Strategies for Enriching the Preparation of Future Faculty* (Jossey-Bass, 2004), which he co-edited with Ann E. Austin of Michigan State University. He has served in national leadership positions for educational organizations and on various editorial review boards for higher education publications. Don received his undergraduate degree from Montana State University, his M.A. from the University of Montana, and a Ph.D. in instructional communication from the University of Washington.

Wayne H. Jacobson is associate director of the Center for Instructional Development and Research (CIDR) at the University of Washington. He provides leadership for CIDR's day-to-day operations, teaches graduate school courses on teaching and learning in higher education, and consults with departments and faculty in mathematics, science, and engineering. Wayne has more than 20 years of teaching and consulting experience in higher education in the U.S. and Asia. He received bachelor's and master's degrees from the University of Minnesota. He has also received a master's degree in counseling psychology and a Ph.D. in adult education from the University of Wisconsin–Madison.

Karen Freisem is a senior consultant at the Center for Instructional Development and Research (CIDR) at the University of Washington, where she works primarily with the mathematics, science, and engineering departments. She consults with faculty and graduate teaching assistants, designs and facilitates workshops, and assists departments in planning and implementing curriculum and program assessment. For 10 years before joining CIDR in 1986, Karen developed curriculum and taught in a variety of settings. Her current research interests focus on student perceptions of effective instruction in large classes. She has served as chair of the International Teaching Assistants Interest Section of TESOL (Teachers of English to Speakers of Other Languages). Karen received her M.A. in Slavic linguistics and her M.A.T. in English from the University of Washington.

Deborah H. Hatch is a senior consultant at the Center for Instructional Development and Research (CIDR) at the University of Washington, where she has worked with faculty and graduate students on teaching and learning issues since 1987. In addition to her work at CIDR, she taught for 15 years in the University of Washington's Interdisciplinary Writing Program, an experience that made her particularly aware of the role of disciplinary contexts in student writing. Her publications and presentations are in the areas of student writing, teaching portfolios, and the scholarship of teaching and learning. She teaches a graduate school course on teaching and learning in higher education and regularly contributes her expertise to university curriculum committees and task forces. Deborah received her B.A. from Swarthmore College and her Ph.D. in English from the University of Massachusetts.

Margaret Lawrence is a senior consultant at the Center for Instructional Development and Research (CIDR) at the University of Washington. She is also the designer of and instructor for training courses in China-America Personnel Service's Teaching English as a Foreign Language Program. She has been teaching for 20 years and has been a consultant at CIDR for the last 14 of those years. In her role at CIDR, she works with faculty, graduate teaching assistants, and departmental administrators in the foreign language, humanities, and social sciences departments. Her recent research has focused on student interpretations of student ratings form items and the implications of those interpretations for faculty practice. Margaret received her B.A. and her M.A. in English from the University of Oregon.

 *Lana Rae Lenz* is a senior consultant and coordinator for program development at the Center for Instructional Development and Research at the University of Washington. In her consulting, she assists administrators, faculty, and teaching assistants with the design, implementation, and assessment of courses and instructional programs, primarily in the arts, humanities, and social sciences. In her coordinator role, she assumes leadership for the development and implementation of special projects undertaken by CIDR as a part of its mission within the university. For 37 years she has been actively involved in teaching, training, and consulting for community professionals in all levels of education and in business, media, mental health, and public service. Lana Rae received her B.A. in English and education and her M.A. in speech communication.

About the Contributors

Alka Arora is a Ph.D. candidate in the Department of Women Studies and an instructional consultant at the Center for Instructional Development and Research at the University of Washington (UW). She has taught and developed curriculum in women studies and assisted faculty and graduate teaching assistants across campus at the UW with issues of teaching and learning. She is currently completing her dissertation on spiritual practice and social engagement in the lives of feminist women. Her other major areas of teaching and research focus on critical and feminist pedagogies. Alka holds a B.A. in mathematics from the University of Southern California.

Klaus Brandl is senior lecturer in applied linguistics and specialist in foreign language pedagogy in the Department of Scandinavian Studies at the University of Washington. In addition, he holds adjunct positions in the Language Learning Center, the Teacher Education Program, the Spanish Language Program, and the Department of Germanics. He has authored several multimedia programs and published on a wide variety of topics in areas such as language teaching methodology, teacher training, and technology and language learning. Klaus received his Ph.D. in applied linguistics/foreign language education from the University of Texas–Austin.

Lisa M. Coutu is senior lecturer in the Department of Communication at the University of Washington, having joined the faculty in 1997. Her research and teaching interests center primarily on the ethnography of communication and issues of language, culture, and communication. Each year, she also teaches a large introductory course of 450 students that surveys areas of human communication. In 2003 she was honored with the University of Washington's prestigious Distinguished Teaching Award. Lisa received her B.A. from the University of Massachusetts and her M.A. and Ph.D. in speech communication from the University of Washington.

Kimberly Emmons is director of composition and assistant professor of English and rhetoric at Case Western Reserve University. Her research focuses on composition and rhetoric, discourse analysis, and rhetorical approaches to health/healthcare. Her recent publications include a co-edited volume (with Anne Curzan) titled *Studies in the History of the English Language II: Unfolding Conversations* (Mouton de Gruyter, 2004) and an article on student reflective practices titled "Rethinking Genres of Reflection: Student Portfolio Cover Letters and the Narrative of Progress." She is currently working on a book-length project examining the circulation and manipulation of discourses surrounding women and depression in the United States. Kim received her undergraduate degree from Princeton and her M.A. and Ph.D. in English language and rhetoric from the University of Washington.

Carla W. Hess is Chester Fritz Distinguished Professor Emerita of Communication Sciences and Disorders at the University of North Dakota (UND), Grand Forks. For 33 years, she has taught, published, and researched in areas as varied as child language development and disorders, teaching and learning, assessment, and research methods. She also served as chair of communication disorders and as chair of the faculty senate at UND. She is currently CEO of HB Associates, a private firm that provides consultation and evaluation for state and federal health and education programs. Carla received her B.S. from Montana State University, her M.S. from the University of North Dakota, and her Ph.D. in speech and hearing sciences from Ohio University.

Sheila Edwards Lange has worked in higher education administration for many years, in both academic and student affairs. She is currently associate director for research in the Center for Workforce Development at the University of Washington. In that position, she manages the Faculty Graduate Mentoring Program for women in science and engineering. She earned a bachelor's degree in social ecology from the University of California–Irvine and a master's degree in public administration from the University of Washington.

She is currently a doctoral candidate in educational leadership and policy studies at the University of Washington. Her dissertation topic is the master's degree as a critical transition in science and engineering doctoral education.

Clarisse Messemer is visiting assistant professor in the Department of Economics at Lewis and Clark College. Areas of her teaching and research include macroeconomics, statistics, econometrics, and the relationship of income inequality—across race and gender—to economic growth. Prior to teaching at Lewis and Clark College, she was an instructional consultant at the Center for Instructional Development and Research and taught courses in the Department of Economics at the University of Washington. She also worked previously as a researcher for Exxon International Company. Clarisse has a B.S. from Drew University and a Ph.D. in economics from the University of Washington.

Bonnie O'Dell was an instructional consultant at the Center for Instructional Development and Research at the University of Washington for four years, working primarily with international teaching assistants. She also collaborated extensively with Catalyst, a University of Washington unit that specializes in developing instructional technology, and co-wrote a teaching guide for the Catalyst online discussion board called EPost. She is currently contracted to Microsoft, where she conducts user query data analysis. Bonnie received her M.A. in language and literacy and her M.A. in library and information science from the University of Washington.

Lois A. Reddick is a doctoral candidate in the Department of Teaching and Learning at the Steinhardt School of Education and a visiting consultant at the Center for Teaching Excellence at New York University (NYU). In her consulting, she has worked primarily with instructors at the Courant Institute of Mathematical Sciences and the Stern School of Business. She is presently pursuing research interests related to issues of diversity and inclusiveness in science, technology, engineering, and math courses. Prior to moving to NYU, she was an instructional consultant at the Center for Instructional Development and Research and taught public speaking in the Department of Speech Communication at the University of Washington. Lois received her M.Ed. from the University of Washington.

Susan Rich is a faculty member at Highline Community College, where she teaches writing, literature, and global studies and serves as the chairperson of the Coordinated Studies Program. She is the author of *The Cartographer's Tongue: Poems of the World*, published by White Pine Press (New York) and

Snailpress (South Africa) and winner of the 2001 PEN West Poetry Award and the Peace Corps Readers and Writers Award. Her second collection of poems, *The Exile Reconsiders,* is forthcoming. Recipient of a Fulbright Fellowship to South Africa, she previously taught at the University of Cape Town and is currently also on the M.F.A. faculty of Antioch University. Susan received her B.A. from the University of Massachusetts–Amherst, her M.F.A from the University of Oregon, and her Ed.M. from Harvard University.

Debra-L. Sequeira is professor of communication and associate dean in the College of Arts and Sciences at Seattle Pacific University (SPU). During her 21 years at SPU, she has taught a variety of courses in communication, served as chair of the Department of Communication and Journalism, and published nationally and internationally in the areas of communication and language studies. In her role as associate dean, she works closely with faculty and administrators on issues related to assessment of learning and teaching effectiveness. Debra holds a B.A. and M.A. from San Francisco State University and a Ph.D. in communication from the University of Washington.

Laurie Stephan is curriculum specialist at the National Workforce Center for Emerging Technologies, a National Science Foundation funded center housed at Bellevue Community College (BCC) in Seattle. She supports faculty in instructional technology research and development of curriculum for online and classroom contexts. She also has served as a delegate in a partnership between the U.S. Department of Education and the Danish Ministry of Education exploring best practices in technology education. Prior to her work at BCC, she was an instructional consultant at the Center for Instructional Development and Research at the University of Washington. Laurie holds a Ph.D. in applied language studies from the University of Washington.

Contents

Foreword

This book rests on the assumptions that teaching and learning are complex, that the context of higher education changes continually, and that the enhancement of teaching and learning requires knowledgeable, sophisticated, reflective, purposeful approaches. It contributes both to our understanding of the teaching and learning process, and subsequently, to its enhancement.

The volume is distinctive in several important ways. First, the view of teaching and learning is grounded in a conceptual, research-based framework: the alignment model. Twenty years ago, Donald H. Wulff derived the model from case studies of highly acclaimed, award-winning university professors. The professors taught in different disciplines, had unique styles of teaching, taught classes of various sizes, levels, and formats, and structured their classes in disparate ways. Although one cannot generalize from case studies, the differences among the outstanding teachers examined were substantial enough to warrant the construction of a model that incorporated the consistent behaviors, categories, interrelationships, and patterns that emerged.

Second, just as the participants in the original research study were award-winning instructors, so too was the researcher. Dr. Wulff, author of *Case Studies of the Communication of Effective University Instructors,* had received accolades for his own effectiveness as an instructor. He was known then, as he is now, on the University of Washington campus as one of the finest scholars of teaching as well as an outstanding practitioner. This prominence and expertise gave him unique insights for conceptualizing and developing a model of teaching and learning.

Third, since its development, the alignment model has been utilized widely, tried, and tested across varying educational contexts, content, settings, styles, instructors, and students. From these 20 years of scrutiny—formal and informal—the model has emerged as reliable, valid, and valuable. The consultants and researchers at the University of Washington's Center for Instructional Development and Research, whose perspectives are represented in this volume, have drawn upon the alignment model in thousands of consultations, workshops, and training sessions with faculty, graduate teaching assistants, and students to improve the quality of teaching and learning on the campus. Graduate students and colleagues of Dr. Wulff have taken the model to their own campuses across the country and utilized it in their environments. Additionally, he and other professionals, including myself, have adapted this model successfully to training programs in business and industry.

Thus, the alignment model has a two-decade record of providing a conceptual basis for the improvement of teaching and learning, both in higher education and in business and industry. This book, the culmination of years of research and practice, provides readers with an array of applications and strategies for enhancing teaching and learning.

Finally, on a personal note, this book is distinctive in that it is a celebration not only of the contribution of the alignment model to the teaching and learning process, but also a celebration of the contributions of its creator, Donald H. Wulff, to the understanding and improvement of the process. Don Wulff was my first doctoral student at the University of Washington and has been my colleague, collaborator, co-researcher, and friend for 25 years. In these years, I have learned far more from him than I ever taught him. He and his alignment model have shaped my thinking, my perspectives, and my practice of teaching, consulting, and training—all for the better. I commend this volume to you. Your thinking, perspectives, and teaching practice will be enhanced by the expertise and experience of Dr. Wulff and his fine colleagues at the Center for Instructional Development and Research.

Ann Q. Staton
Dean of the College of Arts & Sciences
Texas Woman's University
(Professor of Communication, University of Washington, 1997–2002)

Preface

This volume is the culmination of 20 years of work in which we at the Center for Instructional Development and Research (CIDR) at the University of Washington have engaged in teaching and instructional development based on an alignment model of teaching and learning. The model is grounded in original research on teaching effectiveness that Donald Wulff conducted. Since the completion of that research, hundreds of colleagues and students at this campus and other institutions have contributed to our thinking within the alignment perspective.

Overview of Contents

As Wulff explains in the opening chapter of the volume, the alignment model is a framework that emerged from the need to capture more fully the complexity of teaching and learning. The model illustrates how the key components of context, content, instructor, and students all interact to shape learning. Wulff suggests that effective instructors constantly make adjustments at the interface of these various components and use communication strategies to assist in the process. In this volume, we have combined that perspective with our years of experience as instructors, instructional development specialists, and administrators to produce a practical volume on teaching and learning.

Our Purposes

In the past two decades, there has been increasing emphasis on the diverse needs of students, students' learning, faculty roles and rewards, and issues of accountability. We have based this book on the premise that, given this changing context in higher education, it is crucial that faculty, instructional developers, and administrators seek innovative ways of thinking about how to approach the complexity of teaching and learning. Thus, we have written the book to provide the following:

- A perspective that captures the complexity of the teaching/learning process by focusing on the interrelationships among contextual, student, instructor, content, and learning variables and the potential of those interrelationships for improving teaching effectiveness

- Practical applications using the perspective in a variety of instructional settings

- Recommended instructional strategies and approaches for enhancing teaching and learning on all types of campuses based on the perspective in the volume

Intended Audiences and Uses

Because the volume is about teaching and learning, we intend that it will have broad appeal for anyone interested in thinking about instruction in higher education. The ideas it contains can be applied in an array of instructional settings and in a range of institutions including research and master's comprehensive institutions, four-year baccalaureate colleges, two-year colleges, and various specialized institutions in medicine, law, art, etc.

Foremost, for *faculty and future faculty,* the volume provides a perspective that can help them think about how to approach teaching effectiveness systematically. After reading examples and applications in the volume, faculty members will have a more comprehensive view of the teaching/learning process and of specific strategies that can help them enhance teaching and learning in their work.

Second, for *administrators,* the book provides opportunities for reflection about the processes they engage in to support and evaluate teaching effectiveness. It can be particularly useful in helping them think about the range of instructional issues that instructors must confront.

Third, the book demonstrates for *instructional and faculty developers* additional ways to think about their own work with faculty and administrators on campuses. Specifically, it provides some basic tenets about teaching effectiveness that they can apply in working with individual instructors, departments, schools or colleges, and institutions on issues of teaching and learning.

Finally, the book provides fertile ground for *researchers* interested in theoretical perspectives on teaching/learning, the communication involved in the teaching and learning process, and the various ways of implementing the model or applications of the model in the current scholarship of teaching and learning movement.

Organization for the Book

We have organized the book into five parts. We begin with an introductory chapter and conclude with a chapter that provides synthesis and conclusions. In between are three sections that illustrate various applications of the alignment model.

Part I: The Alignment Model serves as the guiding framework for the rest of the volume. In the only chapter in this section, Donald Wulff draws upon his longstanding interest and experience to explain the alignment model of teaching effectiveness that emerged from some of his original research and its major underlying tenets.

In **Part II: Alignment in Design, Assessment, and Evaluation,** Wayne Jacobson and Lois Reddick address the importance of inclusive teaching and learning in Chapter 2. In Chapter 3, Wayne Jacobson and Donald Wulff discuss the use of the alignment model in designing courses. Wayne Jacobson and Karen Freisem focus on using assessment in support of alignment in Chapter 4, and in Chapter 5, Wayne Jacobson and Margaret Lawrence address alignment issues in evaluation.

In **Part III: Alignment in Specific Contexts,** authors from a variety of institutions use their institutional knowledge and experience to illustrate the application of alignment in various instructional contexts: large classes (Chapter 6, by Karen Freisem and Lisa Coutu); team teaching (Chapter 7, by Deborah Hatch and Susan Rich); mentoring (Chapter 8, by Lana Rae Lenz and Sheila Edwards Lange); courses in math, science, and engineering (Chapter 9, Karen Freisem, Clarisse Messemer, and Wayne Jacobson); foreign language courses (Chapter 10, Margaret Lawrence and Klaus Brandl); socially transformative courses (Chapter 11, Alka Arora); courses that incorporate writing (Chapter 12, Deborah Hatch and Kimberly Emmons); and courses online (Chapter 13, Margaret Lawrence, Bonnie O'Dell, and Laurie Stephan).

Part IV: Alignment in Teaching as Scholarship illustrates how the alignment perspective can be useful in thinking about alignment and scholarly approaches to teaching and learning. In Chapter 14, Wayne Jacobson and Deborah Hatch discuss using alignment to advance the scholarship of teaching and learning. In Chapter 15, Donald Wulff, Carla Hess, and Debra Sequeira draw on their expertise as instructors and administrators to discuss the role of alignment in faculty reward systems.

Part V: Alignment: Synthesis and Conclusions consists of a final chapter that provides synthesis and key considerations in the application of alignment and some final thoughts on the future use of the alignment perspective.

Acknowledgements

We are indebted to a number of individuals who have supported our efforts in preparing for this volume.

First, we would like to acknowledge James Anker, for recognizing the importance of addressing the complexity of the teaching and learning process and for supporting our efforts in this volume. We also appreciate the work of the Anker Publishing staff, particularly Carolyn Dumore, in providing editorial assistance and ongoing guidance for getting our ideas published.

We also wish to thank two special individuals who have contributed in significant ways during the last 20 years to our work with the alignment model. We thank Ann Q. Staton for her insights and guidance during the original research, her commitment through the years to the alignment perspective as a conceptualization of teaching effectiveness, and her willingness to write the foreword for this volume. We also thank Jody D. Nyquist, the original director for instructional development at CIDR, who provided leadership, guidance, and support that enabled us to apply the model on a daily basis in our work.

We express special appreciation to our colleagues at CIDR who have supported us throughout our work on this project. Brenda Kelly, Randy Siler, Paul Bronson, Patricia Hadfield, and Sarah Espe have helped us in various ways from providing office support to proofreading and preparing materials for the final manuscript.

We also are indebted to the contributing authors. They spent much time helping us to conceptualize and write the chapters for the volume. They have all contributed to our thinking about alignment, either through their collaboration as former employees at CIDR or as faculty colleagues whose mutual interest in issues of effective teaching and learning brought us together.

Finally, we want to acknowledge each other as colleagues. We have spent many hours in preparation for this volume, through both the years of application of alignment in our work and the months of planning and discussion that were part of the writing process. We are grateful for the collaborative spirit that helped us to bring the final product to fruition. We are indeed fortunate to have the long-standing relationships with each other that have made such a project a reality.

Donald H. Wulff
Wayne H. Jacobson
Karen Freisem
Deborah H. Hatch
Margaret Lawrence
Lana Rae Lenz
University of Washington
July 2004

Part I

THE ALIGNMENT MODEL

1

Using the Alignment Model of Teaching Effectiveness

Donald H. Wulff

When I first became interested in issues of teaching effectiveness, much of the research still focused on the teacher characteristics and/or behaviors that contributed to successful instruction. From my own experience as a teacher and a scholar, I knew teacher characteristics and behaviors played a role in the teaching and learning process. At the same time, my ongoing interactions with faculty suggested that there had to be more to it.

Through the years, I became increasingly intrigued by questions about teaching effectiveness: What is it that contributes to success in teaching and learning? What can we learn about the teaching process by studying it more fully? The research and factor analytic studies had identified some of the categories of teacher behaviors associated with teaching effectiveness, but previous models seemed inadequate. This lack of sufficiently complex models presented challenges as I helped others with their teaching and as I worked to improve my own teaching. As a communication scholar, I also became particularly interested in exploring the role of communication in the questions about teaching effectiveness. To begin to address those questions, I conducted the research that helped me further understand teaching effectiveness and ultimately led to the development of the alignment model.

This chapter explains what I learned from my original research and how the ideas have evolved since then. It highlights the alignment model that emerged and explains the related underlying tenets for this volume.

What Is the Alignment Model of Teaching Effectiveness?

The alignment model from my original research is a framework that incorporates instructional components and general communication strategies into a representation of teaching effectiveness. It suggests that for teachers to be

3

effective in achieving learning goals, they must engage in an ongoing process of aligning the content, themselves, and students in a specific context. In working toward alignment, effective instructors engage in communication strategies in the broad categories related to rapport, structure, engagement, and interaction (see Figure 1.1).

Figure 1.1
An Alignment Model of Teaching Effectiveness

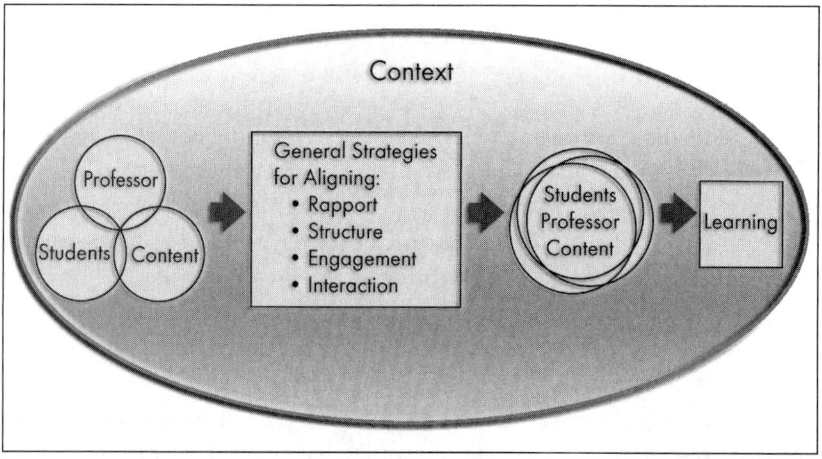

An essential point of the model is that the components and their interrelationships are dynamic and ever changing as opposed to fixed or static. For example, the amount of overlap that may exist at the beginning of a course among the content, the instructor, and the students is dependent on previous exposure. The professor is the expert in the field, so the degree of overlap between the professor and the content will reflect the professor's specific level of expertise and experience with the content. To the extent that students have had previous engagement with the content of the course through related courses or their own reading, there may be some initial overlap between the content and the students. Regardless of the degree of overlap at the beginning of a course, however, the degree of commonality at the intersections of the key components will be constantly changing throughout the academic term. As the model suggests, a course with effective alignment reflects significant overlap of the main areas as the instructor and students get closer to achieving course goals for student learning.

What Is the Research From Which the Alignment Model Emerged?

The model for this volume is grounded in case study research that I conducted in the 1980s to examine the communication of effective university instructors.[1] To complete the study, I enlisted the participation of four faculty members at a major research university. Those faculty members had consistently
high student ratings, had each won the university's distinguished teaching
award, and had been identified by their department chairs as the best, or one
of the two best, instructors in their departments. I observed in the instructors'
classes, interviewed them each several times throughout the academic term,
reviewed their instructional materials, and interviewed their students. The
results of that research changed my view of the teaching/learning process and
led to the alignment model that gave me new insights into what effective
teachers do.

How Has the Model Been Extended?

Since that research, my colleagues and I have substantiated and applied the
alignment model in individual consultations with faculty and graduate teaching assistants, feedback sessions with students, and ongoing discussions with
each other. During hundreds of individual consultations with instructors and
literally thousands of midterm interviews with classes of students, we have
used a research perspective to collect, analyze, interpret, and translate data
from student interviews in ways that have added to our understanding of the
original research (Nyquist & Wulff, 2001). Through the interactions with
faculty and students, we have gained not only new understandings and applications for the original research but also a broad repertoire of strategies that
effective teachers use to promote learning. Based on the original research and
our experiences, we now have a much more comprehensive understanding of
what it is that effective teachers do and how we can use those insights to
improve teaching and learning.

What Does the Model Tell Us About What Effective Instructors Do?

Among the important insights about effective teaching that we have substantiated as a result of the original research and our ongoing work are that effective instructors:

- Focus on key components in the instructional process

- Strive to align those key components in the teaching/learning process

- Use four main categories of communication strategies to assist them in developing appropriate interrelationships among the key components

The next section of this chapter briefly explains the basis for these three contentions.

Effective Instructors Focus on Key Components in the Instructional Process

A more complete understanding of teaching effectiveness begins with what the original instructors viewed as the important components of the instructional process.

Analysis of the professors' comments initially revealed four key areas that were particularly important in thinking about teaching effectiveness. The first was *student learning.* When asked to discuss elements of their teaching that made them successful, all four professors in the original study focused on their students' learning—what their students were going to know or be able to do by the end of the course. A second key component of the teaching and learning process was *content* around which the learning in the professors' courses revolved. For these instructors, content was a key variable affecting teaching and learning in their courses. A third dimension of the instructional process was the *students.* All of the professors talked about the importance of considering who their students were. Fourth, the dimension of the *professors* themselves emerged as an important component. As one professor put it, "(for students) it's just information, often in a book, without someone there to interpret it for them."

A fifth significant component in the framework is the *context.* Although I approached the original research with the assumption that the context is important, contextual issues have emerged even more fully as we have worked with issues of teaching effectiveness since the original study. In a variety of ways, our ongoing work has underscored the interrelationships between specific courses and the broader contexts of physical, social, instructional, and societal factors in which the courses exist. Through the years, the contextual component has emerged as so significant that I placed the entire framework in one large oval to represent the potential influences related to contextual factors in a specific course. For example, the availability of technological tools or the use of technology in online courses affects the choices an instructor makes for methods in a course. Similarly, standardized board examinations requiring that students have certain knowledge or skills can determine the content choices an instructor makes, even the way a course is structured. The place of the course in the overall curriculum also influences the content and the way the instructor and students strive to make links between previous courses or courses that follow.

On the surface, each of these components—context, instructors, students, content, and learning—is important in its own right. That they would emerge in research about teaching and learning is logical to anyone who studies issues in instruction. What has been significant, though, first in the original research and now in our ongoing work, is not that the separate components have emerged but rather that the components are *interrelated* in ways that demonstrate what effective instructors do in their teaching.

Effective Instructors Strive to Align the Key Components in the Instructional Process

Understanding the interrelationships among the key components of the alignment model begins with acknowledgment of natural tensions in teaching and learning. Instructors encounter a number of natural tensions in any instructional context. Those tensions arise from the interactions among the components—the particular content the instructors teach, their own needs and expectations as experts and professionals in their fields, and the needs, preferences, and expectations of the specific students. When all of these factors converge within a specific instructional setting or context, questions arise. For example, how do instructors find a reasonable balance between making a course challenging and making it accessible? How do instructors provide the level of informality some students prefer while maintaining appropriate authority and structure in the course? What does it mean for teaching the course when some students say they enjoy small group instruction while others say they do not? In any instructional situation, such questions create tensions that pull the instructor in seemingly competing directions that require examining the factors involved and making decisions—sometimes on the spot—about how to proceed. Such a process requires a focus on important learning goals and a strong belief that effective teaching is primarily a matter of responsive decision-making and effective balance.

In the original study, instructors responded to such tensions by continually adjusting the content, themselves, and students in an effort to achieve the overall goal of learning. I explained the process of adjustment in terms of what I called "alignment." Since that research, other scholars have used the term *alignment* in a variety of ways, especially to emphasize the importance of aligning course goals, methods, and evaluation or faculty rewards with departmental guidelines and institutional missions (e.g., see Diamond, 1999). Bastick (2002) developed an "alignment model" as a diagnostic approach to align instructor and student expectations more fully in a course. I originally used *alignment,* though, to describe a comprehensive approach grounded in the questions about what teachers do that makes them effective. As I characterized alignment, the instructors worked in ongoing ways to align themselves, the content, and the students in their specific courses, so all moved along the same path toward learning.

Effective Instructors Use Rapport, Structure, Engagement, and Interaction to Assist Them in Developing Appropriate Interrelationships Among the Key Components

If effective instructors strive for alignment, how do they go about that process? Based on the original research, I categorized the communication strategies of effective professors into four broad categories: rapport, structure, engagement, and interaction. While working within the model, my colleagues and I have noted an increasing variety of strategies that instructors use to meet the demands of education in the 21st century. With the advent of technology, increasing active engagement of students in experiential learning formats, and demands for greater accountability in teaching and learning, instructors are broadening the numbers and kinds of strategies they use. Even with the burgeoning numbers of approaches, however, the specific strategies still fall within the four broad categories originally identified. The following section is designed to explain those categories briefly as part of the alignment model in the original research and in our ongoing work in improving teaching and learning.

Rapport. Rapport is established through interpersonal communication that creates the working relationships between instructor and students. At the heart of rapport is respect between the instructor and students and among students. For effective instructors, rapport requires acknowledging individual students as persons and being aware of their varied needs, expectations, and perceptions. It means that instructors engage in strategies and activities that allow them to honor and celebrate their own needs, expectations, and beliefs while simultaneously respecting those of their students.

A first step in establishing rapport is creating a respectful context by helping students feel comfortable interacting with the instructor and each other. Instructors accept students as potentially knowledgeable sources, and they act immediately to address feedback provided about course content and procedures. They also establish rapport by sharing their own humanness and providing ways for students to see human elements in each other. Such revelations allow students to perceive their instructors and each other as "friendly" and "real."

As the alignment model suggests, though, building rapport between students and instructors is much more than "just being nice." It requires ongoing thinking and adjustment to determine what kinds of relationships are most appropriate to achieve learning and how instructors can best establish those relationships. Issues related to discussion lists and email in online learning (Chapter 13) or to mentoring partnerships (Chapter 8) provide two examples of contexts in which effective instructors increasingly strive to implement strategies for establishing rapport. As Chapter 2 illustrates, ongoing rapport-building strategies are especially important for instructors to determine how best to teach inclusively with particular content and specific groups of students. The rapport-building strategies function, then, primarily to align students and the professors.

Structure. Behaviors within the category of structure are directly related to efforts of instructors to organize themselves, the content, and the students in relation to each other in their specific contexts. Structure involves ongoing efforts to cluster, clarify, and synthesize ideas and monitor the effects of those efforts in a particular course with a particular group of students. In the original research, instructors provided structure, in part, by clarifying what would be accomplished in each class and by linking the content of one class to material that had been previously discussed and to information that was to follow.

Over the years, we have observed many additional strategies to provide structure while a course is in progress. Some professors use notes or other signposts as reminders to themselves or as signals to the students about how a class is structured. In some cases, instructors establish a guide for the day by providing a precise outline that highlights the agenda for a particular class period. In other instances, instructors use structuring comments, including statements of daily goals, transitions, summaries, and statements that provide a sense of direction to help the students follow the trend of thought, for example, "Let's turn back to . . ." or "Let's just consider what would happen if . . ." Sometimes emphasis is achieved by pointing to or highlighting ideas on the chalkboard, overhead, or PowerPoint or by verbalizing with such comments as "Now, this is important . . ." or "Focus on this for a minute . . ." More and more, instructors are aware of the importance of providing the structure that helps students make the links among course goals, methods used, and assessment.

Using structure as a strategy in alignment is much more than careful planning in a course. Although structure in course or lesson planning is certainly important, the alignment on paper does not translate readily into alignment in instructional practice. When we add the human dimensions of instructor and student and consider the interactions among the actual students, the content, and the instructor in a course, adjustments to the planning may well be necessary. The idea of alignment allows simultaneously for careful planning but also for making adjustments in structure during the dynamics of teaching and learning in the specific instructional setting.

Engagement. Engagement includes strategies designed to stimulate student thinking, motivate students, and involve them in the instructional process. In the original research, for example, all four of the professors recognized the importance of appealing to student interest. As a result, they sometimes used engaging examples, particularly examples that held strong human-interest appeal. In addition, all the professors presented examples in the form of stories with the potential for engaging students through the plot line. Probably the most universally helpful strategies we have noted, both in the original research and in our ongoing work with faculty, is use of what the students call real-life examples. Such examples bring the content alive by helping the particular students apply it to the kinds of issues, questions, and situations that are of interest to them.

Effective instructors also can use course materials and evaluation procedures to engage students in the content of a course. For instance, one of the professors in the original study successfully engaged students with primary sources for outside reading, providing a way, as he said, for students to "do" the subject and "serving to get them involved." Because of the content of his course, there were many primary sources from which he could select appealing information that engaged students.

Taking a different approach, two of the original professors involved students through the testing procedures. Within one professor's system, students could retake each test until they passed it. This evaluation procedure relieved much of the student anxiety that he perceived as a roadblock to his students' involvement in the content of his course. Testing weekly provided a way for another professor to keep students actively engaged in the material. The approach worked well because the weekly topics for the content of the course were discrete and required little carry-over from one week to another.

Having a range of possible strategies is essential for successful engagement in the alignment process. And, over time, we have observed the use of a broader range of strategies in instruction. For example, as experiential approaches such as service learning and problem-based learning have gained prominence, we see instructors and students involved more fully in engaging students through the application and synthesis of information in settings beyond the classrooms. All such strategies send messages to students about the importance of their involvement in their courses and ultimately serve to align the students more fully with course content and the instructors' preferences, needs, and expectations.

Interaction. A fourth category of effective instructor behaviors is related to communication that is interactional or multidirectional rather than linear and one-way. Given the potential for formality in courses where the instructor is the major source of information, it is essential that students realize there are options for communication not only from the instructor, but also from the student to the instructor and from student to student. In some cases, this openness to communication might be expressed in the instructors' willingness to talk to students after class or during office hours and in the way the instructors respond during such interactions. In other instances, it can be the way the instructors listen and respond to questions or discussion during class. In the original research, all of the instructors encouraged student questions in a series of behaviors that included asking for questions, listening carefully, and responding with sincerity.

An interactive approach is particularly important in the alignment model for providing the kinds of feedback that can allow for making adjustments. For this reason, one of the professors in the original study pointed out that although he had a graduate teaching assistant to help with correcting and grading, he always corrected some of the tests himself to obtain feedback about student progress. Such feedback allowed him to adjust himself and the content to student needs. In the same way, feedback to students on assignments and tests can help to align them with the instructor's expectations as well as with the content. Increasingly, we have observed instructors listening to student comments during questions and discussion as another form of informal assessment of students' understanding and as an indicator of the need for further explanation or clarification. Thus, instructors can use interaction to determine not only when they should make adjustments but also whether they should make those adjustments to align themselves and students, content and students, or themselves and the content.

What Are Some of the Basic Tenets of The Alignment Model?

Using alignment as an explanation of effective teaching has provided a more adequate model for understanding the complexity of what it is that effective instructors do. The alignment model captures the dynamics involved when instructors are balancing a number of components simultaneously and when a slight change in one component can affect all other dimensions. Now that we know what the alignment model is, we can focus more fully on what it means to use alignment in teaching and learning. The final section of this chapter summarizes some of the basic tenets of this alignment model.

Alignment Means that No One Component by Itself Determines Teaching and Learning Decisions

The alignment model reminds us that context, content, students, and instructor are all key components in promoting student learning. At the same time, it does not allow for undue emphasis on any of these key components in the instructional process. For example, an undue emphasis on content coverage might make a course inaccessible to some learners; and undue emphasis on meeting student needs might lead to unrealistic demands on the instructor. Thus, instructors must consider each dimension in light of its implications for all others.

Alignment Means Focusing on the Interrelationships Among Key Instructional Components

It is certainly important to focus independently on the context, students, content, instructor, and learning, but it is equally important to consider the interactions among these various components. What happens when the specific instructor meets a specific group of students? What does it mean for a particular group of students when they encounter a certain body of content? How does the context influence what does and can happen between students and instructors? Such questions focus us on the tensions among the various components and on the important questions about the very essence of teaching and learning.

Alignment Means There Is No Single "Right" Way

The alignment framework suggests that effective teaching is a complex process for which there can be few universal guidelines about how to proceed. We can no longer think of teaching as a process made up of a series of separate behaviors that need to be either present or absent in order for the instructor to be effective. Rather, we must focus on generating methods that provide the most effective balance among the specific content, instructor, and students to achieve learning goals in the particular context. The question is not whether a course has multiple strategies that promote rapport, structure, engaging activities, or communication but whether those strategies provide the best alignment of the key components in the instructional process.

Alignment Means Having a Range of Strategies for Achieving Balance

Given that there is no single "right" way and that strategies vary depending on context, content and goals for learning, professors, and students, the alignment model suggests that instructors need to develop a broad repertoire of strategies. Once they have developed that broad repertoire, they need to be able to determine when some strategies will work more successfully than others for achieving balance, to implement strategies that are selected, and to assess why and how some strategies work better than others.

Alignment Means Staying Focused on Student Learning

A major strength of the alignment framework is that it captures the complexity of the teaching and learning process while simultaneously reinforcing the importance of student learning. As my colleagues and I have been reminded again and again through our ongoing work, the goal of any effort to align students, content, and/or instructors in a particular situation is ultimately to have an imact on student learning. Regardless of what the instructor or students do or what the content is, it is essential that the entire alignment process move successfully toward achievement of course goals.

Alignment Means Engaging in Ongoing Reflective Practice

Ultimately, alignment is a matter of continuous assessment and ongoing reflection about what works and what does not work, about what one is willing to change, and what one needs to do next to enhance teaching and learning. Teaching effectiveness, then, is not defined simply in terms of knowing the right techniques but in terms of making informed decisions about appropriate strategies and their impact on student learning.

Alignment Means Communicating Effectively

Instructors who strive for alignment realize quickly that effective communication lies at the center of their success. It is not just that instructors need to create interaction and use communication strategies within the broad categories of rapport, structure, engagement, and interaction. It is also that they must engage in the process of determining how best to communicate with students to obtain important feedback about learning. A key is that instructors develop the language to explain what they are doing, what they need students to do, and why. Such efforts reflect a continuous process of thinking about what language will communicate precisely and directly and how students might interpret each message.

Alignment Means That Efforts to Improve Teaching and Learning Are Always in Flux

The dynamic nature of the teaching and learning process means that it is ever changing and constantly in need of adjustment. Thus, alignment is a lofty goal in teaching, one to which even effective instructors are always aspiring. The reality is that we never reach a point in which we are able to establish alignment completely and sustain it. Even though alignment is an admirable goal, then, much of the value lies in the process of working to achieve it.

Conclusion

In the years since I first developed the alignment model, changes within higher education have made teaching and learning even more complex. The information explosion and revolutionary new technologies, greater diversity among students and faculty, changes in faculty roles and reward systems, and greater emphasis on student learning and institutional accountability are a few of the many changes that have occurred. Those of us involved in this volume have found the alignment model to be a powerful framework for capturing the increasing complexity that these changes have contributed to the teaching and learning process. The following chapters illustrate the power of the model for conceptualizing, analyzing, and addressing such issues in instruction, with implications for all of us who aspire to improve teaching effectiveness on our campuses.

Endnote

1) The alignment model emerged from case study research titled *Case Studies of the Communication of Effective University Instructors,* by Donald H. Wulff, University of Washington, Seattle, WA, 1985.

References

Bastick, T. (2002, February). *In-course optimization of teaching quality.* Paper presented at the annual meeting of the Southwest Educational Research Association, Austin, TX.

Diamond, R. (1999). *Aligning faculty rewards with institutional mission: Statements, policies, and guidelines.* Bolton, MA: Anker.

Nyquist, J. D., & Wulff, D. H. (2001). Consultation using a research perspective. In K. G. Lewis & J. T. Povlacs Lunde (Eds.), *Face to face: A sourcebook of individual consultation techniques for faculty/instructional developers* (pp. 45–62). Stillwater, OK: New Forums Press.

Part II

ALIGNMENT IN DESIGN, ASSESSMENT, AND EVALUATION

2

Using Alignment in Inclusive Teaching and Learning[1]

Wayne H. Jacobson & Lois A. Reddick

Diversity often has been examined in terms of student backgrounds, identities, and expectations in a course; at other times it has been framed as a matter of the instructor's expertise or experience pertaining to diversity (for example, ethnic identity, disciplinary training, or participation in diversity workshops). Another approach has been to focus on the content of the course, its place in the curriculum, or the institutional value assigned to it (for example, which courses are required or which books students read). The alignment perspective requires accounting for all these factors and for the ways they interact with and affect one another to shape learning throughout a course.

The Instructor's Role in Alignment

Though many factors play a role in alignment, it is the instructor who must make decisions about course content, align the course with larger departmental or disciplinary contexts, and address student perceptions that help shape student learning. And it is the instructor who has the greatest control over challenging the assumptions on which his or her decisions about teaching are based. Of all the factors that influence learning in a course, it is the instructor who is the primary agent of alignment.

In our work with instructors, reviews of research, and observations of teaching, we have identified instructor misperceptions that often seem to be the basis for decisions about teaching. A similar review of research and interviews with students reveal corresponding student expectations and experiences that are often contrary to these instructor misperceptions. From the misalignment that results, students may easily conclude that they don't belong in the course—because it is not relevant to them, because they lack ability (at least in the instructor's eyes), or because the instructor is not interested in helping them succeed.

By identifying these misperceptions, we are not suggesting that instructors intentionally seek to exclude students, and in fact, the effect of these misperceptions is the same whether they are held consciously or unconsciously. Rather than leaving misperceptions unaddressed unless or until a problem develops, we propose steps to address these misperceptions proactively. Our goal is to make the misperceptions explicit, weigh them against available evidence, and identify initiatives suggested by the alignment model which will communicate to students that they are welcome in the course and seen as capable, potentially successful learners (Table 2.1).

Table 2.1
Common Faculty Misperceptions and Corresponding Initiatives for Including All Students

Commonly Held Faculty Misperceptions	Initiatives for Including All Students
Perceptions of How Students See Instructors "All students can see that they have equal opportunity to succeed in my class. I treat everyone the same."	*Establishing Rapport* Convey respect, fairness, and high expectations
Perceptions of What Is Required for Learning "I focus on what students need to know. I expect them to know how to learn it."	*Providing Structure* Support student success
Perceptions of Student Participation "Some students participate and some don't. I can't do anything to change that."	*Engaging Students* Foster equitable class participation
Perceptions of Teaching Practices "This is the way we teach in this discipline." "It worked for me when I was a student."	*Responsive Planning* Diversity in teaching

Perceptions of How Students See Instructors

Most instructors view themselves as fair and equally committed to all their students, but evidence suggests that students' perceptions of equity can be at odds with the instructor's. For many instructors, the operating assumption is, "All students can see that they have equal opportunity to succeed in my class.

I treat everyone the same." Indeed, 50 years after *Brown v. the Board of Education,* instructors must offer students equal opportunities to learn. However, recent studies have suggested that attempts to treat all students in exactly the same way may not result in an equitable education (Atwater, 2000; Bianchini, Cavazos, & Helms, 2000).

Treating all students the same assumes that students enter classrooms with similar expectations and will respond to instructor behaviors in similar ways. Research conducted by Ferguson (1998) suggested that these assumptions are not accurate. Ferguson found that teachers' perceptions, expectations, and behaviors differed across racial and ethnic groups, and that students' responses to instructor behaviors varied similarly. In another study, Marx, Brown, & Steele (1999) noted that some populations of students have experienced bias in the educational system and have come to view classroom settings as untrustworthy. Gonzalez (1994) noted how students' experiences in a class are greatly influenced by the messages they have received throughout their earlier education. Thus, even in the absence of explicit disrespect, bias, or expressed doubt in students' abilities, not all students recognize a course as "neutral ground" for learning.

Instructors must also realize that their own identities are not neutral. Consciously or unconsciously, students' responses to an instructor are influenced by how readily students think the instructor will be able to understand and relate to them, and by previous experience (or lack of it) with people whom they identify with the instructor. Since it is clearly not possible to influence students' previous experiences, instructors need to be ready to take active steps to shape the perceptions they want students to form about them. Higginbotham (1999) wrote that faculty need to recognize their own

> . . . social location and its impact on the classroom. . . . For example, faculty of color challenge the status quo by their mere presence in front of the class, but they might have to actively and repeatedly demonstrate their right to define the subject matter they teach. (p. 474)

Considering the complexity of how student and instructor experiences and identities shape their interactions in class, it is clear that an instructor's unstated intentions to treat students fairly may not be sufficient to bring students' expectations into alignment with the instructor's commitment to creating a welcoming, constructive environment for learning.

Establishing Rapport: Convey Respect, Fairness, and High Expectations

Because students and instructors may come into class with these very different unstated preconceptions, an instructor who wishes to establish rapport with students should be ready to take the initiative to shape student perceptions by conveying respect, fairness, and high expectations for student learning in the course. A number of strategies are available to help faculty implement this initiative.

Communicate expectations for success. Several studies have indicated that when faculty proactively communicate high expectations for success and identify ways that individual students can demonstrate the ability to meet those standards, the learning environment is viewed more fairly. This perception has a positive impact on students' performance and effectively combats students' perceptions of the classroom as biased against them (Ferguson, 1998; Marx, Brown, & Steele, 1999).

Communicate how diversity will be valued in the course. Instructors can explicitly state their respect for diversity and their intentions to treat all students fairly. It may be appropriate in some courses to include in the syllabus a statement of course goals pertaining to diversity. Instructors can also provide examples of how diversity will be recognized in a course; possibilities include the use of examples, perspectives represented in course materials, and activities that bring together different experiences, strategies, and perspectives.

Consider students' prior knowledge. Early in the course, instructors can identify students' relevant prior knowledge, perhaps by giving an ungraded diagnostic test or surveying students about previous experiences. This helps students to identify challenges they can legitimately expect to encounter when they first try to learn the material. Based on this information, instructors can acknowledge the challenges of the course and that students can expect to find it difficult at times—not necessarily because students are doing something wrong or the instructor is teaching poorly, but because it is a difficult subject to master. Hearing an instructor openly acknowledging these challenges can give students more confidence to face challenges and raise questions; on the other hand, comments that minimize challenges, perhaps even with the intention of encouraging students (e.g., "It's easy to see...") can give the impression that something is wrong with students who find the material difficult.

Orient students to ways of teaching in the course. The same approach to teaching can be interpreted differently by different people; for example, quick, intense interactions might be engaging for some, but intimidating for others; open-ended discussions might stimulate some students' thinking, but leave others feeling lost. Thus it can be very helpful to align student perceptions of class activities with the instructor's by showing how a particular way of teaching contributes to course learning goals. When instructors are explicit about their decisions and their alignment with course goals, then teaching is no longer a matter of the instructor's personal style or what has been done in the past, and students have a clearer sense of how to meet expectations.

Use inclusive language. The words used to introduce material and provide examples have powerful effects on student perceptions of whether the instructor is fairly considering all students. Instructors may think that specific wording has little overall effect on the point being made. However, the language used signals to students who the instructor has in mind when talking about the subject matter. To cite an example, if the instructor, most of the students, and all of the examples are referenced with the pronoun "he," then students may conclude that the instructor thinks women don't belong in a serious discussion of the subject matter.

Each of these strategies can help align students' perceptions with instructor intentions to treat students fairly and expect the best from them, regardless of student backgrounds or prior experiences in the education system.

Perceptions of What Is Required for Learning

For some faculty, considerations of how students learn may seem to extend beyond the scope of their job requirements and are considered the students' responsibility. We might hear faculty emphasize, "I focus on what students need to know. I expect them to know how to learn it." We propose that this misperception can also be a source of misalignment. Though we agree that students must play a primary role in their learning, we also recognize the importance of faculty expertise and involvement in helping students learn both the practices of the discipline and how to be successful in it. Breslow (2001) identified several behaviors that distinguished novice from expert problem-solvers, and noted that students' mastery of these behaviors required explicit modeling and demonstration by expert thinkers. Still, many instructors think of their expertise primarily in terms of course content and may not be consciously aware of the expert practices they regularly employ in their work.

Other instructors may have great interest in helping students succeed, but find it a challenge to know how to help students who may be struggling to learn something that the instructor has not struggled to understand for quite some time. Wineburg (2003) noted that, "As teachers, we need to remember what the world looked like before we learned our discipline's ways of seeing it. We need to show our students the patient and painstaking processes by which we achieved expertise. Only by making our footsteps visible can we expect students to follow in them" (p. B20).

Providing Structure: Support Student Success

The message of respect, fairness, and high expectations will be clearer if it comes with the message that the instructor is structuring the course in ways that support students in their efforts to succeed. Otherwise, instructor messages of high expectations for learning can easily come across as "sink or swim."

For an instructor, it may be necessary to begin by realigning understandings of the subject matter to include not only the propositional content presented in course materials ("what students need to know"), but also the skills and practices students need to learn so they can engage with the course content and take full advantage of learning opportunities in the course. Specific strategies for supporting student success can then help instructors align student expectations with an understanding of what is required for learning, and with their commitment to helping students meet high expectations in the course.

Help students learn strategies for successful studying in the discipline. In addition to expert practices of the discipline, students may still be learning more general study practices such as taking on lengthy reading assignments, dividing tasks among group members, or anticipating the amount of time required to complete a project. Instructors can support student success by identifying these strategies as skills that need to be learned and by providing explicit directions and coaching to guide them in their learning (e.g., Felder, 1997).

Let students know what you have done to become a successful learner in the discipline. Many people associate ability with identity, assuming that success as a learner somehow "came naturally" to an instructor. If instructors show students how they have put time and effort into learning, it can help students see that they can also be successful by making similar efforts, even if they think they have little else in common with the instructor.

Make sure assignment guidelines and grading criteria are clearly communicated. Instructions for an assignment can be structured in ways that guide students' work on the assignment, since students often interpret grading criteria as a means for communicating what the instructor values most (whether or not that is the instructor's intention). These criteria can also help align student expectations with the nature of the course content; for example, showing that learning is demonstrated by more than memorization, and requires application, analysis, or synthesis of material. By making these guidelines and criteria explicit to students at the very beginning, instructors can help them learn more successfully through the work that is assigned.

Take steps to establish good working relationships among students in the class. Students may be confident of the instructor's efforts to support their success but not see respect or fairness in ways other students interact. For instance, student learning teams may be an important means for achieving course goals, but teams may operate in ways that are biased against some students: Who determines team membership? How are roles on the team assigned? Who influences team decision-making? Challenges like these can be proactively addressed by structuring ways that teams are expected to work together, for example, or assigning roles within groups.

Remind students of resources available for help. In addition to the help offered through the course or department—for example, office hours, study sessions, and tutoring centers—instructors can remind students of resources beyond the course, such as writing centers, campus services for students with disabilities, or resources for non-native English speakers that might be available. Instructors can support student success by acknowledging the importance of these resources and letting students know there is no stigma attached to getting extra help.

Each of these strategies helps make instructor commitments to supporting student success more visible, aligning students with instructor expectations for what is required for learning in a course.

Perceptions of Student Participation

There are many ways to participate in class, and not all students are likely to participate in the same way or the same amount. Indeed, many faculty have observed this pattern and concluded, "Some students participate and some don't. I can't do anything to change that." Though it may not be necessary or realistic to expect all students to participate equally, it is essential to make sure that no one is kept from participating as a result of how the course is taught. For example, students may conclude that their participation is unwelcome or not valued if it appears to them that the instructor is partial to interacting with a particular group of students, such as students from a certain social or ethnic group or students who sit in the front row. Montgomery and Barrett (1997) examined classroom environments for women in science and engineering and found that the high proportion of male participation and interruption patterns contributed to a less than supportive and perhaps untrustworthy climate for women students. Sadker and Sadker (1992) found that instructors who viewed videotapes of their own teaching were surprised at biases apparent in their responses to student questions and comments, showing that they were unaware of these biases at the time of the interactions. These patterns of interaction can easily inhibit participation by conveying to students that certain backgrounds, life experiences, and even gender, disqualify them from serious consideration as learners.

These perceptions by the instructor and students can be addressed when an instructor more accurately understands why some students don't participate (beyond a lack of preparation or a lack of interest), and when instructor and student perceptions of what counts as participation, what role it plays in learning, and how it is valued in a course, are aligned.

Engaging Students: Foster Equitable Class Participation

Student engagement in class is greatly influenced by the expectations that instructors set for classroom behavior, teaching strategies that are employed, and ways student interactions are structured during class. The following strategies can help to set the stage for more equitable class participation.

Plan ahead. It may seem obvious to say that instructors should plan ahead. However, we find that many instructors think of planning in terms of what they will be teaching and participation as something that spontaneously happens during class. But equitable class participation rarely happens by accident, and the range of possibilities to consider when planning ahead (see Table 2.2) makes it clear that class participation can be planned in many ways, for many purposes. Making these decisions in advance, and making them explicit to students, can contribute toward aligning student expectations with instructor goals for more equitable class participation.

Use the first day of class to set expectations. One way for instructors to communicate expectations is to add a statement to the syllabus and talk with the students on the first day of class about the role of participation in the course. Chapter 3 provides an example of expectations one instructor sets during the first class meeting.

Provide feedback. Provide feedback on the nature and quality of participation you observe in the course. Instructors can let students know what their participation is adding to the course and whether students need to make changes in their patterns of participation. This feedback can help the instructor align students' expectations by communicating how the instructor

Table 2.2
Considerations for Planning Ahead

Goals for Participation—*possibilities include:*
- Discovering new material
- Exploring different perspectives
- Inviting students to relate relevant experiences

Types of Participation—*possibilities include:*
- Large group discussion
- Small group activities
- Face-to-face or online

Student Preparation—*possibilities include:*
- Reading assignments
- Reflective writing
- Small group work to prepare for large group interaction

Facilitating Participation—*possibilities include:*
- Managing "wait time" in a discussion
- Acknowledging student contributions
- Incorporating student input into following instruction

Assessment of Participation—*possibilities include:*
- Communicating expectations to students
- Providing assessment criteria
- Providing clear feedback

---

perceives students' work, rather than relying solely on self-assessment or assumptions based on experiences in other courses.

Seek feedback. Seek feedback from students on their perceptions of participation in the course. Do they perceive that they have opportunities to participate? Do they see how their participation contributes to their learning? This direct feedback can help the instructor align teaching practices with student perceptions of their opportunities to participate, rather than relying on inferences from student behavior or facial expressions to direct teaching practices.

Honor student diversity. It is easy for students to believe they are not welcome in a class when they hear comments that seem to reveal or perpetuate stereotypes that they don't share. Even an impersonal comment not directed at students in the course can become a distraction that prevents students from engaging in the class. One student noted, "One day the professor started class with a joke about people with accents. Chances are he didn't mean anything by it, but it's all I thought about for the whole hour. I might as well have stayed home for all I was able to pay attention to the lecture."[2]

Most people respond even more strongly to stereotypes directed at them. Social identities are strongly held, but people also want to be recognized as individuals—as members of certain social groups, but also as unique individuals within those groups. For this reason, students can easily conclude their participation is not welcome if either dimension of identity is overemphasized or disregarded. Instructors may inadvertently communicate disrespect for other types of student diversity as well. Students may get this message if their commitments to family, work, or other obligations are dismissed as unimportant in comparison to course work. They may also get this sense if instructors respond to student disabilities, language or cultural differences, or struggles with the course content in ways that suggest they are not interested in helping students meet these potential challenges to learning.

Beyond avoiding direct expressions of stereotypes and taking care to consider students' life experiences, an instructor can take a number of specific steps to help foster equitable class participation by honoring student diversity.

Develop a broad repertoire of cases and examples. Instructors can communicate indirectly (by the examples given, the scholars cited, or the problems identified as important) that some perspectives on this work are more valid than others. If validity appears somehow to be judged on identity preferences rather than on the merit of the work under discussion, then students may easily conclude that the instructor is unfairly excluding views that may matter greatly to them.

Set the stage for potentially sensitive material. Rather than assuming that all material can be presented as value-neutral, instructors can anticipate material that may lead to heated discussions. Controversy can then be handled in a way that doesn't cause some students to conclude that their perspectives are automatically discounted by the instructor or by other students. One approach is to establish ground rules for class discussion, providing a common reference point for reminding students of mutually agreed upon ways of interacting respectfully.

Respond promptly to discriminatory remarks. An instructor's failure to respond promptly to discriminatory remarks or other kinds of disruptive behavior may be seen as tacit approval of the comment or behavior.

Be careful not to diminish students' strong reactions to negative comments from other students. A comment that may be intended as value-neutral or simply descriptive may sound very different to students who have been the targets of discrimination, and these students may react in ways that are surprising to people who have not had similar experiences. Bell, Washington, Weinstein, and Love (1997) noted,

> Dominant group members . . . are often oblivious to the effects of their language . . . and in fact are often shocked to realize this effect. Thus the potential for breakdown in communication, hurt feelings, defensiveness, and recriminations is high. (p. 302)

Recognize that students may not appreciate being asked to speak solely as representatives of the groups to which they belong. Asking students to speak on behalf of entire groups often rests on unstated assumptions about students' identification with these groups, asks students to make unsupported generalizations about them, and puts students in the position of being valued for membership in a group rather than for individual abilities or ideas.

Through these steps, instructors help align students' expectations with instructor intentions to ensure that all students recognize their presence in class is valued and their contributions to class are welcome.

Perceptions of Teaching Practices

It is understandable, perhaps unavoidable, that instructors base their decisions about teaching on their previous classroom experiences. In fact, the knowledge base of these experiences is a rich resource for any instructor. However, some instructors have rejected alternative approaches to teaching and defended their traditional approaches with arguments such as, "This is the way we teach in this discipline," or perhaps, "It worked for me when I was a student." It is not always the case, however, that an instructor's personal experiences are representative of teaching practices in the discipline or of learning preferences in the general student population. In other contexts, drawing broad conclusions from an individual case is known as "generalizing from N = 1." To some extent, the social and cultural contexts of students' earlier learning experiences (Nelson, 1996) shape learning styles, suggesting that an instructor's approach to teaching may reflect his or her experiences in life and in school more than it reflects the nature of the content being taught. Thus, to some extent a way of teaching may be biased in favor of students who share educational experiences and social identities similar to the instructor's.

Handelsman et al. (2004) argue that many instructors "demand rigorous proof for scientific assertions in their research [but] continue to use, and indeed, defend, on the basis of intuition alone, teaching methods that are not the most effective" (p. 521). Instructors may suggest a variety of reasons, including a lack of knowledge about alternatives or evidence of their effectiveness. Similarly, since many instructors' vision of their discipline is limited to its propositional content, they are less likely to recognize that disciplinary expertise also includes practices, conceptual frameworks, and commitments that students rarely learn only from lectures or textbooks. Thus instructors who see only a narrow range of options for teaching and learning need to align their understanding of the discipline by appreciating the complexities of disciplinary expertise and by being better informed about approaches to teaching and learning that may differ from their personal classroom experiences.

Responsive Planning: Diversity in Teaching

To plan for greater diversity in teaching, instructors must examine their practices and the assumptions on which decisions about teaching are based. The alignment model presents planning and teaching not as a "linear and one-way" delivery of knowledge, but as an interactive process, adapting to shifting contexts, demands of content, and student input. For example, how responsive are instructors to student input and challenges that emerge during the course? How well does their teaching represent the complexity of the discipline and the social realities in which it is situated? To what extent might ways of teaching perpetuate power imbalances or exclude students from socially marginalized groups? [3]

Planning for diversity in teaching must also account for the reality that individuals do not all learn in the same way and that any group of students will include a variety of approaches to learning. It may not be possible to predict or even discover the various learning styles represented among a group of students. Even if course content allows for some variety in teaching approaches, course goals may necessitate helping students adapt to certain types of classroom experiences. From the alignment perspective, the goal is to teach in ways that support learning. This requires monitoring student progress and responding to student input—which could mean teaching differently or helping students benefit from and understand the value of the teaching strategies used. Strategies for diversity in teaching can be divided into two categories: considering *how* you teach and *what* you teach.

Consider how you teach. The strategies identified in this chapter will help diversify a teaching style by employing a wider range of classroom practices that give students a variety of options for learning and demonstrating what they have learned. One way to monitor the alignment of teaching practices and student expectations is to invite students to provide feedback on their perceptions of how they are learning in a course. At times their feedback may reflect challenges posed by difficult content, but other times challenges may be related to the style used to present the content. Consider the following example from an instructor's perspective:

> I like to move around the classroom a lot and ask lots of questions, showing my own excitement about the topic. I don't write a lot down because it really interrupts the flow. In each class I've had a few who don't like to talk. They complain that they don't get anything out of class and the lectures are disorganized. I think they just want me to tell them everything.

From the instructor's perspective, this particular way of teaching may be well-suited to the content being taught or to the instructor's own personal style, but the following statements from students show that they perceive this instructor's ways of teaching somewhat differently:

> He gives us so many details that I never know where he's going with it, so it's hard to know what to focus on. I tried asking a couple of questions and he always said we'll get to that later. So I don't ask questions anymore.

> I try to take notes but he goes so fast and jumps around so much, it's hard. I wish he would write stuff down sometimes but nobody else seems to need him to do that. I don't ask questions because I don't even know where to start. Maybe I'm just not good at this stuff.

In cases like this one, it is not a matter of identifying whose perceptions are more accurate, but rather, of finding ways to align the instructor's and students' expectations so that students are able to learn what the instructor expects them to learn. Alignment in this case might require orienting students to the instructor's ways of teaching (conveying respect, fairness, and high expectations), and providing students with strategies for successful learning in this situation (supporting student success). There are also a variety of ways to set expectations for student participation (fostering equitable class participation), all of which contribute to helping students see what they are expected to learn and how they can most effectively learn it in this type of situation.

Consider what you teach. Another way to make teaching more diverse is to ensure that course content thoroughly and accurately represents the discipline. For example, instructors who focus on isolated, abstract principles and do not address the ethical or social relevance of their work may communicate that students who are concerned with these issues do not have a place in the professional or scientific community—one of the reasons identified by Seymour and Hewitt (1997) that some undergraduates choose to leave a discipline. Though there may be good reasons to take some concepts out of their more complex contexts for the purposes of learning, these broader contexts still need to be represented so that students gain an accurate understanding of the discipline. Reddick, Jacobson, Linse, and Yong (in press) present diversity of content as an issue of comprehensiveness, "ensuring that what is taught is rigorously grounded in actual (rather than idealized) conditions."

This attention to comprehensiveness also addresses the extent to which students can see that the curriculum represents voices of people with whom they can readily identify. The goal is to show that people of all types are able to make welcome contributions to the discipline—not (by implication) only the people who can readily identify with the instructor. For example, entering a discipline typically requires that students gain an appreciation of the history and development of the discipline, which should include due acknowledgement of the diverse community of professionals and scholars who have shaped it. Attention to comprehensiveness might also include drawing on a diverse range of experts, mentors, and role models, showing that success in the field depends on ability and effort, not social or cultural identity. Although many instructors might think it unnecessary to go out of their way to make this point, evidence related to student achievement reveals that many students see obstacles to their success because of how their identity is perceived, rather than because of their level of ability. Marx, Brown, and Steele (1999) found that telling a group of African American students that an exam was created at Howard University, a historically black institution, countered African American students' perceptions of standardized exams as biased against them and lessened their fears about confirming negative ability stereotypes about their group. Similar results were also found when women students were exposed to female proctors during exams or were told that a particular exam was "gender fair"; that is, not biased against female students in terms of performance results.

These initiatives to diversify teaching begin with instructors' own experiences in the classroom, but also ask instructors not to limit themselves to making decisions on that basis alone. Rather, a more diverse approach to teaching is one that recognizes the complexity of the content instructors are teaching, the learning challenges this complexity poses for students, and the potentially wide range of possibilities for meeting those challenges.

Conclusion

In this chapter we have identified faculty perceptions that can exclude students, accidentally or intentionally, from opportunities to learn. When these perceptions are explicit, it is possible to identify initiatives that are strategically important for helping faculty maintain alignment and communicate through their teaching practices that students are welcome in the class and seen as capable, potentially successful learners.

Endnotes

1) Sections of this chapter are adapted from the Center for Instructional Development and Research's Inclusive Teaching web resources, originally developed by Wayne Jacobson, Nancy Emery, Margy Lawrence, Clarisse Messemer, Bonnie O'Dell, and Yoosun Park. Additional resources can be found at http://depts.washington.edu/cidrweb/inclusive/.

2) Faculty and student quotes are based on confidential faculty consultations and anonymous student surveys. Therefore, original sources for faculty and student quotes are not cited.

3) Arora (Chapter 11) also examines this question from the perspectives of critical and feminist pedagogies.

References

Atwater, M. M. (2000). Equity for black Americans in precollege science. *Science Education, 84*(2), 154–179.

Bell, L. A., Washington, S., Weinstein, G., & Love, B. (1997). Knowing ourselves as instructors. In M. Adams, L. A. Bell, & P. Griffin (Eds.), *Teaching for diversity and social justice: A sourcebook* (pp. 299–310). New York, NY: Routledge.

Bianchini, J. A., Cavazos, L. M., & Helms, J. V. (2000). From professional lives to inclusive practice: Science teachers and scientists' views of gender and ethnicity in science education. *Journal of Research in Science Teaching, 37*(6), 511–547.

Breslow, L. (2001). Transforming novice problem solvers into experts. *Teach Talk, 13*(3). Retrieved November 30, 2004, from the Massachusetts Institute of Technology, Teaching and Learning Laboratory web site: http://web.mit.edu/tll/published/transforming_novice.htm

Felder, R. M. (1997). Who needs these headaches? Reflections on teaching first-year engineering students. *Success 101,* 2. Retrieved November 30, 2004, from http://www.ncsu.edu/felder-public/Papers/headaches.htm

Ferguson, R. F. (1998). Teachers' perceptions and expectations and the black-white test score gap. In C. Jencks & M. Phillips (Eds.), *The black-white test score gap* (pp. 273–317). Washington, DC: Brookings Institution Press.

Gonzalez, J. (1994). Once you accept, then you can teach. In H. Roberts & Associates (Eds.), *Teaching from a multicultural perspective* (pp. 1–16). Thousand Oaks, CA: Sage.

Handelsman, J., Ebert-May, D., Beichner, R., Bruns, P., Chang, A., DeHaan, R., et al. (2004). Scientific teaching. *Science, 304*(5670), 521–522.

Higginbotham, E. (1999). Getting all students to listen: Analyzing and coping with student resistance. In B. A. Pescosolido & R. Aminzade (Eds.), *The social worlds of higher education: Handbook for teaching in a new century* (pp. 472–479). Thousand Oaks, CA: Pine Forge Press.

Marx, D. M., Brown, J. L., & Steele, C. M. (1999). Allport's legacy and the situational press of stereotypes. *Journal of Social Issues, 55*(3), 491–502.

Montgomery, S., & Barrett, M. C. (1997). *Undergraduate women in science and engineering: Providing academic support* (Occasional Paper No. 8). Ann Arbor, MI: University of Michigan, Center for Research on Learning and Teaching.

Nelson, C. E. (1996). Student diversity requires different approaches to college teaching, even in math and science. *American Behavioral Scientist, 40*(2), 165–175.

Reddick, L., Jacobson, W., Linse, A., & Yong, D. (in press). An inclusive teaching framework for science, technology, engineering, and math. In M. Ouellett (Ed.), *Teaching inclusively: Diversity and faculty development.* Stillwater, OK: New Forums Press.

Sadker, M., & Sadker, D. (1992). Ensuring equitable participation in college classes. In L. L. B. Border & N. V. N. Chism (Eds.), *New directions for teaching and learning: No. 49. Teaching for diversity* (pp. 49–56). San Francisco, CA: Jossey-Bass.

Seymour, E., & Hewitt, N. M. (1997). *Talking about leaving: Why undergraduates leave the sciences.* Boulder, CO: Westview Press.

Wineburg, S. (2003, April 11). Teaching the mind good habits. *Chronicle of Higher Education,* p. B20.

3

Designing for Alignment

Wayne H. Jacobson & Donald H. Wulff

It is interesting to ask faculty developers to explain just what it is they do. There are affirming answers (acknowledging all the wonderful work faculty are doing), politically astute answers (for example, "contributing to the university's commitment to excellence in undergraduate education"), and simple descriptive answers ("helping instructors who are working on improving their teaching"). But in an unguarded moment, in response to fellow faculty developers, rather than to faculty, campus leaders, or legislators, one faculty developer offered this memorable, succinct description of his work: "helping faculty teach as though there are students in the room."

This characterization of those of us who teach leaves much room for discussion, but it captures an important element of teaching and learning that was once articulated by Angelo and Cross (1993): "... there is no such thing as effective teaching in the absence of learning. Teaching without learning is just talking" (p. 3). Angelo and Cross suggested in brief what Barr and Tagg (1995) examined at length in their discussion of the learning paradigm—challenging faculty no longer to see themselves primarily as lecturers but as "designers of learning methods and environments" (p. 17). In the learning paradigm, teaching is defined not in terms of what instructors say in the classroom, but in terms of what students learn.

Approaching teaching in this way makes course design a matter of alignment. It requires careful consideration of contexts for learning, course content, and instructor expertise while keeping these elements in balance with an understanding of who the students are, what they should be able to do by the end of the course, how you will know what they can do, and what activities will help them learn. The alignment of these dimensions is dynamic and ongoing throughout a course, but this alignment over time is greatly facilitated when a course is designed to take these dimensions into account from the very beginning.

Context, Content, and Instructor Expertise

An important first step in designing a course for ongoing alignment is to examine instructor perceptions of the context for the course. Examples of these perceptions include how the instructors see the course situated in the department and in the discipline, the level at which the course is offered, and requirements of subsequent courses for which their course is expected to prepare students. In addition, some courses are perceived to belong uniquely to the instructor; others are expected to reflect curriculum goals, accreditation requirements, or other factors over which the instructor has little control. Instructor perceptions of these contextual factors set parameters for the course, and it may take considerable time and effort to select and organize content appropriate for introducing students to the body of knowledge defined by these parameters.

However, the content of a course is not determined by these parameters alone. Within these parameters, instructors have their own areas of interest and expertise, that directly influence what they see as most important for students to learn, how they organize the material, and what range and type of examples they are able to include in their teaching. Instructors also make decisions about how they present the material based on their prior teaching experience, assumptions about student learning, and familiarity with particular methodologies or technologies that might be appropriate for the content they are teaching.

Furthermore, instructors are not always assigned to teach courses that fit neatly within their areas of expertise. Changes in the department or the curriculum might require them to teach different courses or add new material to the courses they regularly teach, so they must adapt content or become familiar with new ways of teaching on relatively short notice. Simply keeping courses up-to-date in response to emerging content and changing contexts may require all the time that an instructor can spare from the demands of teaching and other responsibilities.

So it is not a small accomplishment for instructors to align themselves with course content and the larger context in which it occurs, helping them determine topics appropriate for presentation in the course. However, one professor's experience tells how students look to instructors for much more than their ability to select topics for presentation. Earlier in the term, he had to miss a day of the introductory survey course he was teaching. The course presented a standard set of topics well-known in the discipline, and he could have easily arranged for a colleague to teach the content scheduled for that day. But because the library owned a video series on the topic, he arranged for students to watch a video from it during his absence. On his next day back, students unanimously expressed appreciation for the video. Were there other videos they could watch, they asked, so that they would be able to understand the rest of his lectures? Though he was glad to know that his students found the video helpful, their question motivated him to ask his own question, "If what I know can be so easily replaced by a video, then why am I here?"

He is not the first person to ask this question or questions like it with regard to textbooks, lecture slides, or web-based materials. If effective teaching were only about experts and their expertise, it might be difficult to answer this question. However, the alignment model defines an instructor's role as far more complex than providing students with information from an expert. It is also the instructor's role to consider who the students in the course will be and how they can be brought into alignment with the content and the instructor's ways of teaching it.

Who Are the Students?

To design a course for ongoing alignment, an instructor begins by identifying the context into which a course fits and the content it addresses, then asks who the students in the course will be. Asking this question does not mean that student needs somehow overrule instructor decisions or contextual factors that shape the content of the course. Rather, by answering questions about the students, the instructor can address many other questions along the way (see Table 3.1). The goal is to know who the students are well enough to identify how they can begin to gain access to the content, determine strategies for helping them learn, and provide meaningful feedback on their learning.

Table 3.1
Who Are the Students?

Before class begins, find out as much as you can about the students. Use your own experience as a source of information, as well as that of fellow faculty and staff in your department.

- Are students new to the topic? To the university?
- What are students' reasons for taking the course?
- What can you expect students to know before they come to the first class?
- What range of student backgrounds and experience is typically represented in the class?
- What problems do students typically have with this material?

A number of sources are available for learning about students who are likely to be in a course. An instructor may have taught the course before or may be able to consult with colleagues who have taught this course or similar courses (including courses preceding or following it in a sequence). In many departments or colleges, there are advisors who get to know students as the advisors help the students select courses. Most importantly, there are the students themselves—not that a course can't be designed effectively until the instructor meets the students, but rather, that interactions with students during the first class meetings can facilitate the process of maintaining alignment throughout the course.

Chapter 2 discussed the importance of assessing students' prior knowledge and experience with the subject matter. This pre-assessment can be valuable in a variety of ways for maintaining alignment. For example, if students' prior knowledge is different from what was expected, an instructor may have the option of revising plans for the course. If the curriculum does not allow such flexibility, however, this information will still be valuable for helping the instructor communicate points at which students may face challenges or need additional resources to help them learn. This pre-assessment can also help students self-assess their readiness for the course. Although students are likely to have some understanding of the course based on its title and place in the curriculum, their expectations can vary widely for what (and how) specific topics will be taught, what students will need to do to learn successfully, and how they can expect to demonstrate their learning.

Instructors who are aware of their students' expectations can more clearly communicate their own expectations and bring instructor and student expectations into alignment from the outset. Don Wulff has developed his own list of expectations and information that he routinely addresses on the first day of his courses to help establish and maintain alignment immediately (see Table 3.2).

This ability to appreciate who the students are, what they are expecting, and how they are learning provides instructors with the knowledge to align students with instructor expectations and with the course content. Using this information to foster better alignment is one of the most compelling answers to the professor's question identified earlier, "If what I know can be replaced by a video (or textbook, or web tutorial), then why am I here?"

Table 3.2

Aligning Expectations on the First Day of Class

In addition to using the syllabus as a source of information on the first day of class, I seek ways to let students introduce themselves, list their expectations for the course, and tell me how they think they learn best. I also tell them what I expect and under what circumstances I do my best teaching. Topics that I address to align myself and students on the first day include:

- Respect for each other and each other's ideas
- The value of their backgrounds and experience in helping them learn and in helping me learn at what level to teach the course
- What the course is about and not about based on expectations they have identified (to align our mutual expectations)
- How the course fits into the larger context and goals of the department and the university
- How the course is structured
- The role of participation as a significant part of learning in my courses (a participation grade based on coming to class so they can participate, coming prepared by having done assigned work, and participating willingly in class activities)
- The kinds of instructional methods (lecture, discussion, problem solving, small groups, etc.) they can expect as I teach
- The role that reading and out-of-class assignments will play in their learning
- My commitment to a good balance between high expectations for the learning tasks and a relaxed classroom atmosphere
- My expectations for high-quality work from them and my suggestion (if this is an elective course) that this term may not be the best one for them to enroll in the course if they have other commitments that will detract from their engagement and participation
- My use of their questions and their responses to my questions as a form of feedback—to hear how they are progressing and what I need to do to assist them further
- My expectations about deadlines for assignments and exams
- The role of office hours in the course and what students can expect when they come to office hours
- My plans to gather student feedback systematically in order to help understand their perceptions of their learning during the course
- My commitment to hearing their perspectives so I can make adjustments in my approach and the content as a way to enhance learning

What Should Students Be Able to Do
by the End of the Course?

The next step to help instructors make decisions about designing for alignment is to ask what students should be able to do by the end of the course (see Table 3.3). Answers to this question are often a matter of alignment with the context in which the course is offered and specific departmental or disciplinary expectations. Given where this course fits in a larger sequence or program, what does this course need to prepare students for? The question also refers to an alignment with students. Given where students are starting, where can they reasonably expect to be at the end?

Table 3.3

What Should Students Be Able to Do by the End of the Course?

Considering who the students are, what should they be able to do at the end of the course that they couldn't necessarily do coming into it?

Use terms that emphasize student abilities you can assess or easily recognize. For example, it is more difficult to assess abilities like "know" or "understand" than it is to assess abilities like "identify," "differentiate," or "produce."

Within the boundaries established by these opening questions, the next step is to identify what students should be able to do as a result of learning in this course. It is not to suggest that all learning has behavioral outcomes, but that goals should be expressed in terms that are identifiable. If goals are expressed primarily in terms of content to be presented, a course syllabus might look very much like the table of contents for a textbook on the topic. However, the knowledge one acquires is difficult to establish outside of what one does with it, and for this reason it is helpful to define goals in terms that make learning visible (and therefore, more readily assessable) for the instructor and for students. Specifying identifiable goals may mean making explicit what is already assumed: a lab or project that is a standard part of a course, for example, shows what students are able to do with the knowledge presented in the course. In other courses, specifying objectives in these terms can lead to entirely new ways of thinking about them.

In one science department, most faculty agreed that many students were not prepared for senior-level courses, and decided to redesign their junior-level courses. When the curriculum committee began to consider ways to address this problem, they quickly determined that students were not ill-prepared so much by a lack of content knowledge as by a lack of scientific skills which faculty agreed were essential for learning in their courses. Their solution, therefore, was not to identify new or different scientific content, but to develop courses to address specific scientific skill areas, as identified in Table 3.4.

Table 3.4

Learning Goals Identified for a Junior-Level Sequence of Science Courses

---

1) Relate one piece of information to several layers of larger context (be able to move between levels, systems)
   - Be able to define where information fits into the big picture and draw connections between different pieces of information (concept maps are useful here)
   - Know how (and why) to organize information and realize that there is more than one way to organize it
   - Be able to define issues/problems and devise new hypotheses based on information available
   - Be able to distinguish major points from trivial details
2) Understand how experimental evidence is developed
   - Be able to design experiments; take a problem and break it into manageable parts
   - Be able to analyze and interpret data and graphs
   - Be able to evaluate support for a hypothesis
3) Read a scientific paper and relate its content to #1 and #2 above
   - Be able to interpret new information in the context of what a student already knows; understand the significance or relevance of this paper to larger and smaller questions
   - Understand hypothesis testing and be able to critique methods used or conclusions drawn
   - Identify unanswered questions (realize that not all is known)
4) Understand/apply known methods to new situations
   - Be able to identify unanswered questions, develop hypotheses and predictions, and design experiments to test those hypotheses
5) Communicate knowledge
   - Use writing as a tool (be able to make clear, logical arguments and summarize important points)
6) Identify gaps in their own knowledge/skills; self-assess
7) Use available resources to answer questions
   - Be able to do database searches
8) "Play well with others"—know how to work as part of a team in a collaborative effort
   - Be able to do peer evaluation

This emphasis on what students will be able to do does not replace the disciplinary content of the course, but asks instructors to make explicit what they expect students to be able to do with that content. Wineburg (2003) argued that history professors, for example, do not want their students to learn only what historians know, but also how they come to know it. But, he noted, if that is the goal, then there are direct implications for ways of teaching.

> Students who believe that knowledge bursts Athena-like from the professor's head may never learn to think like historians, may never be able to reconstruct past worlds from the most minimal of clues.... Historians can model in class how they read by having students bring in unfamiliar texts and demonstrating how to interpret and assess them. With a companion document, they can show the strategies they use to corroborate evidence and piece together a coherent context.... By sharing their mental habits, historians could teach students skills they would find useful every time they faced a take-home exam or research paper: how to get started when they lack necessary information, how to prepare their minds to deal with new topics, how to develop a hunch. (p. B20)

Articulating to students what they should be able to do at the end of a course is an important step toward aligning their expectations for what they will learn in a course, how they will be learning it, and how their learning will be assessed.

How Will You Know What Students Can Do?

The next question to help instructors design for alignment follows closely from previous ones: How will you know what students can do (see Table 3.5)? If learning goals are stated in identifiable terms, then learning is demonstrated by achieving those goals. This goal needs special emphasis, though, because many traditional forms of assessment only work to assess what students can *remember,* and assessment decisions are too easily shaped more by course logistics or traditions ("the way we've always done it in this course") than by consideration of students and course learning goals. However, defining assessment in terms of what students are able to do can be a way to monitor student learning that is more effective and more efficient.

Table 3.5

How Will You Know What Students Can Do?

Considering who the students are and what you want them to be able to do, what will provide you with reliable evidence during the course that they are learning and, at the end of the course, that they have learned?

Weekly quizzes?

Original research?

Objective tests?

Reflective papers?

Open-ended tests?

Presentations?

Team reports?

Performance?

For example, a professor once posed a question of test design: How could he assess students' knowledge of when to use particular statistical tools that had been presented in class? He was satisfied from homework and class discussions that they knew *how* to use the tools, but he wasn't sure students could analyze a novel situation and select the most appropriate tool. The problem was further complicated by the length of time required to perform the statistical operations. During a typical class session, there would not be time to answer more than two test questions. Thus, he felt students wouldn't have time to demonstrate their ability to apply these tools in the potentially wide range of situations in which they might be used. In the end, he developed an assessment that provided a set of problems, asked students to identify which tool to apply in each case, and asked them to write a rationale for their decisions. However, he did not ask students to implement the tools fully. For the professor, this approach represented a fundamental shift: He had not previously assessed students' decision-making about when to use these tools, even though that was a primary goal in the course; prior to that he had only assessed how students used them. However, by specifically identifying what students needed to do, he was able to create a more strategic assessment (a short-answer essay exam). This approach was very different from what he had traditionally done in his quantitative courses, but it helped him to assess how well students had learned the higher order skills of knowing *when* (not simply *how*) to use the tools.

An added benefit of assessing students in terms of what they can do is that it helps students more accurately self-assess their learning. Lacking the instructor's level of disciplinary expertise, students who are asked to *know* something may have relatively little skill in determining how well they know it. The ability to achieve objectives specified by the instructor tells students how well their learning strategies align with the instructor's expectations for engaging with the content of the course. Objectives that are vague or inconsistent with how they are assessed—for example, a course which appears to emphasize creative problem solving, but in which grades are based on recall of factual information—can understandably send a mixed message to students about what content the instructor considers important for them to learn.

What Activities Will Help Students Learn?

After instructors have established goals and assessment plans, the next consideration in designing for alignment is to ask: What kinds of experiences, activities, and materials will help students achieve the learning goals that the instructor specified (see Table 3.6)?

Table 3.6
What Activities Will Help Students Learn?

Design the course to include activities that are most likely to lead students toward defined goals. Some goals can be achieved by listening to lectures or reading assigned texts. Others require more active experimentation, practice, or discussion. For example:

Writing

Problem sets

Design projects

Online discussion

Service-learning

Case studies

Field work

Learning teams

Thinking about course activities is often what initially prompts instructors to think about change. They ask, for example:

- "How can I improve my lectures?"
- "How can I develop better assignments?"
- "How can I get students to write better?"

- "How can I put my course online?"

However, it is also at this point that some insctuctors express objections:

- "If I add active learning, I won't have time to cover the content…"
- "I tried group work once, but students didn't like it…"[1]

Sometimes these questions prompt instructors to think differently about their teaching, but from the alignment perspective, it is premature to start with these questions. Instead, we ask first about the course content and the instructor: What goals are lectures or assignments designed to help students accomplish? What is the instructor's experience and comfort level working online? How much time will the instructor have for responding to student writing? Questions at this point in the design process are almost always answered with, "It depends"—on course content, on the instructor, and on prior questions of who the students are, what the learning goals are, and how to identify that they are able to learn.

Questions about course activities also depend to some extent on course context. For example, what are the department's goals for this course? Will there be administrative support for innovative practices that might require time to put in place and fine tune? How will students' experiences in other courses be affected by decisions made about this course? Courses rarely exist in a vacuum, and broader contextual factors such as these may play a critical role in determining what can happen in a course.

Therefore, selection of course activities, assignments, and materials is guided by the alignment of multiple factors that contribute to learning, rather than solely by an instructor's experience or students' preferences. For example, whether or not students *like* the use of small groups is secondary; the primary question is what students will *learn* through a small group activity. Instructors' decisions about teaching are not solely decisions of *how much* content to present, but *how well* students are likely to learn it in the way it is presented.

Professor Dean McManus (2002) wrote of the challenge he faced in thinking about course goals and class activities in terms of what students need to do.

> In lecturing I always thought in terms of "the students ought to know *this* about marine geology." … *This* was some bit of information, some fact, some kind of research, some discovery, some equation, some concept. Now I had to think in terms of "the students ought to be able to *do* this." They ought to be able to observe keenly, compute

accurately, reason cogently, describe results clearly, hypothesize, and to test hypotheses rigorously. They ought to be developing "a scientific habit of mind."

This change of goals led to a number of other changes: In what had traditionally been a survey course taught as a lecture, students wrote and presented summaries of articles in order to teach one another material, worked in teams to gather and interpret data, and reported findings to the class as a whole. McManus explained that his goal in redesigning this course was "not for the instructor to narrate more information, but for the students to learn better how to think as scientists." Thus, he designed learning activities in alignment with his goals for learning, students' prior learning, and their reasons for taking the course. The result was an exceptional learning experience, for both himself and the students. McManus concluded, "I have never enjoyed teaching a course so much, nor received such high student evaluations, nor had students 'earn' (their word) such high grades in my thirty years of teaching."

What Are the Likely Challenges to Student Learning?

There is a final consideration that can help the instructor design a course in ways that will facilitate alignment as the course is being taught. Based on the instructor's knowledge of who the students are, goals for the course, and learning activities designed for it, instructors can also ask, "At what points are students likely to encounter challenges with this content area?" (see Table 3.7).

Table 3.7

What Are the Likely Challenges to Student Learning?

Which aspects of the course are likely to present the greatest challenges for students, and how will you help them meet those challenges? For example:

Challenge = _____

Ways you can help students meet this challenge through:

- Materials:

- Assignments:

- Activities:

- Assessments:

For students, a challenge in a course can easily be perceived as a problem that may or may not be theirs to solve. For example, students may regard low grades as a personal failure ("maybe I'm not smart enough") or as an instructor's problem ("the professor didn't prepare us well enough for the test") rather than recognizing that the material is significantly more challenging than they had anticipated. For instructors, the recognition that particular aspects of their course may pose problems for students but that contextual factors such as curriculum or graduation requirements limit their flexibility to address these issues can be a challenge. Instructors can help align students' expectations by clearly communicating the amount and type of effort required in their courses, by indicating where students are commonly challenged by the subject matter, and by telling students how course activities and assignments have been designed to help them meet those challenges. There are many ways to identify and approach these challenges, but the importance of doing so is well documented: Research has shown that a central element of effective teaching from the students' perspective is the instructor's effort to connect the content of the course to the students' prior learning and to empathize with them about the challenges in trying to learn it (Beyer & Fisher, 2002; Carson, 1999).

One common challenge is that students often request real-world examples to help demonstrate the relevance of the material they are studying. Instructors usually have a clear sense of the larger context to which new material relates, but for students who don't yet see that bigger picture, it can be challenging to learn new material without somehow relating it to familiar concepts or experience. Planning for alignment in this situation might include preparing more examples with which students can readily identify, or it might mean demonstrating how students can learn successfully at the level of abstraction at which the instructor is teaching the material. One economics professor, after explaining a series of supply and demand curves, responded to a student's request for real-world examples by saying, "But this *is* the real world. Let me show you what I see when I look at these curves . . ."—not necessarily giving students what they thought they needed, but helping align their expectations for learning by giving them different ways to think about the challenge they perceived.

At times it can be difficult for instructors to identify these challenges because they are teaching ideas that they have already learned successfully, perhaps even easily grasped. In some cases it may be difficult for instructors to remember what it was like *not* to know the content of their courses, making it all the more difficult to identify challenges for learners. Brookfield (1995) identified this challenge for instructors when he observed that the "best learners . . . often make the worst teachers. They are, in a very real sense, perceptually challenged. They cannot imagine what it must be like to struggle to learn something that comes so naturally to them" (p. 62).

When University of Washington mathematics faculty revised their calculus sequence, one challenge they observed was that students often did not have realistic expectations for the demands of college-level calculus. As the faculty worked to revise and assess the curriculum (Perkins & Freisem, 2003), they identified common student misperceptions about learning calculus, then outlined what was typically required for students to succeed in a calculus course. To help address these common misperceptions and align student expectations, faculty developed "A Note to Students" (outlined in Table 3.8) and posted it on the department web site so that each instructor could easily refer to it in class and link it to his or her course web page.

Table 3.8

Outline for the Department of Mathematics "Note to Students"

A Note to Math 124 Students from the Department of Mathematics

---

Welcome to Math 124. This is an introductory course in calculus.

What makes this course interesting?

What makes this course difficult?

Five common misconceptions

- Theory is irrelevant and the lectures should be aimed just at showing you how to do the problems.
- The purpose of the classes and assignments is to prepare the student for the exams.
- It is the teacher's job to cover the material.
- Since you are supposed to be learning from the book, there's no need to go to the lectures.
- Since I did well in math, even calculus, in high school, I'll have no trouble with math at UW.

How do I succeed?

What is the course format?

What resources are available to help me succeed?

Note. For the full text, see http://www.math.washington.edu/~m124/math124student note.html

These efforts to anticipate challenges help demonstrate to the students that the instructor wants to help them succeed, not by making course content somehow less rigorous, but by more explicitly preparing them to negotiate obstacles to learning. It is one more way to maintain alignment by communicating to students expectations for learning the content of the course, the instructor's desire to see them learn, and the efforts required in order to learn.

Conclusion

"Teaching as though there are students in the room" is a continuous balancing act, and a well-designed course helps facilitate this balance from one day to the next as the course proceeds. Carefully considered, the guiding questions presented throughout this chapter can lay the groundwork for the day-to-day work of alignment that students and the instructor undertake together throughout the course.

Endnote

1) Oddly, one rarely hears, "I tried lecturing once, but students didn't like it, so now I'm doing something else."

References

Angelo, T. A., & Cross, K. P. (1993). *Classroom assessment techniques: A handbook for college teachers* (2nd ed.). San Francisco, CA: Jossey-Bass.

Barr, R. B., & Tagg, J. (1995, November/December). From teaching to learning—a new paradigm for undergraduate education. *Change, 27*(6), 12–25.

Beyer, C. H., & Fisher, A. T. (2002). *What do your professors do that leads you to think they care about your learning?* Retrieved November 30, 2004, from the University of Washington Study of Undergraduate Learning, Office of Educational Assessment web site: http://www.washington.edu/oea/0209.pdf

Brookfield, S. D. (1995). *Becoming a critically reflective teacher.* San Francisco, CA: Jossey-Bass.

Carson, B. H. (1999). Bad news in the service of good teaching: Students remember ineffective professors. *Journal on Excellence in College Teaching, 10*(1), 91–105.

McManus, D. A. (2002). *Changing a course from lecture format to cooperative learning.* Retrieved November 30, 2004, from the University of Washington, Center for Instructional Development and Research web site: http://depts.washington.edu/cidrweb/CooperativeLearning.html

Perkins, P. T., & Freisem, K. (2003, June). *Multiple sources of data to assess changes in curriculum and structure of first-year calculus.* Paper presented at the American Association for Higher Education Assessment Conference, Seattle, WA.

Wineburg, S. (2003, April 11). Teaching the mind good habits. *Chronicle of Higher Education,* p. B20.

4

Using Assessment in Support of Alignment

Wayne H. Jacobson & Karen Freisem

Many instructors have experienced the challenge of assessment when asked to provide evidence for effects of their teaching, only to realize that no single assessment adequately portrays what they observed in class from one day to the next. Others have observed that the class was not going as expected but did not know how to assess what might be causing the problem or what might improve the situation. Alignment helps instructors meet challenges like these by focusing assessment on each component of alignment and on the interactions among them over time, helping instructors assess more strategically the dynamic complexity of teaching and learning.

From the alignment perspective, it's not surprising that instructors may find it difficult to assess the effectiveness of their teaching. Effectiveness is not a matter of finding a "right way" to teach that can be expected to work the same in every situation. Rather, effectiveness rests on choosing a course of action, monitoring its effects, and continuing or adapting it based on the effects observed. However, effects of teaching are not always immediately visible or uniform across a group of students. Because of the inevitable challenges of assessing the effects of teaching, many have agreed that assessment is most meaningful when it is based on evidence from multiple perspectives, at different points in time (Braskamp & Ory, 1994; Lewis, 2001; Nyquist & Wulff, 1996). This chapter will show that different perspectives on teaching offer unique insights to alignment and provide evidence to help instructors address issues of misalignment in perceptions, expectations, and outcomes. Figure 4.1 identifies different perspectives on teaching to consider for this purpose.

Figure 4.1

Perspectives on Assessment of Teaching

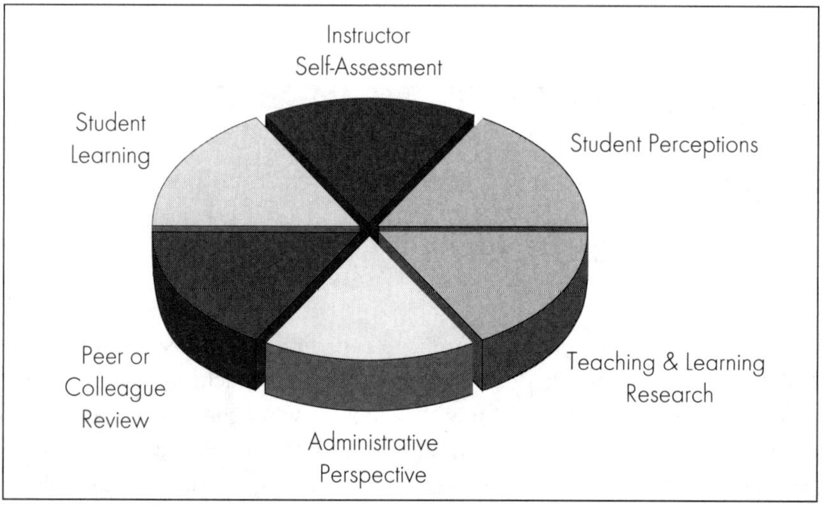

Note. Adapted from Nyquist and Wulff (1996).

After briefly identifying how each perspective can contribute to alignment, this chapter provides three case studies showing how multiple perspectives taken together provide more accurate and meaningful assessment than any one perspective by itself would have been able to provide.

For this chapter, the process of *assessment* refers to gathering data for the purpose of making claims about outcomes. It is to be distinguished from the process of *evaluation,* gathering data for the purpose of making claims about quality. In this sense, assessment is the broader term, since documenting outcomes does not necessarily imply making value judgments about them. However, judgments about quality are most solid when based on accurate information. Assessment and evaluation may in fact use similar means of data collection and analysis, but they lead to different ends. Chapters 5 and 15 will examine issues of evaluation at greater length.

Student Learning

The first perspective to consider is student learning. The student learning perspective is most useful for aligning student expectations with an instructor's goals for teaching and with the demands of course content. If students are not learning as expected, then instructors may need to align students with course content by addressing expectations for what students should be doing in the course. Instructors may also examine goals, assignments, and ways of teaching in terms of how well each is aligned with course content and student expectations. In either case, student learning becomes a source of data for assessing teaching (rather than only for evaluation of students) that can inform instructor efforts to teach more effectively.

To assess what students have learned in a course, an instructor needs to account for students' prior learning. Most instructors start a course with some assumption of what students know about the content of the course, based (accurately or not) on course prerequisites or on the presumed interest levels of students who select the course. However, practices vary greatly regarding the extent to which these assumptions are tested or documented, and the range of prior knowledge and preparation for a course may also vary greatly across a group of students. Efforts to account for students' prior knowledge will provide a more certain basis on which to start the course and a useful point of reference for comparing students' apparent learning at later points in the course.

To identify learning that occurs as a result of teaching, instructors also need to state their goals in assessable terms (as discussed in Chapter 3), and activities and assignments need to be designed in alignment with these goals. Learning may be primarily accumulation of knowledge, but it also may include a change of perspectives, acquisition of skills, or greater depth of understanding, to name just a few—and each can be documented through a variety of measures such as pretests, reflective writing, and surveys, as well as through assignments, projects, and tests that are designed into the course. If an instructor has a reliable sense of students' starting points in the areas they are addressing, then the learning gains that are identified can be an important source of data for assessing the effects of teaching in each of these areas.

Instructor Self-Assessment

A second, distinct perspective for assessment is the instructor's self-assessment. By documenting ongoing self-assessments, instructors are better prepared to align their own perceptions of teaching and learning with stated goals and with student performance and expectations. Noting how students respond to a class activity may help shed light on students' later work that is based on that activity, for example, or may help the instructor to align the activity with content and students in future courses, if a similar activity is used.

There are limits to how much instructors can assess their own practices, although Schön (1987) has argued that this sort of reflection-in-action is a central feature of a professional's expertise. Few things contribute more to the effectiveness of a class session than the instructor's in-the-moment decisions about best ways to proceed, and it would be difficult to gain access to these decision processes from any other source than the instructor. However, due to how much an instructor has to be aware of and the selectiveness of memory, instructors also need to find ways to document their perceptions so those perceptions are available for reflection and systematic consideration together with other sources of alignment data.

Some instructors have been successful in documenting their decision-making by maintaining a teaching journal, which provides a log of the course and their perceptions over time. Others report greater success accomplishing this same goal by maintaining an email conversation with an interested colleague (who provides a more active audience than an individual's journal can provide). Still others use a sticky note model, placing reminders in their class notes for a given day so that when they reach that portion of the course in the future, memories of their immediate reflections and observations can be more accurately remembered. For many instructors, a teaching portfolio can become the collection point for these various forms of instructor self-assessment and reflections on activities and materials that have been used.

These instructor self-assessments are by no means a comprehensive assessment of teaching, but they can provide a distinct and complementary perspective when combined with data on student learning gains or data of other types described in this chapter.

Peer or Colleague Review

A third perspective for assessment of teaching is the perception of peers or colleagues who know the same subject matter and perhaps have taught the same course or the same group of students. Peers and colleagues offer additional insights on an instructor's teaching, observing and identifying issues that the instructor might not be able to focus on while engaging in all the other activities of teaching. These observations of peers and colleagues are a unique source of insight for aligning instructor expectations with the content of the course and the broader context into which it fits.

Some have pointed out limitations of using peer review for evaluative purposes, such as a formal promotion file, since faculty may hesitate to provide constructive feedback to colleagues that might appear to signal a problem to someone reviewing the file at another time. This limitation is less of a problem when peer review is used as only one part of a more comprehensive assessment portfolio that also includes information from a variety of other sources, including the instructor being evaluated. Independent of its uses for formal review, however, informal peer review as a source of assessment between colleagues provides a unique perspective on teaching and can be an important component in the overall assessment of an instructor's teaching.

Student Perceptions

A fourth perspective for assessment comes from student perceptions of their experience in a course—that is, as distinct from student learning gains. Students typically are not experts in the subject matter or on teaching effectiveness. As a result, they will not see things in the same way as the instructor or the instructor's peers and colleagues. There is also some limitation on viewing students as a source of data for identifying their own learning; they may have learned but may not fully appreciate what they have learned or know what value to assign to it. However, students are uniquely qualified to comment on their experience in a course, and gaining a better understanding of student perceptions can help an instructor align his or her own understandings with students' perceptions of what seems to be going well for them, what obstacles they are encountering in their efforts to learn, and how and why they are responding in the ways that they do during class.

For example, many instructors have found it helpful to make use of the Small Group Instructional Diagnosis (SGID), or similar forms of midterm formative student feedback. In the SGID process, students are asked to identify what is helping them learn in a course and what suggestions for change the students would like to make. Student perceptions are collected by a third party (in order to allow students to remain anonymous) and reported to the instructor. At times the instructor may respond to students by making changes they identified, but at other times the instructor may choose to address student perceptions by discussing with students why the changes they identified won't be made. In either case, this midterm student feedback creates an opportunity for greater instructor-student alignment by making these perceptions and expectations explicit so they can be acted upon.

Other instructors have gained similar benefits by using Classroom Assessment Techniques (Angelo & Cross, 1993) on a regular basis. These techniques contribute to alignment by providing frequent checks on student understanding and perceptions, thus allowing instructors to make adjustments or address misperceptions in their immediate context rather than, for example, finding out after a test that students had an inaccurate understanding of what they were expected to know.

Another well-known (and much debated) source of student perceptions data is the use of end-of-course student ratings. The form these ratings take and their intended uses vary greatly from one institution to another, but it is safe to say that they are an increasingly common feature of most institutions of higher education. As one colleague has said, "They're not going away" (A. Linse, personal communication, April 2004). Student ratings are discussed at greater length in Chapter 5, but at this point it is important to note that they are a source of student perceptions data that, alongside other sources of data, can contribute to an instructor's efforts to align students and content when the instructor is planning for future courses.

Administrative Perspective

An administrator who is assessing teaching may draw on any or all of these sources of data and also has an administrative perspective that becomes a fifth source of data. The broader perspective an administrator contributes can provide data for aligning an instructor's teaching in a particular course with the larger context in which it occurs. For example, while an instructor and a given group of students focus on the single course they are experiencing, an administrator considers how the course fits within a broader curriculum, how this instructor's teaching practices fit into a broader faculty career, and how the learning experiences of these students contribute to their longer-term experience within the department. For this reason, an administrator will consider assessment of individual courses and also their integration into a broader curriculum. In addition to surveys of student perceptions at the end of a course, an administrator also will be interested in exit interviews with graduating students to learn their perceptions of an entire program. Rather than considering only student grades, an administrator will be interested in a portfolio of student learning outcomes that demonstrates the knowledge and skills students are developing or taking with them as they leave the program. For instructors, this administrative perspective is an important source of data for aligning themselves and their course content with the larger contexts of the department and the institution in which they are teaching.

Teaching and Learning Research

Teaching and learning research provides another perspective for assessment that can play an important role in alignment. For many instructors, evidence of the effects of their teaching will not always be readily definable during the time that they have opportunity to gather data from students. For instance, one key indicator of learning might be relative success in a subsequent course. Other effects may not be clear until students have completed their degrees or have gained a certain amount of professional experience.

For example, a number of studies have looked at attrition from science and engineering majors, in particular for students traditionally underrepresented in these majors. Among the findings, investigators determined that certain types of classroom experiences influence students' decisions to remain in the major. However, there are very few claims that instructors can make about long-term retention in the major based solely on the data they can collect from their current students. For instructors whose goal is to make their classes more inclusive, one option for assessment could be to indicate how teaching practices that have been shown to encourage retention are designed into the course, demonstrating that "research on teaching and learning tells us 'x' is important . . ." and "my practices are consistent with 'x.'" This research perspective can provide important data for aligning an instructor's plans for a course with the context of current issues and emerging questions in the discipline or in higher education more generally.

Resources for instructors who want to identify research relevant to their teaching might include their campus teaching and learning centers and their own professional organizations, many of which have divisions, interest groups, or listservs dedicated to teaching and learning issues. Subject specialists in campus libraries can also provide a wealth of information on these topics, making the task much more manageable for instructors. Offices of institutional research or minority affairs, development offices, and accreditation review committees may also have relevant data; for example, what are employers of our department's graduates saying? What are alumni saying in 5-year- or 10-year-out surveys? Being able to say "this is what our graduates tell us they need," and "this is what my class provides" can be a useful (and strategic) approach to assessment that students themselves might lack the perspective to offer at the time they are in the class.

Another form of assessment from the research perspective is the instructor's own scholarship of teaching and learning, as discussed in Chapter 14. An instructor may want to confirm or expand on self-assessments or other observations by posing a question and collecting data systematically; for example, not simply "How did students do on the assignment?" but "How did changing the assignment parameters affect student performance, compared to that of previous groups of students?" The classroom can be a place of enquiry where instructors can use findings that emerge to support their efforts to align themselves, students, and the content of the course.

Cases of Assessment in Support of Alignment

Much has been written about assessment based on each of the perspectives represented here. What we add here for the purposes of alignment is the importance of integrating data from multiple perspectives. The three cases that follow illustrate situations in which data taken from any single perspective could have led to a very different understanding of the situation, making it much more difficult to foster alignment, or perhaps even creating misalignment, in each of the cases.

Case 1: Effects of Curriculum Change

When the University of Washington Department of Mathematics took steps to revise its calculus sequence (as noted in Chapter 3), the department also developed a composite assessment plan that included data from multiple sources, gathered at different points in time (Department of Mathematics, 2003; Perkins & Freisem, 2003). Changes included class size, length of class periods, textbook, and the structure of review sessions with TAs. Because changes were instituted within the same window of time, the department recognized that no single measure would provide an adequate assessment of the effects of these changes.

Once the department initiated program changes, it began tracking student perceptions of specific changes by adding customized questions to end-of-term student ratings and instituting a midterm student feedback session (the SGID) for each section of calculus. Data were reported confidentially to each instructor and compiled across sections for issues that were related more to the structure of the course than to the individual instructor for each section. These data gave administrators a way to track how ongoing changes affected student perceptions, over time and across sections, and also provided individual instructors with ways to analyze their own feedback within the context of the course as a whole. Instructors could immediately see, for example, that all students appreciated being in a smaller class. They also saw areas where they needed to address student perceptions that differed from theirs. Through this student perception data, the department was able to identify, address, and monitor student perceptions of the issues—thus moving students, instructor, and content toward alignment.

In addition to student perceptions, the department used other assessment measures to help identify instructional components that were out of alignment. To monitor student learning, administrators analyzed course pass rates and also assessed students' demonstrated problem-solving skills in the context of homework and in-class assignments. These data provided instructors with information for continued improvement of course materials—crucial in aligning students with content. To create a forum for group reflection, problem solving, and self-assessment, the department also instituted regular meetings of calculus instructors and weekly workshops for graduate teaching assistants new to teaching the course. These meetings were useful in aligning the instructors with themselves, a necessary step before instructors could align themselves with students and content in the context of the course.

In addition, administrators sought feedback from client departments on how the revised calculus sequence was serving them. They found that, in general, client departments believed that calculus served their needs, that students in client departments complained less about math, and that the departments appreciated the opportunity for interaction with the math department. Gathering this perspective helped the department view the course in the broader context—and this helped the department become better aligned with client departments. Finally, more informal assessment data also provided a more complete picture, in that administrators reported favorable feedback from faculty on their experiences teaching the course, a wider range of faculty interested in teaching the course, and the relative absence of complaints from students (compared with the number of complaints before changes were instituted)—data that indicated better alignment among students, instructors, and content.

What was gained by this composite assessment? The many different perspectives have given the department a broad picture of how the course revisions have affected student learning and perceptions. If the department had chosen to use only student perception data, there would not be enough specific data to target changes in materials and methods. If the department had chosen only to use instructor perceptions, then administrators would not have benefited from students' perspectives on the effects of the changes. If the department had only chosen to assess the course as a whole and not gather data about individual sections, it would not have been possible to determine which student perceptions were course-based and which were instructor-based. In addition, because the department has published annual progress reports on the web, there is increased visibility in the university community of the curriculum revisions and the effort invested by the department. From an alignment perspective, we can see that this curriculum revision project, in its design and implementation, included a composite assessment plan that informed the department efforts toward balancing instructional components—students, instructor, and content—to achieve learning goals. The alignment perspective would also tell us that, even after the trial period for the curriculum changes, balancing components in individual courses will be ongoing.

Case 2: Effects of Innovative Teaching Practices

One instructor chose to change her teaching based on her understanding of teaching and learning research. In a field where male students outnumber female students, this instructor wanted to learn if changes in her entry-level large lecture course might help create a better learning experience for the female students. Research suggested that changing the traditional large lecture format to include opportunities for peer instruction, self-assessment, and more open-ended discussions would make the class more welcoming and engaging for the women students. As she incorporated these changes into her teaching, she used a variety of classroom assessment techniques to document student responses to the alternate activities and also tracked student learning gains in relation to these activities. She recorded her own observations that students who had previously appeared disengaged and rarely participated (both male and female) now appeared to be more active and also appeared to have a better understanding of the concepts she was introducing. From these perspectives, the changes appeared to be fostering achievement of the goals she had originally set, and research would suggest that students in her class would be more likely to explore further classes in the discipline based on this experience.

However, even as the instructor noted these changes in one group of students, she also observed increasing dissatisfaction among another group of students. Although the first group of students appeared to appreciate her new approaches, the students who had traditionally done well in the large lecture survey course did not appear to be invested in the new activities, and they frequently complained that the activities were "a waste of time." Student ratings at the end of the course were bimodal, with one group strongly appreciating the changes she had made in the course, and another group expressing strong dissatisfaction.

What did she gain from these multiple sources of assessment? First of all, if she chooses to use similar alternative activities in a future offering of the course, she will be better prepared to align student perceptions with the purposes of approaching course content in this way—for example, noting that collaboration and communication are not simply things she likes to impose on students when she teaches, but are valuable academic and professional learning goals for all students, including those who might express preferences for individualized learning in a traditional lecture format. Similarly, she can make this learning more visible to students by noting successes on collaborative projects that demonstrate that students have acquired valued skills through collaborative work. Her assessments also gave her a clearer picture of the cross-section of student perceptions in the course, revealing the extent to which an individual comment represented a larger group of students or just that individual. This insight enabled her to align herself more effectively with students. More comprehensive assessment did not remove the diversity of student learning preferences and previous experiences, but it did allow her to be more strategic in her decisions about aligning herself with the students and aligning students with the course content.

Case 3: Effects of Considering the Context

One department had an introductory course for students newly admitted to its major. This course had been notoriously difficult to teach. Students found the class difficult, and faculty disliked teaching it. Even faculty members who were well-known for teaching effectively reported high levels of student dissatisfaction in the course and received atypically low ratings from students when they taught it.

One summer term, the department assigned this course to an adjunct instructor who was teaching at the university for the first time. A new instructor may expect to encounter challenges in any course, and an especially difficult time in a course that more experienced instructors had found challenging to teach. However, in this particular quarter, it was noted that students were performing well on assignments and tests, and there was a higher quality of participation in the course. A midterm assessment of student perceptions revealed a high level of student satisfaction with the course and with the instructor, and end-of-quarter student ratings were consistent with the midterm assessment. Student performance remained high, and students as a group received relatively high grades in comparison with comparable groups of students in previous offerings of the course. The instructor himself reported a positive experience teaching the course and had a generally good impression of students in the course. These various forms of assessment individually and together indicated a course that appeared to be well-aligned with respect to students, instructor, and course content.

However, the instructor teaching the subsequent course in the sequence during fall term began to observe that students who took the prerequisite course during the summer had a distinctly different preparation for the course than students who had taken it earlier. The fall term instructor's questions prompted him to review the summer syllabus, and he discovered that the summer term instructor had taught roughly three-fourths of the material assigned to the course. When asked about this, the summer-term instructor responded that because he didn't think he would have enough time for the full set of topics, he chose to drop the final one-fourth of the material and go into greater depth with the remaining topics. The instructor and students reported satisfaction with this approach, and documented learning outcomes suggested that students had learned the material satisfactorily. From an administrative perspective, however, the instructor's decision presented the department with the dilemma of a group of students who lacked a significant chunk of information that courses for the remainder of the program used as a foundation.

The administrative perspective on this assessment could lead to a variety of outcomes. Apart from the immediate need to help the summer term students more fully prepare for subsequent courses, one possible outcome might be to realign the amount and type of course content with the backgrounds and abilities of newly admitted students taking their first course in the major. Until that sort of change could be made, or if for other reasons the curriculum couldn't be changed, this experience could also provide insights for the administration to pass along to future instructors. With this information, instructors would be better able to identify in advance the challenges their students would likely have in the course, helping them align both themselves and the students with the content they will be studying. In this case, the assessment did not provide a single answer, but the case demonstrates how any single perspective—the instructor's, student learning, student perceptions, or colleague review—would have been incomplete apart from the administrative perspective on the course.

Conclusions

Alignment is a continual balancing act, accounting for multiple perspectives and interpretations influencing the balance, based on a steady supply of reliable information and ongoing reflection-in-action as balances shift from one point in time to the next. The cases in this chapter illustrate briefly that although alignment cannot be simply or easily assessed, assessment is vitally important nevertheless. Assessment helps inform and prepare the instructor for dealing with the inevitable complexity of the classroom. In light of this complexity, we suggest three important implications for using assessment in support of alignment.

Because Assessment From Any Perspective Is Limited, Seek Assessment Data From More Than One Perspective

Though any single source of data may be accurate as far as it goes, no single perspective can provide a comprehensive assessment that accounts for all the dimensions of alignment.

Because of the Complexity of Alignment, Seek Assessment Data That Shed Light on More Than One Component of Alignment or on the Intersection of These Components

Identifying student learning gains tells the instructor something different from student perceptions of a course, but both look at alignment from the position of students; peer or colleague review provides a distinct perspective from an instructor's self-assessment, but both look at alignment from the vantage point of an instructor. Assessment practices will provide greater support for alignment if they account for more than one of these perspectives or the intersection of different perspectives. Thus, an observer who also interviews students can provide a more informative assessment than an observer with only his or her own perceptions from observing; looking at student learning gains in comparison with students' prior knowledge will be more useful if learning is examined in alignment with the larger contexts of what students are expected to learn by the time they complete the program or enter the profession.

Because Alignment Is Never Fixed or Final, Seek Out Assessment Data on an Ongoing Basis

Any assessment is at best a snapshot of alignment at a particular point in time. As a course proceeds, new content is introduced, students learn more, and instructors ask students to do more with what they have learned. It is always a risk to make decisions about next week's class based on last month's assessment.

References

Angelo, T. A., & Cross, K. P. (1993). *Classroom assessment techniques: A handbook for college teachers* (2nd ed.). San Francisco, CA: Jossey-Bass.

Braskamp, L. A., & Ory, J. C. (1994). *Assessing faculty work: Enhancing individual and institutional performance.* San Francisco, CA: Jossey-Bass.

Department of Mathematics, University of Washington. (2003). *Math 124/5 calculus reform: Summary report for 2002–2003.* Retrieved December 2, 2004, from http://www.math.washington.edu/~m124/Reports/report _summer03_finalversion.html

Lewis, K. G. (2001). *New directions for teaching and learning: No. 87. Techniques and strategies for interpreting student evaluations.* San Francisco, CA: Jossey-Bass.

Nyquist, J. D., & Wulff, D. H. (1996). *Working effectively with graduate students.* Thousand Oaks, CA: Sage.

Perkins, P. T., & Freisem, K. (2003). *Multiple sources of data to assess changes in curriculum and structure of first-year calculus.* Paper presented at the American Association for Higher Education Assessment Conference, Seattle, WA.

Schön, D. A. (1987). *Educating the reflective practitioner.* San Francisco, CA: Jossey-Bass.

5

Aligning Evaluation Practices

Wayne H. Jacobson & Margaret Lawrence

Both evaluation and assessment make important contributions to alignment, and both are most useful when based on evidence from multiple perspectives, at multiple points in time. However, while the terms are often used interchangeably, there are important distinctions in purpose between assessment and evaluation that make it useful to examine each separately. To review, for the purposes of this volume, the process of *evaluation* refers to gathering data in order to make claims about quality. It is distinct from the process of *assessment,* gathering data for the purpose of making claims about outcomes.

Since a primary purpose of assessment is to provide information about outcomes, assessment can be valuable to an audience as small as the one conducting the assessment, solely for the purposes of helping that person make better-informed decisions. The purpose of evaluation, however, is to make summary statements about quality, usually for a more public audience, and often for the purposes of making decisions that directly affect the program or person under evaluation.

As discussed in Chapter 4, the more thorough the assessment, the more useful it is for supporting alignment, but even a partial assessment can be helpful. For evaluation, however, the limitations of the data are a central factor in considering the parameters of the decisions the data can support. For example, if the goal is to help an instructor improve his or her teaching, one place to start is to review student feedback to learn students' perceptions of the instructor. This information might help the instructor to view his or her teaching from a different perspective and identify areas for improvement. But this same information would be insufficient for such broader purposes as deciding whether the instructor should continue teaching in the department.

Lastly, by definition, evaluation communicates values. Assessment tends to be more exploratory, and the value it communicates most strongly is that information is useful for making decisions. Evaluation, however, defines goals—to achieve a passing grade, promotion, tenure, or accreditation, for example—and these goals shape people's efforts to achieve them. Evaluation criteria carry the message of "what counts" more than any other statement of expressed values. For these reasons, evaluation raises additional alignment issues, and the alignment perspective provides a framework for ethical, effective evaluation.

Values of Evaluation

From an alignment perspective, the values communicated by an evaluation present an important set of questions: What is valued, by whom, for what purposes? Instructors communicate what they value in a course by articulating learning goals, shaping the course to help students achieve those goals, and assessing student learning in relation to them. But to what extent are goals, activities, and assessment aligned with departmental goals for the course? To what extent are they in alignment with the broader contexts of the profession or the social context in which it is situated? To what extent are students in alignment with the instructor and with these broader contexts?

Each may evaluate a course differently. Instructors assign grades reflecting the value they assign to students' demonstrated learning. At the same time, they evaluate their experience teaching the course, asking: Will they teach it again? What might they do differently next time? Were the assignments worth the time and effort? Students communicate their evaluation of a course in their ratings at the end of a course, as well as by taking further courses in a department or with a particular instructor. A department's evaluation of a course might include decisions about adapting or retaining the curriculum or about which instructors to teach it. Though each of these purposes is in some way "evaluating a course," the form the evaluation takes and the evidence necessary in each case may vary greatly for these distinct instructor, student, content, and contextual purposes.

Different stakeholders often have compatible purposes and values, so that what the instructor wants is consistent with what the department wants for its students, and both are consistent with what students are expecting when they choose a course in the department. However, this consistency is not always the case: students often express frustration when they perceive that testing and grading practices are not consistent with ways that the course has been taught. Instructors also express frustration when they are asked to make teaching improvement a high priority, but promotion or tenure decisions appear to depend solely on research productivity.

Therefore, although evaluation should account for who values what and why, evidence suggests that people do not always undertake or represent evaluation in ways that account for this complexity. This chapter presents alignment as a framework for identifying four distinct perspectives on evaluation (see Table 5.1), and the points at which values from each perspective might converge or diverge. Learning, the fifth component of the alignment model, is also integral to understanding evaluation; ultimately, the ways in which each perspective considers learning will determine what each looks for in evaluation. In this chapter, we explore the implications of this framework by focusing on two common evaluative activities: grading and student ratings of instructors.

Table 5.1
Evaluation Questions Raised by the Alignment Model

- What does the evaluation mean to instructors?
- What does the evaluation mean to students?
- What does the evaluation mean for this content?
- What does the evaluation mean in this context?

Evaluating: The Case of Grading

We propose that most of us want grades to tell us something about what students have learned in a course. More precisely, we expect grades to tell us something about the extent to which instructors are satisfied with student performance on assessments administered as part of their course, and we expect that grades will be a reasonable representation of what students learned in the course as a whole. We may prefer to have a little more certainty about the meaning of grades than this formulation implies, but Walvoord and Anderson (1998) reminded us that "there is no such thing as an absolutely objective evaluation based on an immutable standard" (p. 11). In the absence of such certainty, we ask instead what grades mean to instructors and to students, for these purposes, in this context.

What Do Grades Mean to Instructors?

Through their grading practices, instructors identify what it is they want students to learn. In reality, they are identifying what they can objectively measure or make defensible judgments about. As mentioned earlier, one of the first alignment issues that arises is the extent to which objectives implied by grading criteria are consistent with objectives identified elsewhere on the syllabus, for example, or during class meetings. Similarly, as shown in one of the cases in Chapter 4, an instructor's stated messages about objectives can be consistent with grading practices and with students' expectations, but out of alignment with departmental objectives for a course.

Instructors sometimes regard grading criteria as representing their standards, suggesting something about the academic rigor of a course. If grades were solely about student learning, a course would be a great success if all students received grades of 100%, but that pattern would most likely be greeted with skepticism rather than with teaching awards. Instructors whose grades are consistently different (higher or lower) from those of department colleagues' might well expect others to raise questions: "If we are teaching the same cohort of students, why is it that they all seem to do so much better (or worse) when you teach them?" There is clearly more than one way to answer this question, but grades alone would not be sufficient support for an answer. To know what an instructor's grades represent, and to determine the extent to which the instructor's standards and practices are in alignment with the rest of the department's, we would have to examine student work, performance measures, grading practices, and students' knowledge base at the beginning of the course. Before we can know what an instructor's grading practices say about expectation for students, we would have to account for these other factors as well.

What Do Grades Mean to Students?

Students may see grades the same way their instructors do, but they often see them in other ways as well. For most students, grades represent shorthand for "how well the instructor thinks I am learning," and while instructors sometimes express frustration that students only seem to care about grades, we propose that many students use grades as the primary source of feedback on their learning. Student decisions about whether or not to study differently, seek help, or continue in a program or major are made on the basis of grades more often than they are on the basis of a self-defined assessment of their own progress as learners. If instructors want to align students' understanding of learning so that the students may see it in different terms, they can provide more frequent feedback of other types that allows students to gain a more complex understanding of their learning. Instructors can also structure opportunities for students to reflect on their learning and develop skills for realistic self-assessment. However, if grading practices are inconsistent with the more complex understanding of their learning that students have gained, most of them will still likely conclude that what matters most is what gets graded.

There is also evidence that students think about grades differently at different points in their academic careers as they become socialized to the expectations of college, and later, to particular departments and majors. Likewise, students in different disciplines may regard grades differently, so that a grade point average in one department might mean something very different from the same grade point average in another. As students move through their academic careers, or take interdisciplinary courses that may be outside their major departments, they often discover that one thing they must learn is how instructors will evaluate them in these different settings.

If an instructor has grading practices that are remarkably different from what students expect, such practices can easily become an obstacle to alignment if the instructor is not careful to make explicit what he or she expects from students. This explicitness is especially important for students who are having to learn in ways that are new for them—for example, moving from an emphasis on recall of discrete facts and formulas to more open-ended design processes or creative work. In these cases especially, the evaluation system is a helpful contributor to learning because it gives students a framework for sorting through the complexity of a task and determining where to focus their efforts.

What Do Grades Mean for This Content?

The content of a course defines the goals with which instructors and students align. Some types of content lend themselves to measurement in discrete, measurable units; others are hard to capture in this way. For example, instructors and students who typically think about learning as an individual effort may find it a challenge to evaluate collaborative projects; instructors and students who are comfortable with traditional lectures may find it difficult to apply evaluation techniques in problem-based learning. In both cases, instructors and students might agree that students have learned a great deal, but it is not a type of learning that can be measured by more traditional forms of evaluating.

Grades in some courses may represent a broader level of mastery in the discipline, while grades in others reflect appropriate incremental progress toward a goal. An "A" in a capstone design course means something very different from an "A" in an introductory survey course. Something as straightforward as use of a grading curve can send mixed messages about students' understanding of the content: If the class average on an exam is 50%, instructors might conclude that students are doing well relative to one another and are learning what is expected at this point in the course. Students may conclude, however, that they have learned only half of what was expected, so something must not be right with what they are doing, what the instructor is doing, or both.

What Do Grades Mean in This Context?

Some contextual values related to grading are strongly institutionalized in admissions standards, regulations regarding academic probation, or means around which grades in a course are expected to be distributed. Other contextually defined values are more subtle: To what extent do students transfer into this major from other departments or institutions—bringing with them a grade point average and set of expectations for evaluation that are already well-established, but in other contexts? Do students in this major tend to apply for graduate or professional school—so that their goals and expectations for grades are based on factors external to the department? These contextual factors set parameters for grading; for example, an instructor cannot usually alter guidelines for admission or academic probation. Sometimes, contextual factors don't directly restrict an instructor's decisions, but accounting for these factors could be necessary for maintaining alignment with student expectations. For example, students who perceive that a course should prepare them for a licensure exam or one of the graduate and professional school admissions tests may be very unsettled by an instructor who doesn't teach or test in ways that appear to value these same goals; instructors who have good reasons to work outside students' expectations should understand that their goal in teaching should include explaining to students why the course is valuable, even though it may not be what many of them expected.

Alignment of Grading Practices

Grading practices can be a great contributor to student learning, but depending on the extent to which instructor and student perspectives are in alignment with one another and with the larger contexts for the course, grading practices can also become an obstacle to learning. We find the alignment model to be a helpful framework for identifying these areas for potential misalignment. Specific strategies for addressing areas of misalignment may vary widely, but the goal is always to bring instructor and student understandings into alignment with one another and with the requirements of the content and the contexts of the course.

In the remainder of this chapter, we propose that the alignment perspective can also provide a useful framework for understanding evaluation when the tables are turned and the instructor is the one being evaluated.

Being Evaluated: The Case of Student Ratings

Like grades, student ratings have a wide range of stakeholders, with a variety of perspectives on and uses for student ratings. Nevertheless, most of us who find ourselves using student ratings want them to tell us something about how effectively an instructor has taught a course. To be more precise, we expect them to tell us students' reported opinions about teaching in response to a series of survey questions asked near the end of the course, and we expect that these opinions will be a reasonable indicator of teaching effectiveness in the course as a whole. We may prefer to have a little more certainty about the meaning of student ratings than this formulation implies, but Centra (1993) has reminded us that "research on student evaluations . . . shows significant tendencies but no certainties" (p. 51). In the absence of such certainty, we must ask instead what student ratings mean to instructors and to students, for these purposes, in this context.

What Do Ratings Mean to Instructors?

There is a wide range of instructor responses to student ratings. At one end of the continuum is a professor who claims his low ratings are a "badge of honor" for holding students to high standards (as one might imagine, this professor was "highly honored" by his students). In fact, studies have found some correlation between student ratings and students' expected grades in a course (Greenwald & Gillmore, 1997). Some have suggested that this correlation shows instructors can improve their ratings simply by increasing students' grades, but it would be difficult to say from this correlation alone that students would rate a class more highly on the basis of low standards for high grades. Ory (2001) has suggested that students who have learned more in a course (thus earning higher grades) are relatively more likely to value the ways that the instructor taught it (thus rating it more highly). In fact, Gillmore (2001) showed that the correlation between overall ratings and the amount of work required for a course was negligible. A much stronger predictor of overall ratings was the ratio between amount of time spent on a course and the amount of that time that students believed was useful for their learning. That is, courses requiring a relatively large amount of time were rated highly provided that the work seemed worthwhile. Overall, students tended to prefer more challenging courses over less challenging ones.

If professors who want to dismiss student ratings can be found at one end of the continuum, at the other end are professors who take them as the definitive measure of their work as instructors. These include professors who put off looking at them for weeks or months because it is truly painful to consider the possibility that not all students saw value in the course; others zero in on particular issues that stand out to them, such as one or two students who responded to most questions negatively, failing to notice that most students rated the class much more positively. Also in this group are professors who summarize their entire teaching experience in a number, as one professor announced in a meeting, "Last quarter was a 3.8."

Researchers who examine student ratings caution against both understating and overstating their value. Those who understate their value would benefit from reviewing the considerable body of research that documents their reliability, validity, and limitations; those who overstate their value would benefit from this same body of research that recommends always evaluating teaching with multiple measures, at multiple points in time, rather than depending on any single measure to fully capture teaching effectiveness.

What Do Ratings Mean to Students?

Like instructors, students also vary in their perception of what student ratings mean. Students in one study (Lawrence & Lenz, 2000) revealed a wide range of opinions about student ratings. Some took the process very seriously and "thought about them all quarter." Others were skeptical about the final impact of ratings because "this kind of form can't give the kind of information I want to give" or "teachers can't change anyway"; some continued to fill them out because "hope is important." Several students made decisions about whether to complete forms at all based on their opinions of the instructor. Some said they filled out forms only if they didn't like the instructor, but others refused to fill them out—in which case, it was noted, the professor "didn't deserve" the student's input.

As part of the same study, 20 students were asked to complete their ratings forms while following a think-aloud protocol, allowing investigators to hear what students were thinking as they completed the forms. One finding of this study was that in many cases, a strongly held impression of their experience in one dimension of the course influenced their responses to a number of different questions; for example, students might explain many of their answers with the same rationale, such as "I'm not getting the big picture"—

suggesting that for these students, the wording of individual questions affected their responses less than an overall impression of the course.

In other cases, students demonstrated a wide range of interpretations for the same question. For example, the item, "Course organization was . . ." generated some predictable comments on how well the course followed the syllabus. However, there were also a large number of less predictable responses. Some students read organization to mean when the class met: "I feel it could have been better organized. Having a class for two hours a day and only two days a week kind of threw my schedule off." Other students interpreted organization as the closeness with which the instructor followed the book. If the instructor skipped around instead of following the order of the chapters, the class was less organized. Still other students rated organization in terms of how well class discussion stayed on track. Six students expressed uncertainty about what "organization" meant or whether one could evaluate it at all: "I'm not really sure what is meant by organization," or "Well it's pretty hard to have a class not organized at college . . . I don't know what an unorganized class would be like." Or "I couldn't think of a 'very good' or 'excellent' rating because organization is one of those things where it either is or isn't poorly organized. I mean it's hard to see degrees in organization."

Interestingly, students always made an evaluative decision even if they felt confused about the item; other times students made decisions based on factors extraneous to the class: "Sometimes when I'm doing these, if I put too many 'excellents,' I think well maybe I shouldn't have so many 'excellents' . . . cause all 'excellents' don't look like I'm thinking very much about it." Others assigned unexpected meanings to the evaluative descriptors: "I'm one of those people if I don't know what I'm doing I'll just, you know, excellent, excellent, excellent, but if it's a real bad class real boring and hard I'd just kinda give him goods you know."

In a second study (Chang, Giurca, & Lawrence, 2003), instructors in a different department asked their administration to review the wording and structure of its customized student ratings forms. In this department, ratings were used to determine merit pay, and instructors believed their non-native English-speaking students might not understand forms in the same ways that administrators or instructors did. With the administrator's approval, a committee of instructors explored student interpretations of key items on the form using focus groups led by an outside facilitator. Initially, students in this second study found some items on the form clear and some confusing, just as students did in the first study. However, additional linguistic and cultural factors sometimes increased student confusion. For example, some of the more surprising interpretations of an item asking about organization included thinking it meant the physical organization of the classroom or the organization of the students. One student said he gave a low rating for organization because he didn't like organization. To him organization meant doing the same thing every day, and he found that boring.

This second study prompted the department to take a series of actions, beginning with refinement of questions used on the ratings form and then a series of additional focus groups until they were confident that they had removed as much ambiguity as possible from the questions. This study also equipped both instructors and administrators with a better understanding of the potential variability in student responses, so that when they interpret student ratings, they will not take them only at face value.

From an alignment perspective, such variation in students' interpretations of student ratings raises many questions. Though some students did read questions on ratings forms in ways similar to what an instructor might expect, it's also clear that not all students read them in this way.

What Do Ratings Mean for This Content?

In addition to this evidence that student ratings can mean different things to instructors and to students, there is also evidence that students rate courses differently based on their experience with the content. At the University of Washington (UW), there is much greater variability in ratings at introductory levels than at advanced levels, for example, or in courses students are required to take than in courses that they choose to take (Office of Educational Assessment [OEA], 1998a)—a discovery that led UW to begin providing statistical adjustments for these factors when ratings are reported.

Students at UW also clearly rate courses in different disciplines differently. Based on a 0–5 scale (with 5 being the highest), instructors in some departments are quite pleased to achieve a rating of 3.5; in other departments anything less than 4.5 is considered embarrassingly low. Does this mean that instruction in some departments is uniformly better than in others? There is clearly more than one way to answer this question, but ratings alone would not be sufficient support for an answer. To provide a basis for knowing what student ratings represent and to determine the extent to which these trends in ratings reflect actual differences in quality from one department to another, we would have to examine classroom practices, student work, performance measures, and students' expectations at the beginning of the course.

One response to disciplinary differences in student ratings has been to look at ratings with respect to different norming groups (OEA, 1998b).

Rather than receiving ratings without any basis for comparison, or comparing them to the ratings of faculty for all other courses, an instructor can compare his or her ratings to those of others teaching in the same department or teaching similar courses in other departments (for example, introductory large enrollment science classes). Norming against courses with comparable content can help separate possible effects of students' responses to the content from their evaluations of the instructor's teaching effectiveness.

What Do Ratings Mean in This Context?

The context of teaching evaluation greatly affects how student ratings are interpreted and represented. Are student ratings used as the primary source of data on teaching effectiveness, or as one among many? Are decisions about the quality of ratings made on the basis of comparisons to others in the department, institutional averages, or trends for an individual instructor? To what extent is student ratings research considered in interpretation and in decisions based on the ratings? This research helps make sense of student ratings, but also identifies other factors that contribute to ratings beyond the individual instructor's teaching effectiveness.

For example, in addition to the disciplinary variation already noted, research has shown that a course tends to be rated lower the first time an instructor teaches it; similarly, a course tends to be rated lower when an instructor first introduces innovative practices or other changes. Without appreciating this greater context of making improvements over time, an instructor or administrator might conclude that an innovative practice should not be repeated (rather than fine tuned and tried again) or that a particular instructor should not be assigned to a course in the future based on a first experience that was not rated highly. If an administrator's goal is to make meaningful decisions on the basis of teaching effectiveness, then it is very important to account for these contextual factors (distinct from teaching effectiveness) that may be influencing the ratings.

Conclusions

It's clear that there are different perspectives on the meaning of an evaluation. Alignment helps identify ways in which these different perspectives might influence interpretations of an evaluation and suggests practical strategies for those who evaluate others or make decisions based on evaluations.

Be Explicit About the Basis for Evaluation

Those who are evaluating need to provide explicit evaluation procedures and criteria, both to give a fair sense of what they expect and to help those who are evaluated structure their efforts and expectations.

Account for the Limitations of Data When Making Decisions

Those who are evaluating need to account for the limitations inherent in any single source of evidence, both to help them avoid overstating conclusions drawn from a single source of evidence and to help identify additional sources of evidence. For example, to make decisions about student learning, instructors might design different types of assignments or tests to address different types of learning (Anderson, 2001), so that grades are not based on any single type of evidence. To make decisions about teaching effectiveness, administrators can identify other elements of a teaching portfolio they will consider with student ratings (Seldin, 1998), to provide a more complete picture of teaching effectiveness than student ratings alone can offer.

Prepare to Align the Perceptions of Those Who Are Being Evaluated

Those who are evaluating may have good intentions and well-designed plans for evaluation but find that others see evaluation plans very differently. For example, students may perceive that "Class meetings didn't prepare us fairly for the test." Faculty may insist that "Student ratings are nothing more than a popularity contest." To help make evaluation a contributor to better alignment rather than an obstacle to it, those who are evaluating should be prepared to respond to these types of perceptions and provide appropriate information about the what, how, and why of their evaluation.

As Part of the Evaluation, Account for What the Evaluation Means (or Doesn't Mean) to the One Being Evaluated

Individuals being evaluated might view what the evaluation means differently than their evaluators. So one strategy might be for them to become interpreters of their own data, rather than assuming that they will interpret the data in the same way as the evaluators. For example, instructors can give students opportunities to comment on what they think their grades mean in office hours, reflective writing, or other self-assessments related to an assignment. Providing these opportunities for students may give an instructor clearer insight on how students see their learning and progress. Such opportunities may prompt students to think more systematically about the work they are doing and how it is contributing to their learning.

Instructors can take similar initiatives when they are being evaluated. In addition to student ratings, an instructor might provide additional data (such as student learning demonstrated in a course or evidence from other sources identified in Chapter 4) or reflective commentary to help guide others in interpreting their ratings. For example, "These student ratings are low compared to the norm, in part because I was trying something new which students in this class struggled with a lot. I see in students' work that they did much better than students in previous years, but that isn't reflected in the student ratings. Here is what I might do differently next time..." Comments such as these provide a more thorough evaluation than ratings alone are able to provide, and also prompt instructors to think more systematically about ways they are teaching and ways they can improve.

References

Anderson, J. (2001, March). Tailoring assessment to student learning styles: A model for diverse populations. *AAHE Bulletin, 53*(7), 3–7.

Centra, J. A. (1993). *Reflective faculty evaluation.* San Francisco, CA: Jossey-Bass.

Chang, C., Giurca, M., & Lawrence, M. E. (2003). *Reworking student evaluation forms in light of diverse contexts.* Paper presented at the annual conference of the Washington Center for Undergraduate Education, Seattle, WA.

Gillmore, G. M. (2001, April). *What student ratings results tell us about academic demands and expectations* (OEA Research Reports 01–02). Retrieved December 3, 2004, from the University of Washington, Office of Educational Assessment web site: http://www.washington.edu/oea/0102.htm

Greenwald, A. G., & Gillmore, G. M. (1997). Grading leniency is a removable contaminant of student ratings. *American Psychologist, 52*(11), 1209–1217.

Lawrence, M. E., & Lenz, L. R. (2000). *Student ratings: What students think.* Paper presented at the annual conference of the Professional and Organizational Development Network in Higher Education, Vancouver, British Columbia.

Office of Educational Assessment, University of Washington. (1998a). *Adjusted medians.* Retrieved December 3, 2004, from http://www.washington .edu/oea/iasadjst.htm

Office of Educational Assessment, University of Washington. (1998b). *IAS norms.* Retrieved December 3, 2004, from http://www.washington.edu/ oea/iasnorms.htm

Ory, J. C. (2001). Faculty thoughts and concerns about student ratings. In K. G. Lewis (Ed.), *New directions for teaching and learning: No. 87. Techniques and strategies for interpreting student evaluations* (pp. 3–15). San Francisco, CA: Jossey-Bass.

Seldin, P. (1998, March). How colleges evaluate teaching: 1988 vs. 1998. *AAHE Bulletin, 50*(7), 3–7.

Walvoord, B. E., & Anderson, V. J. (1998). *Effective grading: A tool for learning and assessment.* San Francisco, CA: Jossey-Bass.

Part III

ALIGNMENT IN SPECIFIC CONTEXTS

6

Aligning in Large Class Instruction

Karen Freisem & Lisa M. Coutu

Imagine that you're observing a large class. You're sitting among students in the back of the lecture hall a few minutes before class begins. So far, about 100 of the 160 students enrolled in the class have taken their seats, and many have retrieved their notebooks and pens from their backpacks and are ready for class. The instructor is standing behind the podium in the front of the class, connecting her laptop and attaching a microphone. You think back to the catalog description of the course. It's an introductory level course intended to provide nonmajors with an overview of the discipline. You know that many students enroll primarily to satisfy distribution requirements, and others enroll because of their interest in the topic. As you look around at the students, you imagine that they represent a variety of backgrounds, knowledge bases, and skills. In addition to the lecture, students meet once a week in a discussion section led by a graduate teaching assistant.

Teaching large classes[1] such as the one described above presents particular challenges to alignment. Because many instructors face these challenges, numerous books, articles, and videos[2] are devoted to the issues involved—and many universities have web sites and programs[3] for faculty teaching large classes. Although the many tips discussed in the literature are useful on their own, the alignment perspective provides instructors with a framework for considering key issues in teaching and learning in large classes and for making decisions about strategies to help students achieve learning outcomes. This chapter explores the additional complexities of teaching in the large class context, identifies key issues in this context, and provides specific strategies for addressing the issues—strategies to align instructors, students, and content of large classes.

The Large Class Context

Let's start by considering how the additional complexities of the large class context can affect the alignment of instructors, students, and content. First, and most important, is the distance in large classes, which poses particular challenges to the interrelationships among the instructional components. The instructor and students are physically removed from each other in a large lecture hall. Because instructors in large classes most often teach broad survey courses—rather than courses in their areas of specialization—we might also describe the instructor and content as distant. In addition, students and content are farther apart because students in large classes are often new to the discipline and thus not experienced with the vocabulary and ways of thinking in the field. So, in the context of a large class, there may be very little overlap at the intersections of instructor, students, and content. A second complexity of the large class context is the imbalance in the relationships among the components. The ratio of students to instructor is much higher than in smaller classes, and there are often multiple instructors or graduate teaching assistants (TAs) involved in teaching large classes. So, in addition to considering ways to align the instructor, students, and content, we also need to account for the interrelationships among the instructors and explore strategies to help align the instructors with each other. Finally, in the large class context instructors need to employ communication strategies more deliberately to address the issues caused by the distance and imbalance.

The Issues

As one reads through the literature on teaching large classes, one finds that the instructional challenges raised mirror the broad categories of communication strategies in the alignment model: rapport, organization, engagement, and interaction. This chapter will examine the application of these four strategies for achieving alignment in large classes. We consider the challenges in closing the distances and countering the imbalance among the components of large classes, and we explore the use of communication strategies to help address these issues. We are hopeful the strategies offered will provide instructors with a range of choices for balancing instructional components to promote student learning in large classes.

Rapport

> *The bell has just rung, and the instructor, looking serious and somewhat ill at ease, is making announcements. A few students enter class late and are talking to each other as they get seated. As the instructor continues, you see other students looking over at those who are talking, and you notice some exasperation in their glances. However, the talking continues on and off through the hour. The instructor occasionally looks towards the noise, but doesn't say anything. When a student asks a question, the instructor listens to the beginning of the question and then interrupts to answer it. You can tell that she has anticipated the question; however, the student who asks the question looks frustrated. Later, the instructor tells you that the talking in the class makes it difficult for her to focus on her teaching, but that she feels it's futile to try to do anything about it.*

In this scenario, we feel tensions in the class atmosphere—a lack of rapport and mutual respect. Instructors of large classes often find it difficult to connect with students; students feel "isolated" (Davis, 1993), the setting is "impersonal" and "anonymous" (McKeachie, 2002), and there's a "heightened sense of personal distance" (Lowman, 1987, p. 72). How might we interpret what's happening in the class described above from the perspective of the alignment model? The students who are talking in class may think the instructor neither hears nor sees them, and may not feel an individual responsibility toward the instructor or toward other students. The students who are bothered by the noise might interpret the instructor's lack of response as indifference. On the other hand, the instructor may interpret the students' behavior as lack of respect for her, and she may not realize that her quick answer to the student's question can communicate a lack of respect for the question and student. These misinterpretations can lead to a lack of rapport. To establish rapport in the large class—and overcome the distance and imbalance of the context—instructors might use the following strategies.

Decide how you can get to know your students as a class. It's often suggested that instructors get to know as many student names as possible. Although this goal is admirable, many instructors find it difficult to achieve and, instead, use ways to get to know the class as a whole. You might, for example, find it helpful to ask students on the first day of class to fill out index cards listing their course goals and previous experience with course content. After looking through the cards and noting themes, you can communicate the themes to the students. Highlight areas that bring together the class as a whole, as well as areas where differing students' needs will impact the way you teach the course. This strategy can show students that you're aware of their varied needs and expectations, thus building rapport.

Find ways to help students see you as a person. Letting students learn about *you* can also help develop rapport. Even in large classes, there are many ways that you can help students to see you as a person. You can talk to students about your personal connection to the course content, and show them your enthusiasm for the subject. You can communicate your interest in helping students learn, and you can talk to them before and after class. If you make a mistake, acknowledge it, correct it, and continue. When students see you as a person, they'll want you to succeed, and will even help you to do so.

Establish the importance of respect in your course. In the large class setting, where frequent informal interaction is more limited than in a small class, promoting an environment of mutual respect takes more direct attention. It's important to explain to students what a respectful environment looks like, to show respect to students, and to expect them to show respect to you and to each other. If you always come to class early and start on time, you communicate respect for the students' time. If you address in-class noise or other distractions immediately, you communicate respect for the students and their

> **Get to Know Your Students as a Class**
>
> "Another way that I try to build rapport is to comment on the uniqueness of the class throughout the quarter. I note when they do something that's different than previous classes—maybe coming up with answers or questions I hadn't expected, or really being successful at completing a particular assignment. This seems to let them know that I've noticed *them* as an identifiable group and that I remember other groups—and may, by extension, also remember them."[4]

> **Help Students See You as a Person**
>
> "On the first day, I tell students that the course is a survey course, so there are some things that I know a lot about and others that I have just general knowledge about. I don't tell them which things fall into each category, but I tell them they'll know when we get to something that I spend my days thinking about in my office (and I usually make a joke that I do this while they're out there having a life!). When I get to areas I do specialize in, I try to let students see my passion about the topics and why I think the material is important for the world. I also communicate my interest in helping students learn by making student learning a theme in the class, talking about it from day one, and then letting them know each time we have an assignment or exam that the TAs and I are there to help them learn the course material."

learning. If you listen fully to a student's question and then paraphrase it for all to hear, you communicate respect for the student and the question—as well as your concern for other students. If you ask students for feedback and respond to it, you communicate respect for students' opinions.

> ### Establish the Importance of Respect
>
> "I do this all explicitly on the first day of class, both orally and in writing (on the syllabus). I have a set of do's and don'ts, and I outline them for the students, telling them that my rules aren't because I'm on some sort of power trip, but because my job is to make sure that people have a good environment in which to learn."

These strategies all help instructors build rapport—a key factor in aligning students with instructors and in aligning students with themselves and with course content. Because establishing a learning environment of respect and rapport is a challenge in a large class, instructors find that planning rapport-building strategies is particularly helpful.

Organization

> *After the announcements, the instructor quickly puts up a slide outlining the day's lecture. She briefly introduces the key points and structure, and then begins with her lecture. Most students are listening and taking notes. As the instructor explains slide after slide, students quickly look up at the screen and at their notes as they write down as much of it as they can. Some students are just listening and not taking notes. The instructor adheres to her outline format, using transitions to help students follow. She appears very well prepared and organized to you. When you talk with her later, the instructor explains that she was happy with her lecture organization until she realized that her structure wasn't reflected in students' notes that she saw. She said students had come to her with questions about the relationships among important concepts in the class. When she saw the students' notes, she could understand why—little of her structure made it into the notes.*

In this class, we see a fairly typical large class situation—an instructor who has carefully prepared and organized a lecture, and students who miss the structure. Large classes raise many such organizational challenges; the number of students adds logistical issues (Brooks, 1987), the need for coordination increases with additional instructors (Civikly-Powell & Wulff, 2002), and the large lecture setting increases the need for clear structure and organization so that students can understand the concepts (Davis, 1993). What, from an alignment perspective, is happening in the class just described? As novices to the discipline, the students might not see the connections among the concepts presented in the lecture. The instructor's outline is probably useful to the students as an advance organizer. However, as the class proceeds, students might not be able to identify the important ideas—perhaps due to the pace and amount of material. As a result, there are two alignment issues: the students are not aligned with the instructor, and they are not aligned with the content. To address these areas of misalignment, instructors can use a variety of strategies.

Find ways to emphasize the organization and structure of a class, and make it explicit to students. In the large class, instructors find that it's particularly important to use organizational strategies—outlines, frameworks, and references to other aspects of the course—to link concepts to concepts and days to days. To give students the opportunity to reflect on what they know and what's coming next, you can begin class with a warm-up problem or a quick review of the previous lecture. You can also write a brief agenda on the board to help focus the class for the students or provide a note-taking outline for students. In addition, because of the complexity of the large class setting, it helps students if you make connections explicit by referring to other aspects of the course. For example, you can clarify how the content of a particular lecture relates to that week's TA section and to assignments.

Work closely with TAs to coordinate lecture and quiz section content so that students see a team of instructors. One of the common issues in stu-

Emphasize Organization and Structure

"Another strategy is to be explicit about how students should take notes in your particular class. I tell students that my lectures, class assignments, and exams are all built around a structure of defining, explaining, and applying course material. That means that students should be taking notes on all three of these things in lecture if they expect to have all three types of material to study for the exams and to complete the assignments. What I often notice is that students only take notes on the definitions, which I write on the overhead, and then put their pencils down while I explain the concept and provide examples. So I stop mid-lecture during the first week of class and tell them they should be taking notes on my explanations and examples. Then I remind them of this consistently throughout the quarter. I also offer to look at anyone's notes to see what kinds of things they might improve on, and I remind them that the TAs are always available for assistance, too. The TAs take notes during class so they can compare their notes to the students' and point to areas for improvement."

dents' perceptions of large classes is the "coordination between lectures and quiz sections/labs"—a perception reflecting the challenge in closing distances in the large class context. Novice students can find it frustrating when their TA solves a problem differently from the instructor, when the TA doesn't appear to know what's happening in lecture, or when the instructor doesn't know what took place in TA section. To align yourself and the TAs, establish clear channels of two-way communication, set clear goals and content for the TA sections, and clarify responsibilities of individuals on the instructional "team," both for yourselves and for the students. You can set up weekly meetings with TAs or communi-

> ### Work Closely With TAs
>
> "I also provide a course-specific TA manual to all TAs. It includes: 1) responsibilities of all course personnel—lead TA, TAs, me; 2) expected time it should take to fulfill responsibilities; 3) grading criteria; 4) articles about leading class discussion; 5) a master syllabus with more detailed information about what I'm going to cover and dates by which assignments should be graded, etc.; 6) class activities for discussion sections (I usually have new TAs, so I try to model for them how to construct activities—rather than have them try to do it on their own); and 7) weekly time sheets—so I can make sure my expectations and their experiences are in line."

cate frequently via email to inform TAs about lecture content and explain how TA sections should relate to lecture. These meetings or emails will also provide you with information about what's happening in sections, how students are learning, and student performance on assignments. You can also visit sections occasionally to interact with students in the smaller, more informal classroom setting. You might even choose to be the instructor of one section so that you can connect better with students and have a clearer understanding of how sections can relate to lecture.

Provide clear structure in advance for assignments and assessment measures. Because there are fewer opportunities for individual questions and more chances for communication to go awry, instructors in the large class find it particularly helpful to clarify—even "overclarify"—their expectations and grading criteria for homework assignments and tests. If the instructor, TAs, and students all have the same information—before students begin an assignment or take a test, and before the instructor and TAs begin their grading—students can more successfully demonstrate their learning, may perceive the grading as more fair, and have fewer questions afterwards. You can use the web for answering common questions and for posting sample test questions and responses. You might also give students a review exam to work on in small groups in TA sections. You could also provide structure for student questions about grading by establishing in advance a process for resolving concerns.

Strategies such as these can help address many of the organizational challenges in the large class context. As instructors and TAs work together to establish clear structures (in the course as a whole, in each class session, and in assignments), to communicate those structures to students, and to reflect on the effectiveness of the structures as the course proceeds, they contribute significantly to alignment among instructors, students, and content.

Engagement

> *Halfway through class, the instructor asks students to apply what they have just learned—what she just lectured on—by analyzing an example. She asks them to jot down some ideas on their own and then compare responses with the person next to them. After three minutes or so, a few students begin discussing the example, but many are sitting back staring into space. When the instructor tries to get students to explain their ideas, only one student responds, while others don't seem to be listening. The instructor later explains to you that her efforts to get the students engaged in the class have, for the most part, failed. She feels that students seem to expect her to lecture the entire class period.*

Here the instructor is trying to engage students in the content, but for most students the approach is unsuccessful. Many authors have written about ways to get student involved in large classes; Davis (1993) discusses how to "capture" and maintain student interest, and Buchanan et al. (2004), Cooper and Robinson (2000), and others describe ways to promote active learning in lectures. How might we interpret what's happening in the scenario above from an alignment perspective? One possibility is that students' expectations of what's going to happen in class differ from the instructor's. Students might think, "Don't ask us to do anything in class. This is supposed to be a lecture." Or it may be that the students are out of alignment with the content. They may not see how the example connects to their "real" lives, or they may not see how what they're asked to do in class relates to what they're asked to do on the assignments and tests. It's also possible that the students aren't aligned with each other. They don't know each other and haven't developed a sense of community, so it's uncomfortable to compare responses, as well as intimidating to speak out in class. The distance and imbalance of the large class context has caused misalignment of instructor, students, and content. To achieve alignment through engaging students in large classes, instructors can use a number of strategies.

Find ways to communicate clear expectations for engagement to students in advance. Make clear on the syllabus and discuss on the first day of class how you expect students to engage with course content; then revisit the topic as the term progresses. Students who enter large classes expecting a lecture format might resist any deviation from that format. If you plan to engage students through in-class activities, tell them so on the first day of class, explain how the activities will help them learn, and describe how the activities will be assessed. If you plan to use examples to engage students, explain how you'll choose examples and how examples will help them learn. If you set up a discussion list, let students know your expectations for online interaction and how you'll assess it (see strategies for online learning in Chapter 13). Whatever means you choose to engage students in the class, make your expectations and rationale explicit, and use the strategy in the first few days of class so that students can practice meeting your expectations and so that you can adjust misunderstandings early.

Choose examples and in-class activities that are relevant to students. In our experience in large classes, we've seen instructors who have carefully planned an in-class activity or used an example only to have the students see it as "useless" and "irrelevant." In the large class, it's essential to make relevance explicit. If you choose to engage students in class by asking them to work in groups, you need to highlight how the type of learning and the content in the activity connect to the kind of thinking expected in the course. If students can see the value, they are more likely to engage with the activity. If you choose to engage students with examples, you can do so by showing an example's relevance to real life or by making explicit its relevance to course content. To find examples that connect with students, you can use information from first-day index cards and then vary examples to reach more students. To show relevance to course content, you can make explicit the relationships between examples and assignments or tests. As students see the relationship of course material to their own lives and to their "lives" in the course, they will be more engaged in the material.

Provide clear structure for activities and monitor student progress. Even with careful planning and framing, an activity intended to engage students can be unproductive. It's important to set a clear task and time frame, and then observe and interact with students during the activity to determine progress. Monitoring student progress allows you to adjust time as necessary and can inform how you choose to "debrief" the activity. The adjustments you make are key to aligning students with you and with the method. If you wait until all groups finish, others might lose focus. On the other hand, if you stop an activity after only a few of the groups have completed the task, the others might feel rushed—and the activity won't be productive. When students feel that the task is clear and that the time allotted is reasonable, they will be able to engage more fully with the content of the activity.

All these strategies can help instructors engage students in large classes. As students become more actively engaged in class, they will be more aligned with each other, with their instructors, and with course content and methods.

Interaction

> *The instructor has just finished a section of her lecture. She pauses and then asks if there are any questions. After a brief, uncomfortable silence, the instructor moves on saying, "Good. You've got it." The class continues on without questions from students. After class, students put their books back into their backpacks and file out of the room. The instructor briefly answers one quick exam-date question, packs up her laptop, and goes back to her office. She tells you later that no one comes to the office hour she holds right after class, and she voices her frustration in trying to provide enough constructive feedback so that students can improve on the assignments.*

Here we see the instructor trying to get students to interact with her, both in class through questions and out of class in office hours, but she's having difficulty getting any response. Books and articles on large classes identify similar challenges; McKeachie (2002) discussed how difficult it is to foster questions and answers in large classes, and Carbone (1998) addressed issues of monitoring student progress and providing feedback on student work. From an alignment perspective, how can we explain what's happening in the class described above? The instructor wants students to ask questions, but students feel little individual responsibility to respond. The instructor interprets their silence as understanding, but the students may still be confused. The instructor wants students to come to office hours, but the students may feel uncomfortable doing so—because they don't know her, and she doesn't know them. These differing perceptions indicate a misalignment of instructor and students. In the large class setting, instructors need to plan, communicate, and implement strategies for interaction to align themselves with students and students with them. The following alignment strategies can help counteract the impersonal nature of the large class and encourage interaction.

Encourage questions in and out of class. Instructors find that there are many ways to encourage questions in large classes. To do so, it's important to let students know in advance that you expect them to ask and answer questions in class, and to give students time to for-mulate questions and responses so that all students—those who need time to think as well as those who might be intimidated in large classes—have the opportunity to interact. If a student asks a question, affirm it, and paraphrase the question before you answer so that all students can benefit from your response. If a question is not relevant to the discus-sion, still affirm it as a good one and tell the student you can discuss it after class or in office hours. You can also encourage students to email you with questions that you'll answer in class— another strategy that allows those students who feel uncomfortable speaking out in class to ask questions. From this give-and-take interaction with students, you can better understand how students are learning in your course and, from that understanding, identify areas of misalignment.

> ### Encourage Questions
>
> "Two other ways I've done this: 1) a 'question box' that I keep in the front of the room so students can anonymously submit questions before or after class; 2) a discussion board where students can ask and answer each other's ques-tions—this board is monitored Monday through Friday by TAs, but the TAs only intervene if the students are off track."

Establish structures for providing and gathering feedback. Instructors find that frequent feedback—both to and from students—is an important step in the alignment process. But how can you do this without being overwhelmed? Make sure criteria are clear, and then, in your feedback, focus comments pri-marily on those criteria. To decrease papers to grade, you can have students work in groups and ask each group to turn in one assignment. You can also use email or find in-class opportunities to provide feedback to the class as a whole. This feedback *to* students helps them understand your expectations for learning. In addition, it's just as important to establish channels for feedback *from* students. Plan a few opportunities during the course to check in with students about their learning. You can gather student perceptions about teaching methods used in the course. You can also use the "minute paper"[5] or a similar strategy to find out what students understand and what they still find confusing. You can also have TAs ask students for feedback about how the TA section is helping them learn. However you decide to get feedback, be systematic in your approach so that responses represent the range of student needs and perceptions, and then consider and respond to the feedback.

Find productive ways to interact with students outside of class. In a large class context, interacting with students outside of class poses a particular challenge, since the potential number of individual meetings or email exchanges can be overwhelming. As a result, you'll want to find ways to balance your own needs and time with students' needs within the context of the course and its content. For example, if you set up an office hour right after class in a public space near the lecture hall, students might feel less intimidated to come with questions, and the group setting for questions and answers is more efficient. Or, you could choose to hold some of your office hours in the department's study center. You can also coordinate with TAs to provide maximum office hours during crucial times of the term. The more one-to-one or small group interactions you and the TAs have with students, the more you'll understand them and they'll understand you.

These strategies for interaction can help instructors discover more about how students are learning in courses and also help students learn more about instructors' expectations. Using what they learn in these interactions, instructors can then make adjustments in courses—adjustments that can bring themselves, their students, and their course content into better alignment.

Conclusion

Alignment that balances the components of instructor, students, and content and that decreases the distance between these components is key to effective teaching and learning in large classes. Instructors who implement strategies to establish rapport with students, communicate strong organization, engage students in course content, and interact with students in and out of class, are well on their way to the kind of alignment that promotes learning. Ultimately, they might find, as Wulff, Nyquist, and Abbott (1987) noted, that effective large classes can, on some dimensions, be just as successful as the best small classes.

Acknowledgment

The authors would like to thank Robert C. Francis, Professor of Aquatic and Fisheries Sciences at the University of Washington, for his input on earlier drafts of this chapter.

Endnotes

1) In much of the literature, "large classes" are defined as classes of 100 or more students (Weimer, 1987). There is some indication that students might consider classes over 75 as "large" (Wulff, Nyquist, & Abbott, 1987).

2) Examples of books on teaching in large classes are Stanley and Porter (2002), Carbone (1998), and Weimer (1987). Books by McKeachie (2002) and Davis (1993) include chapters on large class instruction. There are also numerous articles on the topic, including Buchanan et al. (2004), Litke (1995), and Wulff et al. (1987), and several videos, for example, Schwibs and Hansen (1994).

3) For examples of web sites and programs, see:

   • Pennsylvania State University, Center for Excellence in Learning and Teaching (http://www.psu.edu/celt/largeclass/forum.shtml)

   • University of Maryland, Center for Teaching Excellence (http://www.cte.umd.edu/library/lcn/index.html)

   • University of Washington, Center for Instructional Development and Research (http://depts.washington.edu/cidrweb/LectureTools.htm)

   • UW Collegium on Large Classroom Instruction (http://www.wash ington.edu/oue/academy/collegium.html)

4) Lisa Coutu, second author of this chapter, provided the sidebar comments. For many years, she has taught large-class courses, ranging in size from 200 to 450 students, in communication. She does not claim to be the originator of many of the ideas she offers here. Rather, she considers herself very fortunate to have the resources at the Center for Instructional Development and Research, the Center for Teaching, Learning, and Technology, and her colleagues across the University of Washington to provide her with ideas she could adapt when she has asked, "What can I do about X in my class?"

5) In a "minute paper," you might ask students to answer briefly two questions: "What was the most important thing you learned in class today?" and "What important question remains unanswered?" This strategy and many others are discussed in Angelo and Cross (1993).

References

Angelo, T. A., & Cross, K. P. (1993). *Classroom assessment techniques: A handbook for college teachers* (2nd ed.). San Francisco, CA: Jossey-Bass.

Brooks, R. P. (1987). Dealing with details in a large class. In M. G. Weimer (Ed.), *New directions for teaching and learning: No. 32. Teaching large classes well* (pp. 39–44). San Francisco, CA: Jossey-Bass.

Buchanan, S. A., Reynolds, M. M., Duersch, B. S., Lohr, L. L., Coppola, B. P., Zusho, A., et al. (2004). Promoting student learning in a large general chemistry course. *Journal of College Science Teaching, 33*(7), 12–17.

Carbone, E. (1998). *Teaching large classes: Tools and strategies.* Thousand Oaks, CA: Sage.

Civikly-Powell, J., & Wulff, D. H. (2002). Working with teaching assistants and undergraduate peer facilitators to address the challenges of teaching large classes. In C. A. Stanley & M. E. Porter (Eds.), *Engaging large classes: Strategies and techniques for college faculty* (pp. 109–122). Bolton, MA: Anker.

Cooper, J. L., & Robinson, P. (2000). Getting started: Informal small-group strategies in large classes. In J. MacGregor, J. L. Cooper, K. A. Smith, & P. Robinson (Eds.), *New directions for teaching and learning: No. 81. Strategies for energizing large classes: From small groups to learning communities* (pp. 17–24). San Francisco, CA: Jossey-Bass.

Davis, B. G. (1993). *Tools for teaching.* San Francisco, CA: Jossey-Bass.

Litke, R. A. (1995). Learning lessons from students: What they like most and least about large classes. *Journal on Excellence in College Teaching, 6*(2), 113–129.

Lowman, J. (1987). Giving students feedback. In M. G. Weimer (Ed.), *New directions for teaching and learning: No. 32. Teaching large classes well* (pp. 71–84). San Francisco, CA: Jossey-Bass.

McKeachie, W. J. (2002). *McKeachie's teaching tips: Strategies, research, and theory for college and university teachers* (11th ed.). Boston, MA: Houghton Mifflin.

Schwibs, S., Hansen, E. (Directors), & Burkett, K. et al. (Producers). (1994). *Making larger classes work* [Videotape]. Bloomington, IN: Indiana University, Instructional Support Services.

Stanley, C. A., & Porter, M. E. (Eds.). (2002). *Engaging large classes: Strategies and techniques for college faculty.* Bolton, MA: Anker.

Weimer, M. G. (1987). *New directions for teaching and learning: No. 32. Teaching large classes well.* San Francisco, CA: Jossey-Bass.

Wulff, D. H., Nyquist, J. D., & Abbott, R. D. (1987). Students' perceptions of large classes. In M. G. Weimer (Ed.), *New directions for teaching and learning: No. 32. Teaching large classes well* (pp. 17–30). San Francisco, CA: Jossey-Bass.

7

Aligning in Team Teaching

Deborah H. Hatch & Susan Rich

The alignment model that Wulff presents in the first chapter of this book helps to identify the components—context, content, instructor, student, learning—that comprise effective teaching and learning and encourage instructors to look for and study the strategies that align these components. In team teaching, where there is more than one instructor, each with his or her content, the following needs to be considered: What strategies do faculty teaching in teams use to align their course contents, themselves, and their students to achieve learning in this complex environment? This chapter answers this question by applying the alignment model to a Coordinated Studies Program at a community college.

Applying the Alignment Model to Coordinated Studies

In his definition of team teaching, Davis (1995) described the two ends of the team teaching continuum. On one end are "courses planned by a group of faculty and then carried out in serial segments by individual members of the group. . . . On the other end of the continuum are courses both planned and delivered by a group of faculty working together closely as a team" (p. 7). The program presented in this chapter, Highline Community College's Coordinated Studies Program,[1] falls at the latter end of this continuum. Begun in 1991, it was influenced by the Washington Center for Improving the Quality of Undergraduate Education, whose approach to team teaching asks faculty to work together to develop a single interdisciplinary course, to teach together in the classroom, and to pay attention to student outcomes. The Coordinated Studies courses we examined for this case were "We the Jury," taught by instructors in law and communication, "A Band-Aid Isn't Enough: Global Health Issues," taught by faculty in humanities and physical education and health, and "Women on the Edge: Contemporary Writers, Artists, and Filmmakers," taught by faculty in humanities and writing. The degree of integration in these courses offers faculty opportunities to clarify course content, teaching roles, and student outcomes. The Highline faculty are equipped with strategies to accomplish these tasks.

The first strategy that Highline faculty members use is the Coordinated Studies Application Proposal. Typical applications are five pages long and are jointly written by the faculty team. As the questions reveal, the application asks interdisciplinary faculty teams to address the alignment model components of content, instructors, and students. Question 1 asks applicants to address the student audience for the course. Question 2 asks applicants how they will integrate course content. Questions 3 and 4 ask applicants about their teaching goals: the student outcomes they envision and a sample of work they will ask students to do to reach these outcomes. Finally, Question 5 asks applicants to consider effects on the larger context in which this Coordinated Studies course will be taught (see Table 7.1).

Table 7.1

Highline Community College Coordinated Studies Application Proposal

1) What is the program you are proposing? Please give a one-paragraph description–directed to a student audience–suitable for the quarterly schedule.

2) How will this coordinated study integrate the courses involved, and what are the advantages to offering these courses coordinated rather than as stand alone? Be as precise as possible.

3) Please list the student outcomes for this coordinated study. (Please refer to Highline's Strategic Initiatives, department student outcomes, and college-wide student outcomes before listing your outcomes.)

4) Describe a projected assignment for this coordinated study.

5) How will this program benefit the faculty involved and their respective departments? (If you have already done a coordinated study, respond to how you have applied or will apply any new teaching skill[s] and content from your experience.)

To study more closely what happens in the Coordinated Studies courses that result from this application process and to tap the experience and insights of the Coordinated Studies faculty, we conducted an email survey designed to elicit the strategies faculty use to align content, themselves, and their students. Faculty responded to the following questions:

1) What do you do to:

- Adapt the content of your discipline to the Coordinated Studies context

- Adapt your teaching role to the Coordinated Studies context

- Help students adapt their expectations of teaching and learning to the Coordinated Studies context

2) What are the challenges of these adaptations? How do you meet them? What advice would you offer?

In the sections that follow, we use these questions to organize the results. We provide excerpts of faculty responses to these questions, followed by analysis and interpretation of the patterns that emerged. As part of the interpretation, we emphasize the strategies faculty use to help align the multiple components of content, instructor, and student.

What Do You Do to Adapt the Content of Your Discipline to the Coordinated Studies Context?

In their responses to this question, faculty identified strategies they use to start to align the content from the various disciplines represented. Their responses to this question fell into two general areas: strategies for integrating content from multiple disciplines and strategies for designing writing assignments that encourage students to integrate course content.

Integrating course content from multiple disciplines. The following excerpts begin to reflect strategies faculty use to adapt the content of their courses to a coordinated studies approach:

- "Months before we begin the class, before any syllabi are written, we need to understand the inextricable link between our courses."

- "Spend lots of time with my co-instructor going over the course contents of both classes and discussing ways to integrate."

- "While the concepts that I present are the same ones that I would present in an independent . . . course, I alter the structure. . . . The content is the same, but it is structured in a strikingly different way."

Words and phrases such as *understand the inextricable link, integrate,* and *alter the structure* characterize the strategies faculty use to bring the different content areas closer together. Time emerges as another important strategy, with faculty starting "months before we begin the class" and having enough time to fully understand "the course contents of both classes." And as the response below suggests, the most important strategy for integrating different course contents is straightforward communication.

- "Being straightforward with co-instructor about what is important to cover and how it will be done, either as a separate event or coordinated, and work towards coordination as the preferred model. Occasionally there will need to be instruction that is solely one of the disciplines, but the more you can combine, the better it all seems to work."

Designing writing assignments. Writing assignments play an important role in aligning students with the multiple contents of coordinated studies classes, for it is through writing that students can begin to make the connections that faculty imagined when proposing and integrating the course content. Because Question 4 of the Coordinated Studies Application Proposal asks for a sample course assignment, the process of assignment design begins early and is part of the overall content integration process.

Faculty responses reveal several strategies for joint assignment design. One faculty team member wrote that their strategy is to "consider the outcomes of both classes and incorporate some or all of them into all assignments and projects." Focusing on what each wants students to be able to do in this Coordinated Studies course and what tasks will encourage these abilities, the faculty trade assignment ideas, discuss and revise them, looking for how the assignments and projects reflect and reinforce the learning goals of the course.

Another faculty team member wrote, "As much as possible, the writing and reading assignments I give students link directly to what my colleague is covering in her part of the class." Reading texts from a colleague's discipline and recognizing the conventions and the patterns of argument and evidence of another field are two strategies faculty use regularly when designing writing assignments. They commented that "writing is very easy to adapt" because assignments can focus on "the kind of writing done in the discipline," and that "texts both offer examples of writing within this content area as well as providing the material for students' own writing."

The strategies faculty use to align course content and to design writing assignments that align students with this new content are part of the planning phase of teaching a Coordinated Studies course. As the next section illustrates, faculty use other strategies to align with each other as a teaching team in the classroom.

What Do You Do to Adapt Your Teaching Role to the Coordinated Studies Context?

As one instructor suggested, issues of structure and control are important in adapting the teaching role.

- "I think that instructors in coordinated studies...give up some of their structure and control and this necessarily means they are not wedded to the 'script' that they may be used to in a stand alone class."

What takes the place of this control? Highline faculty answered this question by identifying strategies that allow them to teach as a team.

- "Ideally, I have been able to 'dance' with my teaching partner—playing off each other, challenging each other. For example, my colleague and I have modeled how we have different interpretations of a story (by arguing about it in class), showing how both interpretations are still within the range of the valid."

This response offers a vivid picture of two instructors team teaching in a Coordinated Studies course. The metaphor of the "dance" and the images of "playing" and "challenging" characterize a strategy of back-and-forth communication between the two instructors. Their physical movements in class enhance this communication. They alternate between standing near each other, making eye contact, exchanging ideas, and moving to different parts of the classroom, one out among the students encouraging discussion and comments, the other at the board, recording ideas in support of different perspectives and offering additional comments. Their playful, challenging relationship is not only engaging in itself, it has, as they suggested, the larger purpose of modeling for students different, equally valid, ways of interpreting a text and engaging them in this process. This strategy of modeling inquiry through their interaction represents an effective overlap of their teaching roles. Also, because they are explicit with students about why they are challenging each other and what students should notice, they align themselves and their students.

- "There is more 'flow' and so less coming from me, more coming from the dynamics of learning that includes both disciplines."

- "In the coordinated studies context, because I have a partner who is always present with me, I consciously strive to exemplify the skills I am teaching, especially good listening, cognitive complexity, perspective taking, playing both task and group maintenance roles, etc."

The two instructors represented in these excerpts have team taught a course in communication and the law for many years. Like the pair in the previous example, their strategies come from their awareness of the roles they have created together and their focus on the learning they want students to achieve.

A typical class illustrates the subtle strategies they use to create the flow they described. The law instructor stands in front of the class debriefing a mock courtroom experience they have just completed by asking what students learned about the roles of judges, counsels, juries, courtroom atmosphere. The communication instructor stands to the side, but within eye contact range of her colleague, listening carefully, interjecting questions and summary comments, helping students recognize the elements of their experiences that reinforce what they have learned about communication. The students eagerly share their experiences with each other and the two instructors. Interacting only through eye contact and nods, the two instructors align their roles to encourage students to reflect on and understand their experience. The instructors' willingness to be open to the "dynamics of learning that includes both disciplines" allows them to rely on only nonverbal communication strategies to align their roles and create the learning opportunities their combined disciplines offer.

As we have seen in the analyses of responses to the first two interview questions, faculty team teaching courses have strategies for aligning multiple course contents and multiple instructors and for aligning these components in ways that lead to learning. As the following section suggests, they also have strategies for aligning students with the combined course content and the team of instructors in the classroom.

What Do You Do to Help Students Adapt Their Expectations of Teaching and Learning to the Coordinated Studies Context?

Because Coordinated Studies courses are different from traditional courses, faculty think about how they can help students learn in this new environment.

- "I begin the first class openly examining students' expectations. . . . Then I try to keep this same honest and open, critical approach as we continue through the quarter."

- "We spend some time at the beginning of the quarter talking about how the two classes will come together. As we have taught this class several times, we have been able to anticipate some of the areas that get most frustrating or confusing for the students, and we have worked to spend more time and provide more information and direction in these areas."

In addition to these general strategies of eliciting expectations and providing information and direction, faculty identified course content, workload, grading, and class size as four specific areas where they can help adapt student expectations.

Course content. A key question Coordinated Studies instructors try to answer for their students is, "How will content, usually thought of as separate, come together?" Answering this question explicitly is an important strategy for aligning students with course content and teaching/learning goals.

- "Our syllabus is done in such a way that the students can see what is speech, what is legal and areas where the two come together. This syllabus is something that has evolved over the many times we have taught this class."

Workload. In addition to explaining how traditionally separate contents will come together, instructors need to communicate the new workload requirements accompanying the new course. As one instructor wrote, "One of the challenges for the students is to realize that they are taking the workload of TWO classes." Strategies instructors use to communicate the new workload include emphasizing that the course reading list and the number of assignments represent the work of two courses and reminding students of the number of course credits they are earning.

Grading. Grading is the area that causes most anxiety in a Coordinated Studies setting where there are multiple contents and multiple instructors. Strategies such as establishing, then communicating grading policies that are transparent and fair will go a long way to reduce anxiety. For example, one teaching team uses the following strategy:

- "We have split the grades, so students earn two different grades, which helps them feel more secure. We also include outcomes on the weekly schedule, to show what writing and humanities outcomes they are meeting."

Class size. As is the case with many team taught and interdisciplinary courses in current budgetary climates, having two teachers in the classroom means that each brings his or her regular student load, resulting, in Highline's case, in classes of 50–60 instead of 25–30. Acknowledging the effect of class size on student experience and developing strategies that lessen the impact of size is key to aligning students with content and teaching strategies in ways that enhance learning. Strategies such as individual or small group meetings between the instructor and students allow the instructor to monitor student learning and increase alignment among course content, instructor, and students. Group projects and study groups are strategies that encourage students to provide similar alignment checks for each other. As one faculty member wrote:

- "A student who isn't confident enough to ask for the help they need can really struggle with the larger class size. I schedule mini conferences during class time so that I get to meet with many students one on one. This seems to make a HUGE difference. Once I make a personal one-on-one contact with the student, they are much more likely to come to my office for help."

- "We set-up group projects (where students work together for several weeks) and a study buddy system (someone to call if you miss a class) from the beginning of the class to try and foster student-to-student support systems."

This analysis of Highline Coordinated Studies faculty responses to the questions of how they adapt their course contents, team teaching roles, and student expectations to the Coordinated Studies context reveals that Coordinated Studies faculty have many specific strategies for aligning the multiple contents, instructors, and students. We summarize those strategies in Table 7.2.

What Are the Challenges of These Adaptations? How Do You Meet Them? What Advice Would You Offer?

In their responses to the first of these questions about challenges, Highline Coordinated Studies faculty focused on one area as the major challenge of team teaching: teaching so closely with colleagues. The following summarizes one such response:

- "The biggest challenge for me has been working that closely with a colleague. All warts are revealed, and sometimes I have been disappointed with my colleagues' weaknesses as teachers (as I'm sure they have been disappointed with mine). Because I tend to avoid conflict, I struggle to truly negotiate—I either defer to what the other person wants or take over and do something my way."

Expressing this response in terms of the alignment model, we can say that the biggest challenge of team teaching is getting instructors on the same path.

Table 7.2
Summary of Strategies to Align Content, Instructors, and Students in the Context of Team Teaching in a Coordinated Studies Program

Strategies to Align Contents

- Scheduling enough time to get to know each other's disciplinary contents
- Finding connection points between/among the contents of the teams' disciplines
- Creating a structure for the interdisciplinary course that incorporates the contents of all disciplines on the team
- Communicating each other's content requirements clearly and honestly; working for the greatest degree of coordination but recognize areas where coordination may not be possible
- Considering the outcomes of both classes and incorporating some or all of them into all assignments and projects

Strategies to Align Instructors

- Giving up the control you are used to in a stand-alone class
- Creating a plan for your interaction as a teaching team that includes:
  ~ Back and forth communication
  ~ Physical movement
  ~ Nonverbal communication
  ~ Models of inquiry
- Being open to learning opportunities your combined disciplines offer

Strategies to Align Students

- Eliciting and discussing students' expectations
- Clarifying your expectations
- Communicating workload requirements
- Clarifying grading policies
- Providing guidelines and strategies for learning

In describing how they meet this challenge, Coordinated Studies faculty provided advice for both the individual faculty members and for the faculty team that will help achieve this greater overlap.

For individuals:

- "Think carefully about what you want to do in a class or lesson before you meet with your co-instructor."

- "Spend time with co-instructor to talk about teaching styles."
- "Be very willing to be honest with your colleague—check your ego at the door!!!"
- "Be flexible—doing it 'his or her way' might give you a new way!"

For teams:

- "Meet at least weekly, preferably daily (even briefly), after each class session."
- "Even more than in a stand-alone class, it seems important to revise the curriculum as you go."
- "After you have taught one [Coordinated Studies class], it is good to do it several more times; they really get better as you learn how the disciplines fit together and how the instructors fit together."

This advice for both individuals and teams to be flexible, to take time, to meet often and revise as necessary, to stay with a course beyond the first offering, is all consistent with the alignment model's assumption that effective teaching is an ongoing process of adaptation and adjustment. As Wulff stressed in the opening chapter of this book, you never reach total alignment; rather you are always striving to find a working balance. As one Coordinated Studies faculty member observed, interdisciplinary team teaching is like marriage.

- "The joke at Highline is that you become 'married' to the instructor that you teach a CS class with. Constant discussion and review of what is working and what is not will be the best guide."

And, like marriage, this continual adaptation is what makes interdisciplinary team teaching work and what makes it worth the effort. As another faculty member summarized:

- "Adapting always takes energy. But it is wonderfully creative. If an instructor tends to look actively for challenge, to invite creativity, and to enjoy risk-taking in teaching, coordinated studies is simply great fun."

Conclusion

In studying team teaching, we found that the alignment model was helpful at several stages. It helped us to characterize the complexity of this teaching situation. It helped us to frame questions to ask of faculty teaching in the Coordinated Studies Program. It helped us to collect, analyze, and interpret their responses and to identify the strategies they use to encourage learning. In addition, the strategies we gained from the Coordinated Studies case apply to other team teaching situations, such as large courses taught by faculty and graduate student teaching assistant teams and other courses along the continuum described by Davis (1995). Overall, the alignment model of teaching effectiveness was a valuable way to understand team teaching, a teaching approach that is becoming increasingly popular at all levels of higher education.

Endnote

1) We want to thank Highline Community College Coordinated Studies faculty, Larry Blades, Tracy Brigham, Angi Castor, Barbara Clinton, Allison Green, Joy Smucker, Wendy Swyt, for their email interview responses and for inviting us into their classrooms.

Reference

Davis, J. R. (1995). *Interdisciplinary courses and team teaching: New arrangements for learning.* Phoenix, AZ: ACE/Oryx Press.

8

Aligning in the Mentoring Partnership

Lana Rae Lenz & Sheila Edwards Lange

When the aim of education is understood to be the development of the whole person—rather than knowledge acquisition, for instance—the central element of good teaching becomes the provision of care, rather than the use of teaching skills or the transmission of knowledge. . . . For more than any other factor, it is the partnership of teacher and student that finally determines the value of an education. In the nurture of that partnership lies the mentor's art.

—Laurent A. Daloz

In recent years, our perception of the mentoring role has expanded beyond regarding the mentor as the wise and authoritative source of knowledge for a novice learner. The current conception of the mentoring relationship is learner-centered and grounded in an understanding of the principles of adult learning. It envisions the mentor as a *caring guide* of the novice learner's growth and a *facilitator* of a learning partnership that is often long term.

The mentoring relationship is a special form of teaching and learning. Given the emphasis on learning in the relationship, we wondered what particular insights the alignment perspective might provide for the mentoring process. This chapter explores the ways that the alignment perspective as described by Wulff in Chapter 1 can help us think about mentoring partnerships. For our purposes, we focus on the common mentoring relationship between a faculty mentor and a graduate student. Although we certainly believe that an awareness of the alignment perspective will enhance the mentoring of all students, as well as new faculty or trainees in the workplace, space does not allow for a discussion of all these applications here.

The Mentor Role

Mentoring is something of a mystery, even to those awarded for successful mentoring. Those who study and write about mentoring point out that models for this role are found in classical literature, mythology, religion, psychology, and fairy tales. The "first" Mentor, the teacher and guide in whose care Ulysses left his son in *The Odyssey,* is both mortal and immortal, father-figure, wise counselor, and more. Despite such models, however, there is still little agreement on a definition for mentoring. Thus, the first challenge of this discussion is to explain what is meant by *mentoring.*

In a discussion about mentoring, those who have been in a mentoring relationship, either as an experienced mentor or novice learner (mentee), tend to focus on describing the process. To them, mentoring is a process that is extremely complex. It demands that the mentor have skills above and beyond those traditionally associated with classroom instruction. It requires a committed one-to-one relationship that may extend over a long period of time. The purpose of a mentoring partnership is to move the novice learner into and through the learning that facilitates his or her becoming a professional. As this growth occurs, the relationship between mentor and mentee changes as well. The mentee makes the transition from student and/or apprentice learner to colleague. As the mentor is able to release more and more of the control of the learning relationship, the two may become professional collaborators on their work, possibly friends.

In looking at the literature on the practices of graduate faculty (as well as undergraduate advisors, workplace trainers, and others), we find that those discussions rely primarily on description rather than definition. As the literature suggests, mentoring is so highly varied and dependent on the particular context, content, and needs/experiences of the mentoring partners that it is difficult to provide a succinct definition. Thus, in this chapter, we, too, focus on description. We begin by providing a sample of some of the most frequently cited *behaviors* that describe an effective mentor, based on the current literature (see Table 8.1).

For anyone new to the mentor role, perhaps such a list is not as instructive—or as encouraging—as the reflections of successful faculty mentors describing the roles they see for themselves and the satisfaction that this kind of relationship brings. For example, the following comments provided by distinguished graduate mentor award recipients suggest these mentors' perceptions of the role. Among the key features identified by these comments is the importance of the process for providing new and exciting professional and

Table 8.1
Frequently Cited Behaviors of an Effective Mentor

- Provides support for mentee—academic, emotional, and professional
- Challenges, sets high expectations
- Works in a responsive and interactive way
- Provides tools the mentee will use in further skill development long after completion of the degree
- Values two-way communication
- Encourages critical thinking
- Offers alternative viewpoints
- Promotes the mentee's self-discovery
- Fosters a respect for time together

- Provides a vision of the educational and professional journey ahead
- Provides intellectual leadership
- Remains accessible for advice and assistance
- Involves the mentee in teaching, research, and professional activities
- Respects the mentee's goals and collaborates to achieve them
- Advocates for the mentee
- Offers honest feedback and advice
- Models leadership, team, and communication skills

intellectual opportunities in a relationship that is enjoyable and rewarding to both mentee and mentor and that ultimately fosters independence.

- "If I were a graduate student again, how is it I would like to be 'done unto'? I'd like my mentor to . . . be mindful of the fact that I left many potential roads untraveled so that I might journey down this one, and so do everything possible to make my graduate experience as rewarding and enjoyable as possible."

- "What had seemed like a deep secret held by the best mentors is actually simple: surround yourself with excited and energetic students, enjoy the intellectual challenges they put forward, and celebrate the frontiers they conquer. It is so easy it almost seems like cheating."

- "I've developed a set of techniques over the years . . . [and] perhaps the most important—beyond individual meetings on a regular basis—is taking students . . . to major conferences. Other than the people they meet, the key to going to a conference is learning that they are plenty smart enough to make critical contributions to the field . . . that they can compete successfully in the discipline. This confidence, developed firsthand, goes far beyond anything I can provide as an adviser and mentor."

- "For me, mentoring entails working with students, over an extended time, in developing what really constitutes a theory of one's professional self. Mentoring is deeply rewarding; it generates bonds that combine lessons of the academy and our professional lives with the lessons of life."

- "[I] provide students with considerable intellectual freedom, encourage them to follow their noses in research, give them pride and ownership of their degrees, and . . . develop a partnership with students in research and teaching that fosters independence and leads to a win-win situation where they bring to us incredible new perspectives and ideas."

   (Re-envisioning the Ph.D., 2001–2002)

These comments, it is important to remember, are from faculty with many years of mentoring experience, all of them award-winning mentors. They are clearly among those who find that mentoring students is one of the aspects of being a professor that they enjoy most. They have chosen to move beyond the role of advisor in which the emphasis is on the sharing of information (such as program planning, research methodology, and course development). They have expanded the advising relationship into a mentoring partnership. Their comments not only reflect a little of their mentoring methodology, but also tell us something about their enthusiasm for mentoring and the spirit and care that they bring to their practice of it.

When we combine all these descriptive elements, they provide an understanding of mentoring as a unique and complex learning experience for both mentor and mentee. Based on this general description of mentoring, we begin our discussion of alignment in the mentoring process by briefly examining the context of the mentoring relationship.

The Context of the Mentoring Relationship

Effective mentors must make use of a broad range of social, communicative, emotional, and intellectual skills. As in the classroom, mentors marshal and employ these skills in the service of learning. A few key differences in the *context* for learning should be noted, however.

- In the classroom, instructors are primarily responsible for achieving alignment between the students, the content, and themselves. As a mentor, one of the goals is to guide the mentee to a point in his or her growth at which *shared responsibility* for mutual learning experiences is possible.

- In the classroom, the alignment communication strategies are, for the most part, used with students as a group. Mentors tailor their use of the four general communication strategies Wulff identified in Chapter 1 to the requirements of their individual mentees.

- In the classroom, instructors devote their concern and energies to seeing that many students are making progress toward learning the content of the course. In the mentoring relationship, individual mentees engage in a partnership in which they have the opportunity to determine content and define learning goals for themselves. Although not every novice mentee is able to assume this responsibility at the beginning of a mentoring relationship, the mentor monitors the mentee's progress and watches for opportunities to enable and empower the mentee, so that the relationship meets his or her needs.

Alignment at Key Points in the Mentoring Relationship

The literature frequently describes the "life span" of the mentoring relationship as taking place in general phases (Chao, 1997; Kram, 1988; Zachary, 2000). Models such as these provide a combined timeline and framework for the general progress and benchmarks of the developing mentoring partnership. No relationship will be completely predictable; the sequence in which the partners experience the phases will not be linear, and each mentee's learning will unfold at a different pace over the course of the relationship. The "life" of the mentoring relationship is always changing. In our analysis of the phases of mentoring, we have identified four critical points:

- Initiating the relationship
- Developing a plan for working together
- Assessing progress and reformulating goals
- Preparing for closure

Both mentor and mentee should be aware of these crucial points in the mentoring relationship and use them in monitoring the progress of the partnership. The interaction described in the alignment model is indispensable for all of these points. If two-way communication is not happening, the process is not mentoring. The mentor establishes the pattern and expectation for interaction by carefully structuring the first meeting, and then is consistently interpersonal throughout the relationship, including the final assessment. During the relationship, other key strategies for aligning the work of the pair may be used to different degrees, depending on the point in the relationship and the specific needs of the two in the partnership. So, for example, rapport is critical in initiating a successful relationship, while organization and structure become more important in the development of a plan.

Initiating the Relationship

As a new mentoring relationship is about to begin, there is a period of preparation that usually initiates the process. This phase of the relationship may be relatively brief—a few meetings at most—but is crucial. More formalized/ structured programs may bring the mentoring partners together, or the student might approach the mentor with the request that they work together. At this early point in the relationship, it is sometimes the case that either the mentor or mentee, or both, discover that this initial contact has revealed a mismatch in the potential partnership. Perhaps the mentor is unable to provide the kinds of experiences the mentee is seeking or cannot invest the time the mentee needs. Or, the mentee may feel that communication with this particular mentor will be difficult. Meanwhile, the pairing may have served the useful purposes of introducing the mentee into a new situation and to other faculty colleagues, as well as providing insights on the culture of the department or organization and its expectations. When the mentoring pair is not the result of assignment but of choice (frequently on the part of the mentee), there is still time needed at the beginning of the relationship for the mentor and mentee to begin to learn what they need to know about one another.

In the beginning stages of developing a relationship with a mentee, the elements of the four alignment strategies that are particularly important are those of *engagement* and *rapport*. Engagement is nurtured by the gift of regular time together. The mentor is able to listen, to ask questions, to open up possibilities the mentee has not considered, to offer alternatives, to challenge, and to hear and process the mentee's responses. It is also an opportunity for the mentor to begin to enrich his or her own insights and ideas through exposure to the mentee's learning and prior experiences. The opportunity for both scheduled and informal interaction is one significant aspect that is consistently reflected in successful mentoring partnerships. The alignment perspective makes the most of these opportunities for learning by directing attention to the development and use of interpersonal skills, such as attentive and active listening, respecting the silences that will arise in any relationship, and communicating an interest in the mentee's ideas, questions, and areas of concern.

The second alignment strategy especially useful at this point is the establishment of *rapport* between the mentor and mentee. Prior to and during their early conversations, the mentor (and possibly the mentee as well) will have thought about the implications and potential benefits of mentoring and about individual and mutual goals of the partners. As an initial step in the alignment process, this phase is a time for the mentor and mentee to become acquainted on several levels—professional, intellectual, and personal. This stage may require one or more conversations over a period of time. If both individuals in the mentoring relationship determine that there is an opportunity for a fruitful learning experience, they can begin their work together with a commitment to a partnership that they both believe has a strong chance of meeting the mentee's goals and that can result in learning and growth for both partners.

Mutual respect, which is the central aspect of rapport, can begin to develop in these early meetings. Mentors will want to make sure, however, that they and their mentee meet in an atmosphere that is comfortable for each. Relaxed conversation can communicate the mentor's interest in the mentee as a student and as an individual. It is important that a mentor talk with the mentee about the mentee's interests and passions. Sharing stories about graduate experiences or offering some bit of personal information about interests outside of the faculty role can encourage the mentee to share experiences and interests, too.

This preparation phase begins the process of interpersonal alignment between mentor and mentee. Questions like those suggested in Table 8.2 can be useful for gathering and sharing information about general goals, the particular interests and strengths of the mentee, and the educational background and life experience of the mentor and mentee. This initial set of impressions and information provides mentors with the ability to determine at least some of the work that lies ahead and anticipate some of the areas that may require particular support for alignment.

It is not possible at this initial stage of the partnership to answer most of these questions fully. It is, nonetheless, useful for mentors to raise them and listen carefully to the mentee's responses. Such discussion will not only provide important information about the mentee's level of development and self-awareness, but also introduce the questions and content that will serve as a guide for developing timelines and goals.

As mentors facilitate the development of rapport, engagement, and trust in the relationship, the following recommendations might prove useful:

- They should reflect on their own preparation, expectations, and goals related to mentoring.

Table 8.2
Questions for Initiating the Mentoring Partnership

- How close is the match of your communication styles?
- Is there compatibility in your working and learning styles?
- What are the experiences the mentee has had with other mentors/teachers?
- What expectations does the mentee have for this relationship? What is the work he or she wants to accomplish? To what extent is the mentee aware of his or her needs and goals?
- How does the mentee think he or she can best go about reaching these learning goals? (This will reveal the mentee's style of learning and communication.)
- What are the different pressures and stresses in the mentee's life at this point? In your own life? How might these affect your work together?
- In what ways are your background and life experiences similar to the mentee's? What are the biggest differences between you?
- What more do you need to know about the mentee at this point? How can you go about finding out what you need to know?

- They can make use of the information they obtain in initial meetings with prospective mentees to evaluate the potential success of the relationship.
- They should consider providing some questions or exercises for both to think/write about and share during the meeting times. This communicates to the mentee that the mentor values reflection and that two-way communication will be a part of their relationship.

Using the "journey" metaphor for thinking about mentoring, one could see this period of preparation as a time when a mentor and mentee stand at the beginning of the path, each having made the determination to move forward together. This decision takes the process to the next phase and the next opportunity for application of alignment strategies, as the partners begin to organize and create a structure for their work.

Developing a Plan for Working Together

When both mentor and mentee have had adequate time to learn if their relationship is viable and if the commitment is mutual, they move to another critical point in the mentoring relationship: developing a plan for working together. At this point, the mentor and mentee can together structure the content and align joint perceptions of the overall context of their work. This phase ensures that the mentoring process will have the best chance of meeting the needs and learning goals of both partners. The primary work of this phase—while continuing to build rapport and engagement—is to create *structure* and an *organizational plan* for the mentor and mentee's work. Thus, this phase reemphasizes the importance that Wulff (Chapter 1) placed on organization in the alignment process. In this phase, the mentor initiates the efforts to move the content, the mentee, and himself or herself more closely into alignment. To achieve the learning that both partners hope to accomplish, mentors and mentees can consider the following recommendations:

- They should *mutually* develop and define the structure of their work together and develop a written plan (or contract, if they wish) that outlines their agreements.

- Part of this plan should anticipate problems that might occur and outline procedures for addressing them.

- The organizational plan should identify specific learning goals with a flexible timeline for their achievement and include checkpoints for regular assessment of progress.

- Mentors and mentees should reevaluate and restructure the work plan as needed on a periodic and regular basis.

- The mentoring partners should individually reflect on how the *relationship* is or is not working for both partners, and discuss these reflections openly so that adjustments can be made as needed.

As mentors and mentees negotiate their agreement for working together, they set the framework for aligning the components of content, mentor, and mentee. This process considers not only learning goals and expectations and ways to assess success, but also structure for the relationship (for example, accountability, boundaries, and expectations for communication about problems). Table 8.3 identifies possible questions that might guide discussion of these issues.

Assessing Progress and Reformulating Goals

After the mentor and mentee have established the structure for their work, they move into the third important area in their relationship, assessing and reformulating goals. The general alignment strategies of rapport, organization, engagement, and two-way communication that have been employed through-

Table 8.3

Questions for Developing a Plan for Working Together in the Mentoring Partnership

- What are the questions we want to ask? Why are these important to each of us?
- What criteria will we use to evaluate whether we have achieved our intended learning results? How will we measure this?
- What will be the mentor's responsibilities? What will be the mentee's?
- What will be the purposes/questions/plans we have for our meetings?
- What will each partner do to prepare to make good use of the time together?
- What agreements are needed for issues such as active and equal participation, honesty, punctuality, respect for differences, confidentiality?
- How will we communicate with each other about problems as they occur? If either of us wants to end the relationship, how will we approach that possibility?

out the mentoring relationship serve the partnership well when feedback is needed in order to make adjustments in the relationship, the learning goals, and/or the work plan. The structure that the mentoring pair has used throughout the relationship has included assessment and revision as a key element in nurturing the relationship, ensuring progress, and keeping the work on track and responsive to changing needs of mentor or mentee. Among the additional strategies that the mentor and mentee might consider are the following:

- They may develop, as needed, a set of assessment questions that both can think/write about and use as a guide for discussion.
- If only one partner is experiencing problems or feels progress is not being made, each of the partners might choose to write and exchange written thoughts in advance of the meeting.
- They can vary the questions used for assessment to make them more or less specific, depending on the goals and activities that have occurred.
- If some of the pair's work has to do with one or both partners teaching a course, they could consider collecting student feedback, or the feedback of an observer, to enrich and expand the discussion.

During an assessment discussion, there are three key areas on which the mentoring partners can focus. The first is related to the learning process and accomplishment of goals. It may become clear, for example, that the initial, or most recent, goal statement overlooks elements that the assessment indicates are important to one or both partners. Or, the partners may decide that some of the agreed-upon learning goals are no longer as relevant or important as they originally thought or that those goals have been accomplished. A second area for ongoing focus is the relationship. Planning for regular opportunities to assess and discuss relational issues will provide both partners with a sense of forward movement and productivity. It also will allow for both mentor and mentee to identify problems that might not have surfaced before, prompting a discussion about ways to resolve them. Third, assessment reflections and discussion can also be an opportunity to review the organization and structure that the partners have given to their work. Table 8.4 provides some possible questions to guide discussion in these three areas.

The conversations that result from using these (or similar questions) assist the mentor and mentee in making the decision whether to go forward with the relationship and its work. They also can strengthen the rapport and sense of engagement between the partners. However, the result might also be that one or both partners feel that the relationship cannot move forward and that it is time for a change, possibly even to end their work together. Bringing a mentoring relationship to a successful close is the final task we will consider.

Preparing for Closure

It is important that the mentor and mentee maintain the work of alignment as they move into this final significant stage in their relationship—closure for the partnership. The literature on mentoring reminds us that at almost any point in the relationship either the mentor or mentee, or both, may perceive a mismatch in the partnership. Perhaps the mentor feels unable to provide the kinds of experiences the mentee is seeking. Or, maybe the mentee feels that communication with this particular mentor has become difficult or that the mentor is unable to invest the time necessary to meet the mentee's goals. Continuing with the process if one or both individuals have serious misgivings about the alignment of their goals and expertise is likely to be nonproductive. In the early discussions of the structure for the partnership, the mentoring pair should have given some attention to the ways the relationship could be brought to a close. This early attention should have included both an agreement about how the partners would recognize the need to end the relationship and an outline for how to deal with closure when the time came. In imagining the end of the relationship at its beginning, mentor and mentee will have insured that, whatever the cause for bringing the relationship to an

Table 8.4

Questions for Assessing and Reformulating Goals in the Mentoring Partnership

---

Questions for Assessing the Learning Process and Progress Toward Goals

- Do you have a sense that you are achieving your current learning goals?
- What are you most pleased with at this point?
- What is most troubling or frustrating to you?
- Are we working together in the best way to facilitate your learning? If not, what changes should we consider?
- What other resources do you need?

Questions for Assessing the Progress of the Relationship

- I'm interested in your perspective on our relationship at this point—how do you think we are doing as a learning team?
- Are there things we could do to make our relationship stronger?
- What do you think of the quality of our communication with each other?
- Are there problem areas we should be talking about?
- Does anything need to change?

Questions for Assessing Organization and Structure of the Work

- Is the work plan that we agreed on earlier still working for you?
- Do you feel that the frequency of our meetings and the amount of time we have together are appropriate? Would you like to see either of these change? If so, how?
- Are we both participating actively in this relationship, as we agreed to do? Is one of us carrying more of the responsibility for keeping the relationship going? Does this balance need to change? If so, how?
- Do you have any discomfort about the way we communicate our criticism, concerns, or frustrations to each other or about the confidential nature of our relationship? What about this works well for you? What changes might we want to make?

---

end, there is a plan, including some lead time if possible, through which both can prepare for this change.

Long-term mentoring relationships most commonly end (or at least change significantly) when one of the partners is no longer present or able to participate. The mentee will complete his or her studies and move on to another role, another institution, or even another part of the world. The mentor may also move on—to another university, to a position outside the academy, or to retirement. Let us assume that the situation prompting the end of the mentoring work together is a happy one—the mentee, after years of work, will be receiving his or her degree, then leave for a position at a college in another state. Some recommendations/strategies that could be useful at this point include the following:

- In anticipating the change ahead, mentors can bring this issue into conversations months in advance.

- Mentors can assist mentees in thinking about any unachieved goals while time remains for the partners to work on these together.

- The pair can initiate the process of reflecting on the work that has been done together over time, the changes the mentee has undergone, the progress made, and the challenges the mentee has overcome.

- The pair can discuss together the ideas both have about activities that will structure the end of the relationship.

If the mentor has been careful over the course of the relationship to share the "lead," the decision-making process, and significant responsibilities with the mentee, it is important to continue in this spirit to the end. The mentor and mentee will have had time to practice together to prepare them for this negotiation. Questions such as those in Table 8.5 can serve to assist in creating alignment between the mentor and mentee as both prepare for making a change.

Table 8.5
Questions to Assist With Alignment During Closure

- Think back to our original goal for working together—what has been our path since that point?
- What learning have we achieved? What have we left undone?
- When and how can we make the opportunity for at least one meeting in which we share our reflections about the process and content of our learning? What questions should we use to guide that discussion?
- How should we celebrate the learning we have done together?

Zachary (2000) addressed the issue of closure and included a series of useful checklists and worksheets to assist mentoring partners in processing the experience, in celebrating its achievements, and in looking toward the future contacts they might have as colleagues and friends. She encouraged the mentoring partners in this final step by saying that

> ...coming to closure in mentoring is an important part of learning, development, satisfaction and promise. Closure links the present to the future for mentee and mentor.... Good closure should elevate a mentee's learning and catapult it forward, raising the learning to another level. (p. 160)

Conclusion

Effective communication is critical to the mentoring relationship and the learning needed as the mentee moves from novice to professional. Engagement and rapport in the initial phases of their interaction enable mentoring partners to establish a relationship that guides their work together. The organizational plan provides a framework that includes assessment of progress toward the learning goals. As the relationship evolves, ongoing reflection, assessment, and, especially, adjustment are essential. Throughout the process, the lens of alignment offers a useful perspective for examining how to provide for more successful experiences in the partnership, for both mentor and mentee.

References

Chao, G. T. (1997). Mentoring phases and outcomes. *Journal of Vocational Behavior, 51*, 15–28.

Daloz, L. A. (1999). *Mentor: Guiding the journey of adult learners.* San Francisco, CA: Jossey-Bass.

Kram, K. E. (1988). *Mentoring at work: Developmental relationships in organizational life.* Lanham, MD: University Press of America.

Re-envisioning the Ph.D. (2001–2002). *Marsha L. Landolt distinguished graduate mentor award statements.* Retrieved December 7, 2004, from the University of Washington, Graduate School web site: http://www.grad.washington.edu/envision/project_resources/metathemes.html

Zachary, L. J. (2000). *The mentor's guide: Facilitating effective learning relationships.* San Francisco, CA: Jossey-Bass.

9

Aligning in Math, Science, and Engineering Courses

Karen Freisem, Clarisse Messemer, & Wayne H. Jacobson

In our work with a wide range of math, science, and engineering courses[1], we have observed that students and instructors in these disciplines often have different perceptions of learning that can pose obstacles to alignment. Gaining an understanding of these obstacles can help instructors make decisions in designing and teaching their courses—decisions that can better align instructor, students, and content to promote learning.

Research suggests that students learn more by engaging in the processes of scientific discovery than by memorizing the results of scientific investigations (Ireton, Manduca, & Mogk, 1996; Uno, 1997). McDermott (2001) has identified the need for instructors to address students' conceptual misunderstandings explicitly, for students to participate in the construction of conceptual frameworks, and for students to relate conceptual understandings to the real world. These research findings emphasize that students learn by *doing* science—by asking questions, by overcoming misconceptions, and by actively engaging in the process of learning. Though research provides strong support for understanding learning in these ways, we have observed that instructors often do not share this perspective on learning, and that students' understanding of learning is often different both from that of their instructors and from the conclusions of research. This chapter focuses on those areas where student and instructor perceptions of learning differ, and then suggests strategies for bringing perceptions of both into alignment with research findings on learning in these disciplines.

This chapter looks at student and instructor perceptions in three separate contexts in math, science, and engineering courses: 1) gateway courses that are prerequisites for entry into a wide range of disciplines, 2) elective courses designed to introduce students to an academic discipline, and 3) advanced problem-oriented courses in students' major field of study.

In these three contexts, we have observed that alignment issues tend to cluster around two main areas. First, instructors and students often differ in the degree to which they perceive the real-world relevance of course content, and therefore, the purposes for learning course content. A second area where understandings may differ concerns what it means to know and learn the content of the disciplines. For example, does knowing the content mean that students have memorized the formulas or that they can use the formulas to solve a problem in class? If students believe that learning content means memorizing formulas, they may expect that lectures about formulas are more useful than group problem-solving sessions. These differences in perceptions can significantly impact student learning in a number of ways, including students' ability to use prior experience to learn, their motivation to learn, their expectations in terms of depth of learning, and their preferences for what happens in class.

This chapter discusses how student and instructor perceptions of learning often differ in math, science, and engineering courses, and proposes strategies for increasing alignment among students, instructors, and content in the context of such courses.

Courses That Are Gateways Into Other Disciplines

The first context in which we will look at the differing perceptions of learning is "gateway" courses, which primarily serve nonmajor students as prerequisites for other courses and programs in science, technology, engineering and mathematics. How, in courses such as these, do student and instructor perceptions of learning differ?

Relevance and Purpose for Learning

In gateway courses, students and instructors may have very different perceptions of the relationship of course content to the real world, and thus what they consider to be the purpose of the course. To instructors, the links are obvious. In a sense, they see the world through the perspective of their discipline—it's everywhere they look. Students, on the other hand, might not be able to connect a particular topic to their everyday lives.

- "We would like more real-life scenarios or explanations for the reasons we are doing the problem!"

When students perceive course content as unrelated to the real world, they may not recognize the purpose for learning the course content. Novice students often have only a surface understanding of why the course is required, what the course concepts will equip them to do, and how the course fits into their future program of study. They might see the course as just one hoop to jump through so they can gain admission to a major, though, at the point of taking the course, they may have little idea of what will be required for them to succeed in the major. As a result, in gateway courses the students' primary purpose may be just to pass the course.

On the other hand, instructors understand why the course content is important for future courses within the curriculum and have an intrinsic appreciation and love for the discipline. So, often they see little reason to explain to students what is to them, as instructors, self-evident. In these situations, if students do not recognize on their own the relevance of course content and the purpose of learning, we see misalignment.

What It Means to Know and Learn

Another area where students and instructors have differing perceptions in gateway courses is what it means to know and learn the content of the discipline. Students might perceive course content to consist of facts or formulas, whereas the instructor knows, for example, that mastering the content means that students are able to take one concept and apply it to other problems in the course. The instructor might ask students to demonstrate ability or literacy by approaching problems that require application of the course content. However, because they have a different view of what the content consists of, students may comment that the application problems are harder than students think they should be. Such students may see course content as a sequence of procedures, and therefore, they might expect to demonstrate their knowledge only in the context of problems that vary slightly from ones they've already solved, as this comment illustrates:

- "The additional word/application problems on the homework are way too hard."

When students and instructors have different ideas of what it means to know the content of the discipline, they also often have different perceptions of effective approaches to learning the material. For example, students may think that an effective approach to learning the content is to memorize terms, follow predefined lab procedures, or solve discrete problems that are similar to those explained in the text; that is, they approach learning in terms of following a template. Instructors, however, might believe that a very different approach will help students learn. For example, instructors might introduce theory that is broad enough to apply to a number of examples, while students see a trade-off between theory and examples.

- "Deriving equations causes more confusion than clarification. If you say it, we'll believe it."

In addition, while instructors might care more about the application of theory than the routine or obvious steps of a problem, students may feel that it is necessary to work through an entire problem, step-by-step, from start to finish, before they can make the transition to similar problems or concepts.

- "Don't skip so many steps and assume we can finish or fill them in on our own."

One effect of these differing perspectives on learning in the discipline is that students often conclude that the instructor is not aware of, or does not care about, what students really need to learn.

- "There's not much awareness of us on the professor's part."

Instructors in math, science, and engineering gateway courses can increase their "awareness" of their students—and thus improve alignment—by considering these two areas where their own perceptions of learning may differ from those of the students and by developing strategies to address the resulting issues. After we examine two other contexts, we will present strategies that can help instructors bring themselves, their students, and their content into alignment.

Courses That Are Entry Into the Discipline

Contextual factors may contribute to the differing perceptions of learning in gateway courses. Students are required to take a gateway course, and, although it may prepare them for later courses in their major, it is not a subject area that most have chosen as their major. Most students have a novice understanding of their future major, at best, and so they are not necessarily prepared to draw connections to the contexts where they will use the content of the gateway course. Also, because these are often large courses, they present many of the challenges identified in Chapter 6.

However, even when the context changes, many similar issues in alignment arise. In courses that are intended as entry-level courses in the discipline, we again see that students and instructors have different perceptions. Students perceive such courses as not relevant to the real world, so they do not appreciate the purpose for learning the course content. They also have perceptions of what it means to know course content that are different from their instructors', and, as a result, have differing views on effective approaches to learning course content.

Relevance and Purpose for Learning

Since instructors know what comes next in the discipline and students do not, their different views of content often lead to different perceptions of the purpose for the course and its practical application. Students might want courses to be more practical and skill-building, and, as a result, expect to gain hands-on experience.

- "I wouldn't be able to recognize a switch router, or hub, in real life. That is not good."

One example within these disciplines is an entry-level economics course. Students take this course for one of two reasons: first, they may need it for a distribution requirement; and second, they may consider it as a prospective major. Economics instructors were concerned that many of their most talented students did not take additional economics classes. In fact, many students went on to major in a related discipline, business. So, instructors asked students why they made that choice. The most common response was that students preferred classes that were practical and dealt with real-world issues. Theoretical classes such as economics, they said, were more appropriate if you wanted to go on to graduate school than if you wanted a job upon graduation. Many students said that they preferred business school classes that gave them hands-on experience working with everyday problems and that stressed critical thinking skills. The students' responses highlighted an area of misalignment because what the students saw as the usefulness of business courses was exactly what economics instructors had thought they were emphasizing in their courses. Similar to the situation in gateway courses, we see that the students perceived the content to be theoretical, but the instructors viewed it as inherently practical, and, as a result, students and instructors viewed the purpose of the course very differently.

What It Means to Know and Learn

Again, even though students might have different purposes in entry-level classes than they do in gateway courses, students and instructors often have differing perceptions of what it means to *know* in the discipline, and, as a result, have very different ideas of effective approaches to learning. Although students at this level seem to understand and accept that they *do* need to learn theory, student perceptions of effective explanations may still be different from their instructor's. The instructor's approach to teaching may emphasize the theoretical and de-emphasize the practical application, whereas the students believe that many concrete examples will help them to use theory more effectively.

- "The theoretical basis of this class is difficult to grasp. It would help if you did more examples from the book."

Let's look again at the entry-level course in economics. The main goals of this course are to teach students how individuals or firms make choices and to give a broad overview of how the economy works. The beauty of teaching these courses, for instructors, is that students seem to have similar goals–they want to comprehend the business section of the newspaper or gain the skills necessary to start up their own business in the future. However, the methods instructors use may result in misalignment of the student and instructor perceptions of how to achieve their common goal. For example, often the course begins by deriving supply and demand diagrams where the instructor is very specific about the assumptions economists use to derive a model of market behavior. Once these assumptions are accepted, the analysis is straightforward—at least that is how instructors see it. Students, on the other hand, often get caught up in the assumptions. Recognizing this potential obstacle, instructors may devote class time to helping students see that economists use these simplifying assumptions in order to draw refutable implications by analyzing changes in constraints. At this point in the course, one of two things happens, depending on students' sense of what it means to understand economics: Some students are attracted to the elegance of the economic models, while others conclude that economics is the study of unrealistic assumptions about an idealized world.

In this case, we see that some students arrive expecting that the course content consists of practical concepts, but then discover that it consists more of theoretical models—and so are disillusioned. The instructor, on the other hand, delights in using economic models and sees their usefulness and intrinsic interest. In this case, we see that students' perceptions of learning—their perceptions of the content and their perceptions of the teaching approach—can be very different from their instructor's. However, by identifying differing views of content and learning, instructors can move towards alignment of students, instructor, and content.

Next, we examine advanced courses that are structured around problems in the discipline, and then conclude with strategies for addressing issues raised in all three contexts.

Advanced Problem-Oriented Courses in the Discipline

One way to interpret the alignment issues in these first two contexts is to see them as a function of teaching introductory-level courses. Students new to the discipline must begin to think at levels of abstraction they may find challenging. Though students may eventually choose to major in the disciplines represented by these courses, most are still on the periphery, just beginning to appreciate what the discipline offers and how work in the discipline is done.

It is interesting to see, therefore, that similar issues in alignment arise even in advanced courses that focus on problems in the discipline. Some problem-oriented courses may be designed for problem-based learning, with a curriculum organized around cases, students divided into teams, and instructors in the role of facilitating team learning. Other problem-oriented courses are structured in more traditional ways, but still focus on identifying and addressing issues and problems with relevance that students in the major can readily recognize, and that they may have already studied to some extent in prerequisite courses. The students, content, and context for these courses are different in many ways from those of entry-level courses, and yet similar student and instructor differences in perceptions of learning can emerge, resulting in misalignment of instructors, students, and content.

Relevance and Purpose for Learning

In problem-oriented courses, students might still have questions about the relevance of course content and about what their purpose for learning really is. Although the problems themselves are often practical and grounded in contexts that students recognize, it is often a challenge for students to know how well their learning will extend beyond the classroom. Perhaps they have developed credible solutions for the problems presented in class, but will they be able to solve similar problems outside of class? In fact, research on problem-based learning suggests that problem-solving skills developed in class often transfer readily to other contexts as students take more courses or move into a profession in which the skills are required (Albanese & Mitchell, 1993). However, when students are taking the class, they don't always know how to assess or evaluate what they are learning in terms of its application to the context beyond the course, other than recognizing that they have developed their own solution to an isolated problem. This uncertainty can at times become an obstacle to alignment.

Relevance and purpose also become issues when problems fall outside of familiar disciplinary boundaries. In one natural sciences course, the instructor invited a colleague from a social science course to discuss human factors influencing the environmental issues the course was addressing. Although both instructors worked to show connections between the ways that their respective disciplines addressed the problem, many students expressed frustration that they had to "give up class time" for the social science lectures. In a similar course that included field trips, students clearly saw the relevance of the problems they were studying and appreciated the chance to engage in fieldwork, but they reported that it was difficult to see the relevance of what they had read to what they did in the field.

What It Means to Know and Learn

Another area where perceptions of students and instructors differ in advanced-level problem-oriented courses is what it means to know the course content and how to learn it. Problem-oriented courses offer a radical vision of what the content is. Students learn not only information, but also skills. Instead of facts, the content of these courses consists of the process of collecting, collating, and using facts to analyze problems in the discipline. However, because students are trained to focus on facts, they may not even be able to identify the skills they're learning.

Because their perceptions of what it means to know might differ, students and instructors may also have different perceptions of how best to learn the content. In problem-oriented courses, students, even at these more advanced levels, might still see learning as receiving knowledge from the instructor, who is considered the content expert. In this type of course, however, although the instructor's content expertise is still vitally important, part of the instructor's role is how to teach and model expert practices in dealing with the problems of the discipline. Though students may find the problems engaging, they often find this type of learning much less tangible and may not even see it as learning. As students in one senior-level problem-based learning course commented, "We really enjoy chatting about the cases, but the course is more than half over and we haven't started to learn anything yet." From the instructor's perspective, they were delving into the real issues of the field, integrating a wide range of relevant scientific and social information, and posing novel solutions to complex problems. From the students' perspective, they were "chatting about cases."

Another aspect of differing perceptions of the process of learning in problem-oriented courses is the way successful learning is recognized—how do students know *when* they know? One of the goals of these courses is to prepare students for work on open-ended problems they might encounter in the real world of the discipline. Because these problems may not have unambiguous "right answers," it is difficult for students to know how to gauge their progress or recognize what level of competence their solutions represent. Instead of assessing themselves in terms of scores on tests or assignments, students need to rely more on comparison with peers or on self-assessment of their progress. Students will also look to instructors for feedback; yet an instructor may be unsure how much feedback to give, since one aspect of the learning is to develop the ability to deal with the complex, ambiguous, or open-ended nature of the problem. In addition, instructors may face challenges about how to give feedback on students' work: As students present a range of possible solutions to a problem, instructors may be confident in identifying which solutions are relatively stronger or more supportable, but may find it challenging to articulate exactly by what criteria they recognize quality.

We see the same alignment issues arise in these advanced-level, problem-oriented courses. Perceptions of real-world relevance and of purposes for learning might differ; also, because what it means to know the content is very different in these courses, students and instructors can have very different perceptions of effective approaches to learning. Advanced-level students in problem-oriented courses lack confidence in their learning processes as learning becomes "real world," with more complexities and fewer "right answers." In addition, these students may not be confident that the problems they're working with and the skills they're learning are indeed transferable to their professional or graduate careers. These differing student and instructor perspectives point to areas where instructors will want to focus strategies for balancing instructional components.

Strategies for Alignment in Math, Science, and Engineering Courses

Considering how student and instructor perceptions of learning in math, science, and engineering courses might differ, instructors can seek strategies that help align their own perspectives with those of their students. One professor who recognized a need for aligning his perception of course content with his students' adjusted his thinking in this way: "Before, I focused too much on content—on what I was going to say. Now I try to split it 50/50 between content and audience. I try to adapt the content to the audience" (Rethinking the Classroom, 2001). This instructor has found a strategy effective in working toward alignment in his teaching. The strategies outlined below include examples from other instructors.

Relevance and Purpose for Learning

To help students understand the relationship of course content to the real world and the purpose of the course, instructors use the following strategies.

Find out more about students' experience and expectations. As mentioned in Chapter 6, many instructors find it helpful to learn where students are starting from and why they're taking the course. A simple and effective technique is to ask students to write answers to key questions on index cards. For example, an instructor can ask students to note their previous experience with course content and their goals for taking the course. With this information, the instructor can discuss with students his or her own perspective on the purpose of the course and highlight areas where students' perceptions are similar or different. Or, by asking a simple question such as, "What does it mean to learn X?", an instructor can also discover students' perspectives on what it means to know and learn in the discipline. Acknowledging the differences and similarities in perceptions can help instructors align student perceptions with their own.

Express learning goals for the course and purposes for assignments in terms that students will be able to understand and appreciate. To balance students' possible misperceptions of the content and purpose of the course, instructors can be explicit about why the content is important and for whom it is important. For example, students may not know what they will do in the future as engineers, but showing how the course content has relevance to engineering provides a point of contact with students' expectations for learning. Instructors may also have options for restructuring course content to help students see its importance and, thus, help motivate learning. For example, the instructor of a large engineering class, after finding that "students didn't understand where all the apparent 'disconnected' topics fit in until it was too late" (Eberhardt, 2000, p. 19), decided to reorder topics so that the students could see the big picture first. Another example is the use of student misconceptions as a basis for course design (McDermott, 2001). In both cases, instructors adjusted learning goals so that students could better understand and appreciate course content.

Another example is from the instructor of the Principles of Economics course who redesigned the course with the goal of making clear connections between students' understanding of issues and the economic principles presented in the course. To accomplish this goal, the instructor presented issues interesting to social scientists, such as income inequality, discrimination, and unemployment, and demonstrated the tools that an economist uses to analyze these social issues. Upon introducing these topics, the instructor asked students to write down their impressions of policy designed to alleviate a specific social problem. By engaging in this activity, students associated the course material with how they viewed the world around them. After introducing vocabulary and skills necessary for students to achieve economic literacy, the instructor then asked students how, using the tools of an economist, they could propose social policy for change. With this sequence of assignments, the instructor could align the students' need for relevance and skill-building with the instructor's foresight of the tools and theory necessary to continue in the discipline.

Develop a broad repertoire of examples. Knowing that students are looking for points of reference that connect course content with their own experience, instructors can develop a range of examples that will help students make those connections. For example, graduate teaching assistants (TAs) assigned to teach problem-solving sections for business calculus often found it difficult to provide examples and frameworks that would help business majors see the relevance of the material presented in the course. The TAs were mostly from the mathematics department, with little or no experience in the fields of business, economics, or finance. One graduate student, after observing this challenge, developed a handbook for TAs teaching business calculus, providing TAs with a ready set of examples and reference points to help them align content with students' background and purposes for learning.

Another way that instructors place material in a range of contexts is by letting students know how different disciplines might view content differently. For example, an instructor might say, "I look at it this way as a physicist. As an engineer, you would need to . . ." By including other disciplines and making the different perspectives explicit to students, an instructor can help students see how what they're learning fits into a broader context. In addition, instructors can find ways to help students see relationships in course content by being explicit about connections among examples at different levels of abstraction. For example, by pointing out similarities in underlying concepts of problems, instructors can help students develop their own ability to see connections.

What It Means to Know and Learn

To help bring into alignment student and instructor perspectives on what it means to know and learn content, instructors use many strategies, including the following:

Introduce students to the unknowns of the discipline, not just the "knowns." If one of the misperceptions of students is that math, science, and engineering represent fixed bodies of knowledge, then instructors only reinforce that misperception by focusing on widely accepted conclusions and results of scientific studies, rather than by exposing students to the areas that are debated. For example, one instructor designed a life sciences course around the concept of "diseases we aren't able to cure," using unresolved medical challenges as a way to frame what is known about the healthy functioning of selected biological systems. Other instructors have made time in class to discuss their own areas of research—not expecting students to appreciate fully the research that they do, but emphasizing that there are significant and interesting questions that scholars in the field are still exploring. In cases such as these, instructors were able to use the "unknowns" both to frame the concepts they were introducing and to demonstrate to students that knowledge is far from complete in these disciplines.

In the Principles of Economics course described earlier, the instructor introduces supply and demand analysis by asking if mandatory family leave legislation maximizes social welfare. Students read articles written by economists who disagree about whether the policy reflects a shift in the supply curve or in the demand curve for female labor. Using the same tools of analysis but different assumptions, economists can arrive at different forecasts of how the legislation will affect the market for female labor. Students are then asked, based upon their understanding of the opposing views, whether they favor limiting or expanding the legislation. By proposing legislation based on their own analysis, students learn the importance of simplifying assumptions as well as the tradeoffs associated with social policy making. The important idea to highlight for students is that the issue remains unresolved among economists who, using the same tools of analysis, can arrive at different conclusions through different assumptions about what is held constant along the supply and demand curves.

Model ways of solving the problem in addition to teaching the solutions. If one of the misperceptions of students is to focus on getting right answers, then instructors only reinforce this misperception when they limit their demonstration of problem-solving procedures and jump to a final answer. Processes that the instructor can demonstrate with ease may be much more difficult when students try them on their own; skipping steps in a demonstration may save the instructor time, but it may give students an unrealistic and inadequate understanding of how to handle difficulties when they are solving problems.

One instructor described his surprise when students reported to him that one of the best days of his class, from their perspective, was a day that he remembered as one of his worst. What was planned as a brief demonstration of a simple robot quickly took over half the class period because the robot would not work. Without a specific plan in mind, the instructor began trying to fix it, verbalizing his thinking throughout the trial-and-error process of getting the robot to work. The students later told him, "You make everything look easy, but our stuff rarely works the first time we try it. We learned a lot by watching what you do when something goes wrong."

Teach students strategies for self-assessment. As noted in Chapter 5, many students use grades as a primary source of assessing how well they are learning. Though grades may be useful to some extent for students' self-assessment, students will be much more able to align their learning with the course content and the instructor if they are able to assess their own progress on a continuing basis. Self-assessment is important to learning in any type of course, but it is particularly so in the advanced-level problem-oriented courses where students are learning more independently. If students can reliably self-assess their learning, they can make better decisions about how to use their time, how to recognize when they're having problems, and when they may need to seek additional help. For example, as noted in Chapter 3, starting a course with an ungraded diagnostic test is useful, not only for the instructor, but also for students to assess their own readiness for the course and the amount of work it will take for them to succeed in it. In addition, incorporating the regular use of classroom assessment techniques (Angelo & Cross, 1993), as noted in Chapter 4, provides the instructor with ongoing information about students' progress and helps students build skills for reflecting on their own learning.

Conclusion

As discussed in three contexts in math, science, and engineering courses, students and instructors often have very different views of learning in the discipline. Because students and instructors might see the relevance of course content to the real world differently, they might have differing views on the purpose for learning course content. In addition, because students and instructors might have different perspectives on what the content is, they might also have different perceptions of how to go about learning the content. These differing perspectives on learning can lead to areas where instructor, students, and content are out of alignment. If instructors approach the teaching of their courses with these differences in mind, they can make adjustments in how they present the course content and the purpose for learning it—and in how they help students understand what the content consists of and how to approach learning it. As instructors in math, science, and engineering make adjustments in their courses based on these differing areas of student and instructor perceptions, they can better align themselves with students and course content.

Endnote

1) We are defining math, science, and engineering courses broadly to include courses that emphasize quantitative reasoning, experimental design, and scientific methods.

References

Albanese, M., & Mitchell, S. (1993). Problem-based learning: A review of the literature on its outcomes and implementation issues. *Academic Medicine, 68*(1), 52–81.

Angelo, T. A., & Cross, K. P. (1993). *Classroom assessment techniques: A handbook for college teachers* (2nd ed.). San Francisco, CA: Jossey-Bass.

Eberhardt, S. (2000). Airplanes for everyone: A general education course for non-engineers. *Journal of Engineering Education, 89*(1), 17–20.

Ireton, M. F. W., Manduca, C. A., & Mogk, D. W. (1996). *Shaping the future of undergraduate earth science education: Innovation and change using an earth system approach.* Washington, DC: American Geophysical Union.

McDermott, L. C. (2001). Oersted medal lecture 2001: Physics education research—the key to student learning. *American Journal of Physics, 69*(11), 1127–1137.

Rethinking the classroom. (2001, Winter/Spring). *Arts and Sciences Perspectives.* Retrieved December 8, 2004, from http://www.artsci.washington .edu/newsletter/WinterSpring01/longfeaturelong.htm

Uno, G. (1997). Learning about learning through teaching about inquiry. In A. P. McNeal & C. D'Avanzo (Eds.), *Student-active science: Models of innovation in college science teaching* (pp. 189–198). Philadelphia, PA: Saunders College Publishing.

10

Aligning in Foreign Language Instruction

Margaret Lawrence & Klaus Brandl

Foreign language teachers and learners often differ in their views about the nature and value of teaching and learning activities. For example, one area of difference is use of the target language. Many instructors take a communicative approach to language teaching and thus emphasize using the target language as the medium of instruction; however, students frequently experience extensive use of the target language as difficult and frustrating (Brandl & Bauer, 2002).

Another area where students and teachers often differ in their perspective on learning language is grammar. Teachers who follow communicative-based methodologies prefer to treat grammar as a means to an end. They focus on the use of authentic language within situational contexts and seek to provide opportunities for functional and communicative language use that allow the learners to develop communicative and grammar skills simultaneously. On the other hand, many students believe that detailed and explicit grammar explanations help them advance faster in the development of language skills.

A third area where instructors' and students' perspectives frequently differ is pronunciation. Many learners believe that extensive, focused pronunciation practice leads to improvement in pronunciation skills. However, many teachers subscribe to research findings in second language acquisition suggesting that achieving native-like pronunciation is a complex process, largely related to factors beyond learners' and teachers' control (Pica, 1994).

As the preceding examples illustrate, foreign language teachers frequently face alignment issues. To explore these issues in this chapter, we make use of case studies from three first-year language instructors. Based on the data from the case studies, we discuss the alignment process and present some strategies that can help maximize alignment in foreign language learning environments.

Questions About Alignment

We focused the analysis of our data on three key alignment issues:

1) How do these foreign language instructors identify the need for alignment?

2) How do they make decisions about alignment?

3) What does it mean for them to succeed at alignment?

The first question was asked to identify factors that alerted instructors to the need for alignment. The second question sought to examine instructors' decision-making processes as they attempted to foster alignment. To what degree did these instructors anticipate alignment issues and respond with proactive strategies? When they identified misalignment, how did they respond and what kinds of strategies did they employ? Finally, because alignment is an ongoing, evolving process, the third question was designed to determine how instructors assessed whether their alignment efforts were effective.

Data Collection

Our study spanned the period of one academic quarter. In order to document ways in which instructors approached the alignment process, we collected data in the following ways:

- Initial interviews with instructors that asked what aspects of the course they felt were difficult for students, what challenges they were encountering, and what strategies they were employing to address those challenges

- Mid-quarter interviews with students that asked them to identify strengths they saw in the course and changes they would recommend

- A second interview with instructors about the mid-quarter interviews

- Written feedback from students near the end of the quarter on changes they saw in the class

- A final interview with instructors when they received the second set of student feedback and a discussion of how the feedback compared with their own final perceptions of the class

Findings

We begin the discussion of our findings with brief summaries of the cases and then turn to the consideration of our results using our alignment questions.

Case Summaries

In *Case 1*, Sara described in the initial interview a number of strategies that she used to foster alignment and anticipate problems. The only concern she identified was how students might feel about her homework policy, which required them to correct homework after she marked mistakes, then turn it in again.

In the mid-quarter interview, students listed many strengths in Sara's class. They also listed a few suggestions for change that Sara had not anticipated, such as giving homework in English as well as Swedish, using fewer handouts, providing more in-class pronunciation practice, and reminding students to turn in homework at the end of class. They also made a few suggestions for practices that Sara was already planning to implement in the latter part of the quarter or in the following quarter, including: centering vocabulary learning on topics, employing a greater variety of activities, and including more culture in lessons. Sara decided to implement some of these suggested changes, propose alternate solutions for other issues, and discuss with students reasons for not making some changes at all during fall quarter. At the end of the quarter, almost all students reported that they felt Sara had made satisfactory adjustments in the areas they had suggested.

In *Case 2*, Bruce said at the beginning of the quarter that he felt more successful at "inductive teaching" than in previous quarters and that his students seemed to respond well to his attempts to make the class active. He noted that the main challenge in his teaching was that sometimes his explanations weren't clear.

In the mid-quarter interview, students expressed appreciation for Bruce's knowledge, his emphasis on using the target language in class, and his approachability. But they asked for more visual support in the form of handouts or writing on the board, louder, clearer speech, more use of English, even greater rapport with the instructor, and more fun. Bruce decided to ask students for further clarification on some issues, such as the difference between rapport and approachability and the request for more visuals. Other suggested changes, like speaking louder, he decided to address. Still others, such as developing more rapport or creating more fun, he decided were not necessarily aspects of his role as an instructor.

At the end of the quarter, more than half the students reported that class had become more fun and that Bruce "was noticeably more open," even though he hadn't made conscious efforts to change in this area. Bruce attributed this perception to the fact that he naturally felt more relaxed as the quarter progressed, so he met student expectations without actually making a conscious effort. About half the students also perceived change in areas that he had consciously worked on, such as speaking louder and using more English at key points in his explanations.

In *Case 3,* Paula was teaching a first-year language course for the second time. During our first interview, she focused almost entirely on her dissatisfaction with the textbook that the department had recently adopted. She felt that its features and organization worked against designing coherent, efficient language lessons for her students. She was trying to supplement the text with her own handouts and thought she saw some improvement in student performance as a result. However, she still expected that students would complain about the book in the mid-quarter interview.

In the mid-quarter interview, students identified the following strengths: Paula's positive attitude, her organization, and her preparation. They asked for more English explanations, more help in test review, and handouts organized into packets on a weekly basis. Only about half the students found the design of the textbook confusing. All the students were confused by the way the textbook was being used, however. For example, they weren't always sure which parts of the text to focus on in preparation for class.

In response to the feedback, Paula decided to use more English in class. In discussion with us, she decided that the remaining requests reflected the lack of focus brought about by the book's structure. Although she felt she couldn't implement students' requests as they were framed, she developed alternate strategies to address the underlying needs their requests suggested. At the end of the quarter, all students reported they felt the course had changed for the better in the areas mentioned in the mid-quarter interview.

Discussion of Research Questions

In the following sections, we discuss findings from our cases in terms of our three guiding questions on alignment.

Question 1: How do these instructors identify the need for alignment? At least three factors alerted the three instructors to potential or actual alignment issues: their beliefs about learning, student performance, and student feedback. They typically relied on some combination of these factors to help them identify the need for alignment but varied in the degree to which they took each factor into account.

Beliefs about learning. Instructors' beliefs about effective learning play a fundamental role in how they teach. These beliefs are typically based on a blend of pedagogical theory and personal perspectives on teaching gained from past experiences as learners and teachers. As Richards (1998) suggested, teachers normally develop their own "implicit theories of teaching—that is, their personal and subjective philosophy and their understanding of what constitutes good teaching" (p. 51). When student expectations, the text, or curriculum guidelines conflict with the instructor's "implicit theories of teaching," some kind of alignment may be required.

In these cases, the instructors' interpretations of pedagogical theory influenced them to varying degrees in identifying or anticipating misalignment. Sara, for example, believed communicative practice was key in acquiring language and thus required regular classroom attendance. When a few students missed class at the beginning of the quarter, she considered the absences a problem and approached the students individually to encourage them to attend regularly. Paula, on the other hand, believed that an effective textbook should not include material extraneous to a lesson's vocabulary or grammar point focus. She had trouble aligning these beliefs with the more global, whole language approach of the text her department had chosen for the language course she taught. She thus anticipated accurately that some students would feel as uncomfortable as she did with the text.

The three instructors' beliefs about language learning reflected not only pedagogical theory, but also their own previous experiences as learners and teachers. Bruce most often referred to his own experience as a learner to help gauge his alignment with his students and their alignment with the content. For example, as he explained a grammar point in class, he listened to himself, imagined himself as a student, and decided his explanation was confusing. When explaining changes in his teaching, he would sometimes say, "I wouldn't like that if I were a student." In these cases, he assumed that he was out of alignment with his students' expectations based on his own previous experience as a student. Other times, he used his own sense of what it meant for him to align with the content to assess whether students aligned with it. For example, he decided he needed to use more cultural activities in his class because, as he said, "To me, the culture—it's an incredible place. And if I can't give some sense of that to them, then they're not going to have as much enthusiasm as they could."

In addition to drawing on their previous experience as learners, instructors also draw on their previous experience as instructors. Over time, teachers' experiences in the classroom form their perceptions about how classroom activities promote desired learning outcomes (Prabhu, 1987). These perceptions then shape their expectations about how to align most effectively in future classes. For example, Paula reported that her current group of students "could communicate but they made a lot of mistakes on very simple things on tests. They shouldn't." Thus, her previous experiences with student performance helped her decide that there were problems with the current learning experiences of her students. Although previous experience as an instructor can help identify problematic areas, it can also set expectations that decrease the instructor's sensitivity to current issues. For example, Sara was caught off guard when a group of students struggled with the use of numbers, a topic which former students had easily mastered.

Student performance and behavior. Student performance in class and on assignments is another means that instructors use for identifying student alignment with the content. In our cases, Bruce assessed whether students understood his grammar explanations by asking them to summarize what he had just explained. Sara determined students' mastery of questions in the target language by reviewing items during warm-ups at the beginning of class, asking students "How are you?" or "What's your name?" Additionally, all three instructors used performance on quizzes and homework as indicators of student mastery of the content.

Instructors also interpret students' nonverbal behavior as indications of their engagement with the material. Bruce realized that he was speaking too fast or that his explanations were not clear when students "looked confused." He also interpreted students taking notes as an indication that they were actively engaging with the material. If they were just "staring at him," he interpreted that behavior as being less engaged.

Direct student feedback, solicited or unsolicited. In addition to instructor beliefs and student performance, direct student feedback is a third tool for identifying alignment needs. Students who feel comfortable with their instructor may volunteer information about ways in which they feel out of alignment with the course or the instructor. However, often just a few students make such voluntary contributions and are not necessarily representative of the class, even though students frequently frame their suggestions as something "everyone thinks." Thus it is often helpful to check student perceptions through more formal forms of solicited feedback that garner information from the entire class. For example, one or two students told Sara they felt that correcting and rewriting homework was busywork. However, the mid-quarter class interview revealed that, contrary to her expectations and the informal feedback she had received from a few students, nearly all students found making corrections on homework and turning it in for a second time very helpful.

Question 2: How did instructors make decisions about alignment? All three instructors used a variety of factors in determining how to make decisions about alignment. Their beliefs about effective learning continued to

play a significant role in their decisions as did student needs, student suggestions for change, and the time and effort required to make changes. In the
next sections, we discuss the decision-making practices instructors used for
alignment in terms of two broad categories: preactive decisions and interactive decisions (Richards & Lockhart, 1994). Preactive decisions are those that
teachers make as part of their curricular and daily planning by drawing on
their experience and evaluation of preceding lessons or previous teaching
experience. Some preactive strategy decisions are preemptive; that is, instructors employ them to prevent misalignment. Other preactive decisions involve
ongoing planning strategies. These are initiated in response to alignment
needs that surface during the course. Interactive decisions, on the other hand,
are those made as immediate responses to classroom situations. Richards
(1998) noted that these types of decisions are essential to good teaching
because lessons are dynamic, to some extent unpredictable, and characterized
by constant change.

Preactive decision-making. Sara employed preactive decision-making by
using a variety of preemptive strategies, which were grounded in her beliefs
about student-centered learning and her previous teaching experience. Even
before the current course began, she reviewed notes she had made on lesson
plans from the previous year's course and revised plans according to comments she had made about what had and had not worked. At the beginning
of the current course, she handed out a "wish list" questionnaire, asking students what they wanted to learn about the language and the culture. Additionally, in her detailed discussion of the syllabus at the beginning of the
course, she emphasized specific expectations for participation and homework as well as tips on language learning strategies. Finally, she made it clear
to students that she always welcomed their feedback. Thus, by the beginning
of the quarter, she was already using a combination of strategies that enabled
her to align her content and her teaching approach to students' needs and
align students with her expectations and content. Furthermore, her invitation for student feedback helped promote ongoing efforts to align as the
quarter progressed.

One preemptive strategy that Sara wished she had used was giving students the big picture at the beginning of the course. In the mid-quarter interview, her class asked for more culture and more varied activities, developments that she already had planned to implement at later stages of the course.
Sara felt she might have aligned more effectively if she had given a more complete picture in the first week of class to explain how language practice and
cultural discussion would develop over the year.

Because even the most carefully thought out preemptive strategies cannot address all alignment issues, much alignment takes place throughout the term in the form of ongoing planning strategies, such as creating additional materials, slowing the course to provide additional review, or redesigning activities.

Of the three instructors, it was Paula who implemented the most ambitious use of ongoing planning strategies to overcome the unanticipated difficulties she was having with the text. She created numerous supplemental handouts to provide more structured practice for specific grammatical points and align students with the content more effectively. When students made more mistakes on tests than she had anticipated based on her previous experience with the course, she took time for additional review of problematic points. Because Paula was only using parts of the book, she also took extra care to align students with her expectations by clearly identifying which vocabulary words students needed to learn and which parts of the book they needed to study. She also had to align student needs with her own. Students found the large number of handouts confusing and asked to have them distributed in packets a week or two ahead of time, a request she could not realistically fulfill. She let students know she could not fulfill their request, but instead tried to address their underlying need for increased order by taking extra care in labeling, dating, and sequencing the handouts.

Sara took overheads to class from the previous two or three days of lessons so that she was prepared should students need review of a difficult point. Although she came to class with a plan for the day, she was always prepared to adjust the plan in order to realign herself with students and align students more fully with content.

In addition to adjusting activities, creating new materials, and revisiting old material in order to align themselves and the content with students, all three instructors used increased communication to help students align with their expectations or course content. For example, when students asked for more pronunciation practice in the mid-quarter class interview, Sara decided not to change her classroom approach. Instead, she shared her rationale on the teaching of pronunciation and explained how pronunciation skills would develop as an aspect of other activities during the course.

Interactive decision-making. Sometimes instructors must make alignment decisions spontaneously while teaching. In this case, there is little time for the reflection that underlies planned decision-making. Instead, instructors must adjust their assumptions and their previous plans for alignment to address the alignment needs at that moment in the class.

For example, instructors in our case studies responded differently when students were confused by the use of the target language for grammar explanations in class. Sometimes, instructors chose to repeat their point more slowly in the target language. In these instances, they maintained their commitment to teaching in the target language. At the same time, they were aligning themselves with student needs for greater clarity. At other times, instructors used English to clarify either because repetition wasn't working or because they didn't want to use class time for the explanation. In such cases, they compromised slightly on their belief that a language is best learned when everything is taught in that language for the sake of increased efficiency and clarity. Still other times, instructors chose to write on the board or spend extra time clarifying a point. In each of these cases, the instructors made decisions on the spot to align student needs, content demands, and instructor beliefs.

Question 3: What does it mean to succeed at alignment? As all instructors discover, alignment is an ideal that one approaches but never fully attains. Even when a satisfactory level of alignment has been reached with one class, the process of alignment starts anew with a new class, shaped by a new group of students or new course content. If we can never arrive at complete alignment, what does it mean to align successfully?

The alignment model suggests that the amount of student learning, as measured by factors such as assessment of student achievement, ultimately defines success in alignment. However, although evidence of student learning was the ultimate criterion, instructors in our study also measured their instructional success in terms of where the components of alignment intersected. Those intersections included aligning students and content (achieving curricular goals), aligning students and instructor (adhering to methodological principles), and aligning instructor with students (addressing student needs and expectations).

Aligning students and content. All three instructors evaluated their lessons in terms of how well they had accomplished their curriculum goals. They daily assessed the success of activities and students' responses against the immediate plan for the lesson, the larger plan provided by the curriculum, and the goals of their departments. At the end of the quarter, they defined their success by the changes and adjustments made in their teaching that allowed them to align students more fully with curricular goals and content.

For example, Bruce described his curricular adjustments in the following way: "I think giving [my students] an opportunity to work orally together . . . bringing in more cultural activities . . . explaining things more systematically on the board allowed me to be more successful."

For Sara, integrating more cultural information was a curricular change that was suggested by her students, and one she also had set as a goal for herself. At the end of the quarter, she measured her success by the number of cultural activities she had managed to implement: ". . . we've done more songs and modern music as well. . . ."

In describing her achievements, Paula focused on student performance and her curricular goals; that is, the content she was able to cover and how well her students were able to perform in the target language. Curricular goals were particularly an issue for her, as she had been dealing with the challenges of a newly adopted curriculum and textbook throughout the quarter. Although she covered less material, she was still satisfied with the goals that she had reached.

Aligning students and instructor. As instructors' understanding of effective teaching evolves, methodological principles based on these instructors' current beliefs often become the yardstick of what constitutes effective teaching. For example, Bruce felt he successfully balanced his students' needs with his own desire to adhere to certain methodological principles. Although he strongly believed in teaching all portions of the course in the target language, he was able to balance his convictions with student needs when his students requested grammar explanations in English. He said, "I repeated things in English more than I did before." At the same time, he continued teaching mainly in the target language: "But I don't think I actually changed much in terms of how much I spoke French. . . . I think I've gone about as far as I'm willing to go with English explanations."

Aligning instructor and students. Another factor that contributed to the instructors' feeling of success was how well they managed to align with students' needs and expectations. For example, Paula expressed her own success by referring to her students' comfort with the content: "But at least things are solid. It seems like they're comfortable about what they're learning." Sara felt she successfully balanced addressing students' needs with implementing her own curricular goals and teaching philosophy: "I reduced the number of handout interviews and did more questions on the overhead . . . watched a movie and had more discussions about [target language] culture . . . provided homework emails in English and [target language]. . . . I think that helped."

Strategies

The three instructors in our study faced a range of alignment issues and approached alignment in different ways. Drawing from their experience, we offer a set of strategies that others can consider in working towards alignment in foreign language teaching.

Discuss Methodological Approaches and Language Learning Expectations Early in the Term

Students come to class with particular expectations of how they like to be taught as well as personal goals for learning the target language. Instructors also come with certain methodological beliefs and concrete strategies on how to go about teaching. Thus, addressing student and instructor beliefs and expectations at the start of a term becomes an essential strategy for alignment. For example, to see more specifically where she needed to align students with course goals and approaches, Sara used a questionnaire at the beginning of the term that asked students about their learning goals. She included specific questions about what students wanted to learn about culture; what their language learning expectations were; whether they were more interested in focusing on spoken language, grammar, or writing; and how they wanted to use the language in the future. The information she gleaned from this questionnaire helped her align students with her philosophy of teaching and the course content by addressing issues raised in the questionnaires, by giving specific hints for effective language study, and by clearly explaining the rationale for her methodological approach. The questionnaire also helped Sara to identify those areas in which she might modify her own approaches and content to address student expectations.

Encourage Participatory Use of the Language

Language students can more effectively align with the content of the language when they are encouraged to practice communicating with it. In our study, Bruce used video materials to provide authentic and rich input that became a basis for communicative language application. Sara encouraged communicative language use by giving in-class participation points to students. She also explained why oral practice was important and strongly encouraged students to attend class on a daily basis for that reason. In addition, she often emphasized to students that she was accessible through email and during office hours for additional language practice.

Consider Modifying the Use of the Textbook

Language textbooks vary in their organizational and methodological approaches to language teaching; rarely does a textbook completely address the needs of a particular class. The instructor's methodological preferences, student backgrounds and needs, or situational issues like length of term all affect the suitability of a text. In order to align students optimally with content, effective language teachers generally make use of the textbook as a guide rather than as a determinant of the curriculum. If necessary, they modify materials, omit complete sections, or rearrange and adapt outside resources. In our study, Paula's approach to aligning her materials with student needs and her own methodological philosophy demonstrated this principle. She selected portions of the text on which students could focus and asked them to ignore other sections that she felt were less useful in her course. She also highlighted key vocabulary and grammar points, sometimes orally and sometimes on handouts. Finally, she created additional exercises to provide more meaningful and focused practice on those key items.

Consider Multiple Ways of Implementing Methodological Approaches to Learning Languages

In a typical course, there is a wide range of student types with different needs and expectations, so to make alignment possible, instructors may need to find alternate solutions within the context of a particular approach. For example, all three instructors in our study believed that teaching in the target language is the most effective way for students to learn. Yet, in all three cases, students asked for a little more use of English in grammar explanations or homework assignments. The three instructors attempted to align themselves with students in this area in different ways. Bruce repeated more in the target language instead of using more English. Sara continued to send out homework assignments over email in the target language, but she included an English translation at the end in case some students were confused. Paula maintained instruction in the target language but occasionally made very conscious exceptions where grammar points were particularly complex. Thus, all three instructors retained their commitments to teaching in the target language while addressing student expectations.

Conclusion

Our three case studies provide examples of using the alignment process in language learning and teaching. All three instructors identified areas needing alignment by considering multiple factors: their own theories about good teaching, their previous teaching experience, student performance, and student feedback. By attending to all of these sources of information, they developed rich perspectives on areas needing improved alignment. These instructors also implemented numerous combinations of strategies in their attempts to foster alignment. They experienced increased alignment and saw that their students were learning effectively as a result.

References

Brandl, K., & Bauer, G. (2002). Students' perceptions of novice teaching assistants' use of the target language in beginning foreign language classes: A preliminary investigation. In W. Davis, J. Smith, & R. Smith (Eds.), *Ready to teach: Graduate teaching assistants prepare for today and for tomorrow* (pp. 128–138). Stillwater, OK: New Forums Press.

Pica, T. (1994). Questions from the language classroom: Research perspectives. *TESOL Quarterly, 28*(1), 49–79.

Prabhu, N. (1987). *Second language pedagogy.* Oxford, England: Oxford University Press.

Richards, J. C. (1998). *Beyond training.* New York, NY: Cambridge University Press.

Richards, J. C., & Lockhart, C. (1994). *Reflective teaching in second language classrooms.* New York, NY: Cambridge University Press.

11

Aligning in Socially Transformative Courses

Alka Arora

You are planning a new course, "Gender, Race, and Class in Transnational Perspective." You have read and studied a little about critical pedagogy; you consider yourself a feminist; and you have never been in favor of traditional teaching methods where students sit passively trying to absorb the teacher's vast knowledge. No, in your class, all students will be "empowered" to value their own knowledge. They will think critically about issues of power and identity, grasping the links between their own personal experiences, media images, and wider historical and political forces. Students will have a "voice" through lively discussions and debate. You will step back and "facilitate" rather than teach, all the while secretly congratulating yourself for unleashing the potential of such bright and socially committed students.

Suddenly, you wake up. Your blissful reverie is cut short. The quarter has already begun; you need to prepare for another week of class. First, you read some anonymous student feedback: Some students complain that there is not enough structure in class, and they wish you would lecture more. Others write that they think your grading is too harsh and they thought you *wanted* them just to write about their own lived experience. Meanwhile, your department is talking about countering "grade inflation" and improving learning outcomes. Reality provides a stark contrast to your idyllic vision. Although you have been immersed in theories about pedagogy and social change for years, you realize that you have limited practical experience with teaching and learning in a democratic classroom. Are you in over your head?

Teaching a course using critical and/or feminist pedagogical methods—what I call "socially transformative" pedagogies—presents unique alignment issues. First, teaching *method* becomes almost synonymous with course *content* in a socially transformative course. In other words, your course may include an examination of the social interactions in the classroom—between you and students, and among students—as part of the curriculum. The second alignment issue, which follows from the first, is that your identity and perspective as a teacher become particularly salient. Third, students may enter the course further away from both you and the content, given the newer and possibly controversial content and structure of the course. Finally, the institutional context in which your course is situated may constrain some of the ways in which you implement a socially transformative pedagogy.

Fortunately, there are some steps that can help create a classroom environment that, if not quite utopic, is still a place where students, content, and instructor are better aligned in the process of liberatory education. In the sections that follow, I will provide a brief overview of socially transformative pedagogies and address their unique alignment issues by focusing on the four key intersections of the alignment model: those between instructor and content, instructor and students, students and content, and course and context. In addition, I will discuss how viewing socially transformative pedagogy from an alignment perspective can help both you and your students to reach the goal of learning. Students will learn to claim their power to produce knowledge, and you will learn from students and the interactions that take place in the course.

Socially Transformative Pedagogies

There is a vast body of literature on both "critical" and "feminist" pedagogies. Critical pedagogy grew largely out of the work of Paolo Freire, who educated landless peasants in South America. Through this work, he developed a theoretical framework for how marginalized groups can produce knowledge that serves their own needs, rather than echoing the knowledge that serves the needs of those in power. One of his most widely circulated ideas is his critique of the "banking" system of education, where information is "deposited" into students' heads for future retrieval (Freire, 2000). As critical pedagogy has made its way into higher education in the United States, it has evolved and been extensively debated. Most critical pedagogues would agree, however, that a critical pedagogy focuses on the role of power in the context of education and aims to empower students to become knowledge *producers* rather than consumers.

Feminist pedagogy initially emerged out of concerns regarding the ways in which women might learn differently from men, particularly in traditionally male-dominated settings such as the university. In addition, contemporary debates about feminist pedagogy have been largely influenced by critical pedagogy and "examine the political and social mechanisms that have controlled the knowledge production process and have marginalized (or left out) the contributions of women and people of color" (Tisdell, 1995, p. 70).

My own interest in critical and feminist pedagogies has emerged from my experience as an instructor of women studies, from my involvement in developing new women studies courses, and from my role as an instructional consultant. These multiple roles have afforded me an opportunity to see the links between pedagogical theory and classroom practice. Though the theoretical frameworks encompassed under the headings "critical pedagogy" and "feminist pedagogy" are broad, I believe that they share certain key principles. So for the purposes of this chapter, the term *socially transformative pedagogy* will be used to incorporate insights from both traditions and to denote teaching based on the following premises:

- *"No education is politically neutral"* (hooks, 1994, p. 37). Socially transformative pedagogies highlight the relationship between power and knowledge production. Canonical texts or knowledge within a given discipline are not the result of immutable truths. Rather, they reflect the perspectives and experiences of those who have the social and political power to decide what counts as "truth."

- *Students bring an array of knowledge with them to the classroom.* Students bring not only the academic learning from other educational settings, but also their backgrounds, life experiences, and social identities, which together provide a rich source of knowledge. Part of the aim of socially transformative pedagogies is to help students make this knowledge explicit and link them to larger social realities.

- *The classroom is part of the real world.* Students and educators alike often speak of college as a separate, privileged place that prepares students for the real world while standing apart from it. A socially transformative pedagogy, on the other hand, views college life as continuous with other parts of life. It emphasizes "systemic thought" (Shor, 1996, p. 58), or an analysis of linkages among power in the classroom, power in the lives of students outside the class, and power structures at broader levels.

- *Everyday and relational learning is as valued as abstract thought.* Relational learning encompasses two ideas: 1) many students learn better when knowledge is constructed in relation to concrete life experiences and activities, 2) the development of positive relationships among students, and between students and instructor, is conducive to the learning process.

The following sections examine the concrete implications of these pedagogical principles and present specific strategies to help align instructor, students, and content within the particular context of an undergraduate classroom. The strategies offered in this chapter have emerged from the literature on socially transformative teaching, my own experience as an instructor, and the informal interviews I've conducted with other instructors—both colleagues and clients—who are committed to socially transformative education.[1]

Aligning Yourself and Content

As the instructor, you are very knowledgeable about the texts, theoretical frameworks, and facts that comprise the course content you are teaching. However, in a socially transformative course, your identity as a teacher and the ways in which you interact with students are equally important elements of course "content." In order to align yourself more effectively with this content, then, it is essential to do some self-reflection prior to meeting students.

Taking some time to increase your awareness of your socially situated identity is consistent with the critical pedagogical concept of "praxis," or back and forth movement between action and reflection (Freire, 2000). That is, the *action* of teaching a course is best done if it is both preceded and followed by *reflection*, which in turn leads to new action. This interplay among action and reflection is also a key aspect of the alignment model, for the instructor must be mindful of the dynamic nature of instruction and continually adjust course components to maintain alignment.

Reflect on Your Social Identity and Its Relation to Societal Power

The first step towards "eradicating authoritarian practices" and fostering the conditions for student empowerment is "the development of an awareness of one's own location in history, society, and privilege" (Leistyna, Woodrum, & Sherblom, 1996, p. 198). Thus, a socially transformative pedagogy demands that you maintain awareness of your place in classroom power relationships. Your own identity is going to impact your relationship to course content, and, as I will discuss in the next section, the ways in which students relate to you.

Gerschick (1999) raised the issue of instructor identity in his essay "Should and Can a White, Heterosexual, Middle-Class Man Teach Students about Social Inequality and Oppression?" He notes that he was often perceived as distant from the content of his course due to his privileged social identity. His academic expertise on social oppression was therefore necessary, but not sufficient. He also had to reflect critically upon how he benefited from unequal social structures and how he was accountable for creating social change. He concluded his essay with an answer to his title question: "If a white man is willing to confront his status and privilege and to continue to challenge himself as well as the class, then he is in a position to teach such a course" (p. 485).

Of course, members of marginalized groups are not automatically aligned with the content of courses that deal in social inequality. Rather, alignment comes through the interplay of experience, critical reflection, and academic expertise. Notice where course content challenges you and use this as an opportunity for further learning.

Consider How Your Own Educational Experiences Impact Your Teaching Style

Socially transformative pedagogues often speak of creating a "democratic" classroom where students and instructor come together and negotiate power. However, most teachers who attempt to create a democratic classroom have little experience as learners in democratic settings (hooks, 1994). Inevitably, instructors revert to teaching in ways that they themselves learned. As a result, you may find that your teaching is misaligned with the transformative content of your course. Thus, you may find it useful to reflect on your experiences as a student in order to recognize some of the assumptions about teaching that you may unconsciously hold. As one of my clients, a graduate student instructor, noted:

> I have this idea of how I want my class to be student-directed. But, in reality, it's very hard for that to happen. It's much easier to just tell students what to read and what to discuss. They accept it. And, you know, I realize that's how I was taught—even in my most "radical" courses.[2]

Begin Writing Your Teaching Philosophy

Reading some of the literature on critical and feminist pedagogy may help you to start thinking about your philosophy of teaching. Combining that reading with some reflective writing, however, will help you to determine your own stance. For example, the client quoted above was better able to identify her unconscious biases about education through writing about her experiences and ideas about teaching. She could then make conscious decisions about what aspects of her own, more traditional education she wanted to maintain and what she would strive to change.

The strategies identified here can help you begin the process of aligning yourself with socially transformative pedagogies. But aligning yourself to the content of this pedagogy is an ongoing, even lifelong, process. This process is intimately linked to the process of better aligning yourself with students. The next section explores the alignment issues raised for instructor and students in a socially transformative course and offers some concrete strategies to help you achieve greater alignment.

Aligning Yourself and Students

As an instructor, you might expect that students would welcome an opportunity to claim their voice in the classroom. You might also hope that they would appreciate your efforts to divest yourself of power. Therefore, you may be surprised when students enter your course even *further* apart from you than in a traditional classroom. Some reasons that students may resist attempts to create a socially transformative classroom environment include:

- *Discomfort.* Like most people, students are comfortable with what they know and have seen before. Most likely, few of your students will have participated in "democratically" run courses. They may feel discomfort with an unfamiliar classroom environment and new parameters for behavior. If they are resistant to course content (as discussed in the next section), they may be even more likely to resist your authority to teach them.

- *Distrust.* Students may be skeptical of attempts at an egalitarian classroom when they know that, in the end, you are the one with the power to assign grades. Students have learned the hierarchies of the educational system, so may regard you as one of the "elite" class in this system rather than their ally.

- *Lack of structure.* Students may be unclear about what the new environment entails. For instance, if due dates are "negotiable," students may find it a challenge to plan ahead as they wait for the class to reach consensus. If the instructor eschews setting agendas, students may feel lost when it comes to connecting ideas.

- *Increased responsibility.* With power comes responsibility. Asking students to select texts, lead discussions, or in other ways shape the direction of the course structure and content will likely add more time to their workload.

Fortunately, there are several things that you can do to anticipate and deal with student resistance in your class. The following strategies will help you to build rapport and improve classroom structure, thus better aligning yourself and students.

Be Clear About How This Course May Differ From Others They Have Taken

"In the transformed classroom there is often a much greater need to explain philosophy, strategy, intent than in the 'norm' setting" (hooks, 1994, p. 42). As a socially transformative pedagogue, you might find it helpful to make explicit your political perspective, the course process, and your expectation of student responsibilities. According to Jeanette Bushnell, a women studies instructor,

> I tell my students how I try to model the process of my classes to match the content of social critique. I have them read some of Freire and hooks and maybe Rasmussen who critiques Freire as not being critical enough. We talk about learning and teaching and what I think works well for their learning based on my scholarly authority. (personal communication, July 22, 2004)

Be an Authority, Not an Authoritarian

Some instructors believe that a socially transformative pedagogy implies that the instructor "facilitates" rather than teaches, but this is problematic. Even Freire (2000) has stated that he has "never pretended to be a facilitator." Despite your best intentions, you have institutional power that your students do not. Acting as if you are on the same plane as your students can provide an "illusion of equality" (Ellsworth, 1992, p. 487) without really altering the power imbalance between students and teacher. Therefore, you should make clear to students when you will exercise your authority (e.g., to intervene in a heated discussion or to set guidelines for written work) and when you will step back to enable students to make decisions (e.g., what questions will be posed during a class discussion).

Talk About Yourself

Students are naturally curious about their teachers' backgrounds, particularly in courses that deal with nontraditional subject matter. Sharing your own background, perspective, and interest in transformative politics is therefore a key part of aligning yourself with students: "I do not expect students to take any risks that I would not take, to share in any way that I would not share" (hooks, 1994, p. 21). Bushnell shared with me one of the ways she relates to students.

> I tell personal stories and anecdotes about American Indians and having a mom who left the rez and "passed" [as white], so the alienation from that aspect of my heritage. I talk about being heterosexual, a mom, and married for 30 years and living through those heady days of the 1960s and 1970s. I talk about mundane stuff like housework and how difficult it is to talk with car repair guys. I also talk about how my social identity has brought up scholarly questions to which I don't necessarily have answers now, like the whole concept of "nation" which comes up in relation to American Indian sovereignty. (personal communication, July 22, 2004)

Be Open to Student Feedback and Critique

As in any other course, eliciting feedback can help you to align yourself with students in a socially transformative course. Feedback can be used to improve course structure, pacing, or other elements of the course. Keep in mind, however, that some types of "negative" student feedback may also indicate a strength, rather than weakness, of your pedagogy. Shor (1996) discussed this paradox when he wrote that "I felt the democratic process [in my class] succeeded when Stephanie and others felt secure enough to criticize me" (p. 57).

Discuss Issues of Safety and Communication in the Classroom

Many educators believe that the classroom should be a "safe" space for students; however, disagreement arises about what constitutes "safety." For some, a safe space is one where conflict is minimized and difficult or unpleasant discussion is avoided. Some critical educators challenge this notion of safety, noting that "many students, especially students of color, may not feel at all 'safe' in what appears to be a neutral setting" (hooks, 1994, p. 39). From this latter perspective, conflict and discomfort are part of the practice of socially transformative education. Safety, then, does not imply lack of conflict, but rather a level of respect and mutuality from which risk-taking and genuine dialogue can emerge.

"Hear" Silence

Student participation is often regarded as the hallmark of transformative pedagogies. However, you should not only listen to students who are vocal in the classroom, but also pay attention to those who are silent. According to Ellsworth (1992),

> what they/we [marginalized groups] say, to whom, in what context, depending on the energy they/we have for the struggle on a particular day, is the result of conscious and unconscious assessments of the power relations and safety of the situation. (p. 493)

Thus, "hearing" this silence can give you some input into adjustments you need to make in aligning your course. Rather than trying to solve the "problem" of silence by calling on students, or otherwise prodding them to speak, consider whether the content of the course or your instruction need adjustment.

Moreover, it is important to differentiate between encouraging student "voice" and demanding that students share. Talking is not the only way in which students can come to voice. Although you want to create an environment where students do feel safe to speak, recognize that this dynamic is not always in your control. Consider alternate ways that students may have a voice in your course, such as through an anonymous electronic message board, free-form writing, or speaking with you in office hours.

Provide Structure

As the instructor, you still hold most of the responsibility for providing an organizing framework in your course. To align yourself with students, it is important that you provide structure, even if elements of the classroom are open for negotiation. In other words, if you ask students to select texts for some of the course, you still need to set timelines for when those texts should be selected; if students generate content during a particular discussion, you should present a summary of their ideas to the whole class during the next class period.

As the above strategies indicate, there are several ways to bring yourself and your students closer together in the shared goal of learning. In the next section I will briefly discuss potential areas of misalignment between students and *content* and then offer suggestions for aligning these two core instructional components.

Aligning Students and Content

In the same way that students may enter your course further removed from you as the instructor, they may also resist course content that deals with issues of power, oppression, and inequality. These topics are uncomfortable and often undermine students' idea of who they are in the world. Therefore, you should recognize the possible sources that create distance between students and content and employ strategies to create better alignment.

Provide a Space for Students to Air Concerns About Course Content

Most likely, students will enter your course with preconceived notions of what a course dealing with diversity and issues of power will cover. Some students will likely have a positive view of the course content, whereas others may hold a negative opinion about the topics that you are addressing. To align students with content, then, you may find it helpful to reserve some class time early in the term (ideally the first day) to discuss these preconceptions with students.

When I teach "Introduction to Feminist Theory," for example, I start with having students write down a word or phrase that immediately comes to mind when they think of the word "feminist." I compile this list—which often ranges from "angry" and "male-bashing" to "women's equality"—and circulate it among students the next class period. This list starts a discussion about what they already "know" about feminism and through what sources (e.g., media, school). I then explain that we are going to be exploring some different perspectives on feminism in this course. I ask them to try to entertain some of these ideas for the span of the quarter, emphasizing that, in the end, they must make up their own minds.

Make Clear How Course Content Is Relevant to Everyone

Many people—students and educators alike—often assume that a class on "race" deals with the concerns of people of color and may not speak as strongly to white students. Similarly, many assume that a class on "women studies," or even the more encompassing "gender studies," is irrelevant for men. Therefore, it is critical that you emphasize how your course is relevant to *all* students, both those who identify with *and* those who do not identify with a particular marginalized group. For example, brainstorm ways in which "classism" is a concern for people with money. Take note of who your students are as you develop course content and classroom activities. The point to remember is that *all* students in your class should feel aligned with course content so that, as noted in Chapter 2, no students are excluded from opportunities to learn.

Give Students a Voice in Shaping Content

Find out what it is that students are interested in learning, and use this as a basis for at least part of your course. Bushnell, a seasoned instructor, shared the following strategy:

> In one summer class, I let students make their own syllabus with the only caveat that we had to stay mostly with the content of a rather forward-thinking textbook. I had put together two different syllabus options, expecting that they would choose the one that they liked. Darned if they didn't come up with their own syllabus that was different from either of my options. They even negotiated as a class various assignments and multiple options for each assignment and consequences for not doing assignments (grading strategies). I was blown away since most of the students were first- or second-year college students. They decided some things that I would not have chosen but they convinced me that it could work for them—and it did. (personal communication, July 22, 2004)

Bring Course Content Down to Earth

Within the academy, language used to analyze social injustice has become increasingly dense. Postmodern theory, while useful in providing new ways of thinking about social life, has added to the difficulty that students (and instructors!) have in relating to potentially transformative content. Although you should encourage students to tackle difficult texts or concepts, make sure to link such concepts to students' everyday realities.

Avoid Gloom and Doom

Some people shy away from discussions of racial, class, or other types of inequality because, frankly, these are not "fun" topics. Furthermore, courses in which students learn about injustice after injustice can easily lead to despair and apathy—the opposite of the goal of a socially transformative course. To counter this possibility, you can provide examples where social activism has had direct, positive results. Balance careful, critical analysis with an emphasis on human resilience and hope.

By taking steps to improve alignment for your students and content, you can preempt some common areas of student resistance. In addition, strengthening this area will also help align you and your students. The next section examines some of the challenges of aligning your course within the institutional context.

Aligning Your Course and Institutional Context

Within an educational institution, there are contextual factors that must be considered when aligning courses. Colleges and universities require students to take prescribed courses, in a prescribed order, and within a given time period. They require instructors to grade, usually in a way that positions students as competitors. Admissions procedures affect who your students are and what they expect from you and from your course. Therefore, you need to take some steps to ensure that your course is well aligned with the particular context in which you are teaching.

Ease Students Into Sharing Responsibility for the Course

The university context in which you are teaching has implications for students' relationship to transformative learning. It is possible that many students in your classroom are not seeking "empowerment," but rather a passing grade for a graduation requirement. As a result, you might find yourself facing what one instructor has called the "irony of imposing democracy" (Fendler, cited in Jacobson, 1998, p. 137). Moreover, a university usually requires that texts and assignments are selected well before the course begins. These contextual factors can constrain the degree to which students are able to take an active role in shaping course structure and interaction. Consider providing a tighter structure at the beginning of the course and gradually easing students into assuming more power *and* responsibility.

Use Institutional Realities as Discussion Points

As discussed earlier, a socially transformative pedagogy insists that the content of your course be linked to larger social forces. Thus, you can use classroom time to have students critically reflect upon the institutional setting of the university. One instructor shared the following strategy:

I ask students to list the ways that university life is geared towards certain groups of people, and how it may structurally exclude others. The older students in class usually mention that the system is suited towards younger people; moms discuss the difficulties of childcare. We talk about access, and how people of color are underrepresented in higher education. If students don't mention it, I point out the assumption that students be able-bodied, and be able to move and think quickly. After the students have come up with "grievances," I push them to think about why the university is set up the way it is—who benefits from this? Who loses? What would they change and how?

Talk About the Grading Process

Grading is a reality that we all must deal with. You may feel that grading feeds into a hierarchical system of competition and judgment. Yet, you need some way to assess student learning and to ensure that students put time and effort into coursework. Your department's desire to prove the rigor and academic value of your field may add to this dilemma. Discuss this issue with your students. See if you can collectively come up with creative ways of assessment that do not require a competitive system of grading. Consider developing "learning contracts" with students where you collectively negotiate criteria of effort and quality in exchange for particular grades.

Set Realistic Goals

In an ideal socially transformative setting, class sizes would be small to allow for in-depth discussion by all participants, and students would have ample time to reflect upon and process course material. The realities of tertiary education—and the demands of the "rest of life"—don't always allow for this level of time and intimacy. Given these factors, set goals that you and your students can expect to achieve in the span of a quarter or semester, while remembering that the learning process does not stop at the end of the term.

Conclusion

As Wulff suggested in Chapter 1, "any effort to align students, content, or instructors in a particular situation is for naught unless it ultimately is being done to promote learning." Traditional notions of learning place primary emphasis on students' acquisition of new knowledge or skills. "Learning" in a socially transformative pedagogy, however, departs from this view in three ways. First, not only is education focused on learning "new" material, but also on "unlearning" oppressive ways of thinking and being. Second, effective learning implies behavioral change and is linked to the concept of praxis. Third, a socially transformative pedagogy includes *instructor* learning as a course goal. The alignment strategies offered in this chapter can help improve each of these facets of socially transformative learning.

By engaging in the praxis of reflecting on your social location before you teach your course, you are better aligning yourself with course content. As you communicate with students and negotiate power, both you and students *unlearn* undemocratic classroom behaviors and become aligned with each other. When students begin to question status quo ways of behavior and learning as they align with course content, they develop a greater capacity to bring about social change.

Endnote

1) The author extends special thanks to Jeanette Bushnell and Kristina Knoll for the excellent teaching strategies they've shared.

2) This quote and the one on page 159 are based on confidential consultations and anonymous feedback. Therefore, I have not cited the original sources for these two quotes.

References

Ellsworth, E. (1992). Why doesn't this feel empowering? Working through the repressive myths of critical pedagogy. In C. Luke & J. Gore (Eds.), *Feminisms and critical pedagogy* (pp. 90–119). New York, NY: Routledge.

Freire, P. (2000). *Pedagogy of the oppressed* (30th anniversary ed.). New York, NY: Continuum.

Gerschick, T. J. (1999). Should and can a white, heterosexual, middle-class man teach students about social inequality and oppression? One person's experience and reflections. In B. A. Pescosolido & R. Aminzade (Eds.), *The social worlds of higher education: Handbook for teaching in a new century* (pp. 480–486). Thousand Oaks, CA: Pine Forge Press.

hooks, b. (1994). *Teaching to transgress: Education as the practice of freedom.* New York, NY: Routledge.

Jacobson, W. (1998). Defining the quality of practitioner research. *Adult Education Quarterly, 48*(3), 125–138.

Leistyna, P., Woodrum A., & Sherblom, S. A. (Eds.). (1996). *Breaking free: The transformative power of critical pedagogy.* Cambridge, MA: Harvard Educational Publishing Group.

Shor, I. (1996). *When students have power: Negotiating authority in a critical pedagogy.* Chicago, IL: University of Chicago Press.

Tisdell, E. J. (1995). *Creating inclusive adult learning environments: Insights from multicultural education and feminist pedagogy.* Washington, DC: ERIC Clearinghouse on Adult, Career, and Vocational Education.

12

Aligning Through Writing

Deborah H. Hatch & Kimberly Emmons

Writing instructors have long argued that learning to write is a lifelong process that should involve the entire campus community. Two main approaches to campus-wide writing initiatives have developed over the past several decades. The first emphasizes the ways that writing can help students master disciplinary subject matter; the second emphasizes the need for attention to the situated writing practices of individual disciplines themselves. Although these two approaches seem to focus on different goals—one on mastery of content, the other on mastery of genres—the alignment model suggests that both programs' outcomes can be achieved when instructors, content, and students are brought into closer alignment through course structures and communicative practices. As the following case study illustrates, students who are encouraged to "write to learn" the content and ways of thinking in biodemography do "learn to write" in ways that make them members of that disciplinary community of scholars.

As coauthors of this chapter, we share a commitment to writing as central to student learning. While Debby brings years of faculty development experience to this article, Kim offers the insights from her position as writing program administrator at a Midwestern research university. The chapter proceeds in two parts. First, Debby narrates and analyzes a case involving several consultations with an instructor in biodemography at her West Coast research university. As Debby's analysis demonstrates, the alignment model is useful not only for structuring faculty consultations but also for understanding the dynamic nature of the instructor's interactions with her students. In the second part of the chapter, Kim applies recent theorizations of genre and discourse communities to the recommendations developed from the case study. As Kim suggests, the alignment model encourages instructors to promote "writing to learn" in their classrooms, and it also requires them to adjust their instructional methods to suit the context, students, and content of their courses. Such adjustments result in students who "learn to write" in their new disciplines. The chapter concludes by demonstrating not only that the alignment model can be useful for promoting better student writing, but also that the alignment model complements the theoretical work of writing program administrators and other composition scholars.

Using the Alignment Model in Writing Consultations

As a writing consultant, I encourage instructors to look at course content and teaching strategies in terms of the opportunities they offer for helping students to write well. Instructors can structure course content to make explicit the kind of thinking and writing they want students to do, and they can give students constant, conscious practice in this thinking and writing through teaching strategies as varied as lectures, discussions, collaborative activities, oral presentations, and writing assignments. Students become better writers through these ongoing opportunities for practice.

The Alignment Model and Writing Across the Curriculum

This approach to writing consultation has been shaped in part by the writing across the curriculum (WAC) movement but more strongly by the alignment model perspective and its focus on strategies instructors use to align course content, themselves, and students in a writing context to achieve learning. The valuable contribution of WAC has been the idea that faculty in all disciplines should assign writing to help students learn. Thanks to WAC efforts, writing is a teaching strategy that faculty accept much more readily today than they did twenty years ago. However, even when faculty accept writing as a teaching strategy, it can still be challenging for them to integrate writing into the overall design of a course in ways that will help students write well. Faculty designing a course will add a writing assignment to assess student learning but may not consider what prior experiences students bring to the assignment, what they as instructors could do to help students succeed on the assignment, or how the assignment connects to the course content. All of these considerations can affect student writing performance and what students learn through writing.

The alignment model perspective encourages both writing consultants and faculty colleagues talking to each other about student writing to pay attention to the dimensions of student, instructor, and content and to the many teaching strategies that can increase the alignment among them and lead to learning and to better writing. In particular, strategies that help to align students with the course content and the instructor deserve attention because efforts to align this component have the greatest effect on student writing.

A Case Study

The following case illustrates a process of finding strategies to align students with course content and the instructor so that students learn through writing and become better writers. The case began when a faculty member emailed requesting a consultation on revising a course she had taught the previous year.

> Attached is my syllabus. It may give you some idea of the course content and goals. . . . My big thing in teaching is for the students to learn how to learn—to think critically and to ask questions about what they find most interesting, what they want to know more about, how to group brainstorm, etc. I care far less about facts and far more about critical thinking. But, I teach relatively hard science.

The course was an upper-level elective in biodemography for advanced undergraduates and new graduate students. The syllabus the instructor used the last time she taught the course listed course topics in a logical progression from introductions and definitions to cases and applications and concluded with new directions. It also included assignments for individual presentations followed by presentation papers and a term paper. Biodemography, "an interdisciplinary field that examines the biological and ecological mechanisms contributing to aging, mortality, fertility, and population growth and decline, and the life history implications of these patterns," (from syllabus) is a new area of study for most of the students, and the instructor felt she needed to adjust the content to match the level of the students' experience. However, providing students the basic information they needed kept her from addressing the topics that interested her.

Our meeting began with a discussion of course content. I asked the instructor to tell me more about biodemography and what I would learn as a student in her course. She answered by talking about the amount of background material she'd need to cover to introduce students to the field and her frustrations managing all of the content. Shifting my role from student to interested colleague, I asked her to identify the big questions in her field. This inquiry and her immediate listing of four broad research questions were the turning point for our work on her course. Sensing her engagement with these questions, I asked if she could keep the course topics and readings from her draft syllabus, but emphasize how both addressed these big questions. "Yes" was her enthusiastic answer. What appears in the revised syllabus accommodates both her students' role as beginners and her role as expert.

> The course will be run in a seminar format, with a focus on learning how to learn. The course will be designed around the following four broad biodemographic research questions:
>
> 1) What is the mortality pattern and life span of humans today?
>
> 2) What were mortality patterns and life span of humans like in the prehistoric past?
>
> 3) What is the mortality pattern and life span of nonhuman primates?
>
> 4) What is the relationship between nutrition and fertility?

These questions allowed the instructor to begin to align the course content with the students' experience and her expertise, and she was enthusiastic about using the questions to structure her lectures and discussion on course topics and readings. Her goal for students was that by the end of the quarter, they would be able to answer these questions. I was interested in exploring with her additional strategies that would help her reach this goal. What other strategies could reinforce the four broad biodemographic research questions and lead to even closer alignment?

To begin, we imagined that the instructor would refer often to these questions as she lectured and led discussions, helping students see how she was answering them and engaging students in answering the questions themselves. The instructor's modeling and the students' practice would be two excellent strategies for continuing to align students with the course content and the instructor's learning goals. Even more important for the students' success as writers, the ongoing practice with the questions could help them if they were asked to write about these questions. As we neared the end of our meeting, the instructor asked what she could do to test student learning in her newly revised course. I pointed to the four key questions we had just developed to structure the content, and she suddenly realized the answer. She could ask students to write papers in which they responded to the four questions that were now structuring the course. After our meeting, she revised the original term paper assignment, turning it into another strategy for aligning students with the course content and her goals.

The difference between the original and revised versions of the assignment illustrates the kinds of revisions that can turn a writing assignment from a task added on to a course to a task that functions as an important strategy for aligning students with course content and instructor's goals. The term paper assignment from the original course plan asked students to do the sort of writing they may, or may not, have done in the past—literature review, research proposal, or data analysis—and it provided them with some definitions of review and research proposal papers. What the original assignment did not do was encourage students to make connections with the four broad biodemographic research questions that are now structuring the course. The revised assignment addresses this disconnect and functions as an important strategy for aligning students with the course content and the instructor's goals.

> *Your learning in this course will be assessed through two response papers:* The course is built around the four overarching biodemographic research questions listed above. You are required to prepare a written answer to two of these questions, in two separate papers. Each response paper should be 5–10 pages (typed, double-spaced), and summarize the main research topics, issues, methods, and findings of the relevant class readings, the material covered in class, and any aspects of the work that you feel remain unanswered, unclear, or merit further investigation. These papers are due on the last day of class. Each paper is worth 35% of your grade; total = 70% for the two papers.

The revised assignment directs students immediately to the four questions that serve as a framework for the course. It combines the literature review and research proposal tasks of the earlier version but links them to the learning that is going on day-to-day in the course by asking students to answer two of these questions by summarizing: "the main research topics, issues, methods, and findings of the relevant class readings, the material covered in class, and any aspects of the work that you feel remain unanswered, unclear, or merit further investigation." Given on the first day of class and due on the last, this assignment and the day-to-day exploration of the four broad research questions through lectures and discussions represent a combination of strategies that can work throughout the term to help align students with the course content and the instructor's goals.

In addition to the response papers and the lectures and discussions as venues for day-to-day exploration of the four broad research questions, two other assignments function as strategies to align students, content, and instructor: oral presentations and presentation papers that followed them.

The instructor asks students to prepare oral presentations on assigned read-ings before she discusses the readings in class and then to write up these pre-sentations, incorporating any comments or information that come up during the presentation and class discussion. These assignments reflect the instruc-tor's goal, expressed in her first email, "for the students to learn how to learn—to think critically, and to ask questions about what they find most interesting, what they want to know more about." She had given a similar assignment the last time she had taught this course and liked it because it "directly forces engagement on the part of the students." Students had liked the assignment, too. In the previous course, one strategy the instructor had used to align students with her goals and the course content was an informa-tion sheet for each of the components of the assignment. She planned to use these information sheets again, including a section on "tips for a successful presentation" that she and the last class had generated. These guidelines rein-force the expectations and objectives of the assignment and further align the students with the instructor's learning goals.

Several weeks after our initial meeting, curious about how the presenta-tions were going and how the framing questions were working, I sent the biodemography instructor an email.

> I wanted to check in to see how the presentations were going and also to see how those four broad biodemographic research questions are working to structure/focus your course. They seemed like such a good idea at the time, and you used them so nicely in the design of the two response papers. How much do you find you refer to them class to class? Let me know, if you have time. It's always helpful for me to know how ideas play out.

The first part of her response indicates the success of the presentations.

> Well, so far it's going great. A student was telling me the other day that she liked "discovering" on her own the key issues and topics, rather than having them pre-chewed for her. So, the presentations and having them read primary lit-erature before we talk much about a topic is working very well. I am so thrilled that they are discovering on their own—this is what I strive for them to be able to do, and this is what learning is all about! They are doing a pretty darn good job with the presentations, too.

The next paragraphs address the effectiveness of the four broad biodemographic research questions, noting how well they are working but also raising important concerns about whether she is doing all she can to assure student success on the response papers.

> I do keep referring to the four key questions and the response papers, and one thing that is great about organizing the class in this way is that the overarching themes and the interconnections among course materials are constantly on the horizon and are tangible things that the students have to pay attention to.
>
> The only thing that I have yet to see is how well it works: in writing their response papers, the questions might seem a bit vague in that the students can go in several directions for each question. I like this plasticity, but I worry that they will be uncomfortable with it. Another related concern is that the questions don't obviously have them [students] addressing some interesting and/or relevant methodological issues that we are covering in the class. So, perhaps what I need to do is make a handout explaining that these sorts of things can and should be in the response papers. I can't wait to read the response papers; that will be the real test of how this worked.

The instructor's description of the way the four key questions are working reveals how she is using this four-question strategy to align her students with the content and her goals for their learning. Calling students' attention to overarching themes and interconnections and reminding them of the response papers are specific applications of this strategy that will contribute to students' success on the response papers.

Although the four key questions are working well to organize the class and to remind students of the response paper tasks, the instructor is concerned that "in writing their response papers the questions might seem a bit vague." Writing her concerns out as she does here leads her to a strategy that could better align her and her students: ". . . perhaps what I need to do is make a handout explaining that these sorts of things can and should be in the response papers." Like the information sheets she designed for the presentation assignments, this handout is an excellent strategy for aligning her and her students, bringing closer together her goals for their learning and their chances for success.

In my email response, I encouraged her to develop this handout.

> I agree that the response papers themselves will be good evidence for how well these questions have worked. I like your idea of making a handout covering the sorts of things that can and should be in the response papers. I'd be happy to read a draft of this handout if that would be helpful to you. Let me know.

> As I think about this handout/guide, it occurs to me that if you had a little extra class time between now and the end of the quarter, you could arrange students in groups based on one of the questions they plan to address in a response paper, ask them to review the handout/guide, and to tell each other what they are planning to do in their response papers and perhaps what questions they have about writing them. You could listen in on each group as students discuss to give you an idea of what approaches they are taking. They could pose their questions to you, either in writing, so you'd have time to think about them and respond the next day, or in class, where you could respond right away. This small group interaction could serve as a kind of "pre-draft" for students, getting them thinking about what they need to do to write these response papers. I don't think that you'd end up with a lot of papers that sound the same, but rather, that an activity like this would help each student become clearer about what he or she thinks. If this idea sounds good and/or if you'd like to talk about it, let me know.

In an email the instructor sent a few days later, she describes the new strategies that she is adding to the course to align students better with her goals.

> Hi! I did incorporate one class day (the last class day) to talk about the response papers. I call it "Response Paper Brainstorming Day." We will work in groups and as a class. I think this is an excellent idea, and the students voted unanimously in favor of having it. So, thank you very much for the suggestion!

A few days later, she sent the guidelines for writing the response papers. Elements of the guidelines that represent particularly effective strategies for aligning students with her goals include the following:

- An extended example of an answer to one of the four questions that discusses methods researchers have used to answer this question and that argues in favor of one method over the other.

- Suggestions for how to begin and to develop each response paper.

- A statement of her goals for her students' work, stressing her confidence in their ability: "The goal here is to demonstrate your mastery of the material we have covered in this course. I know that you have all mastered some of the material, judging from the level of the class discussions. You have extensive knowledge and perspectives on the topics we have covered, and can be considered near-experts on a lot of this material!"

Her enthusiasm for the quality of the students' work appears in this guideline and in the email that accompanied it. Referring to the presentations students had been giving all quarter, she writes,

> Again, I want to thank you for the idea to organize the course around the theme of answering key questions. It has worked fabulously well to integrate the material. Many of the students, on their own, have in their presentations referred to which of those four questions the papers they are presenting on that day is relevant to. I didn't ask them to think about that (except to tell them to integrate the papers they are presenting into the rest of class material).

This comment as well as her enthusiasm two weeks later when she received response papers that met her expectations are strong evidence that the strategies she developed as she planned and taught this course were effective for aligning the students with the course content and her goals and for enhancing learning. Not only did the strategies for alignment produce an effective learning environment, they also enabled students to improve their writing (see summary of strategies in Table 12.1).

Improving Student Writing Through Alignment

In our case study, the consultant facilitates a closer alignment between the instructor, her students, and the content of the biodemography course by encouraging the instructor to focus on four key research questions. As a composition and rhetoric specialist, I cannot help but notice the crucial role that writing plays in this process: from the instructor's revised syllabus and writing guidelines for students to the students' responses to the course's guiding ques-

Table 12.1
Strategies for Alignment in a Biodemography Course

- Use key questions to organize the course content
- Refer to the key organizing questions throughout the term (both instructor and students)
- Design writing assignments that build on the key organizing questions
- Engage students in figuring out the material on their own and speaking and writing about what they find
- Use guidelines to clarify the instructor's expectations and communicate to students how they can succeed on assignments
- Brainstorm in class to further clarify the instructor's expectations and give students time to practice and to ask questions

tions, writing serves as a mechanism for the alignment of the instructor, the students, and their subject matter. Writing offers more than a channel of communication, however. With each assignment revised by the instructor and with each activity completed by the students, the expectations and strategies of the discipline are better articulated. In other words, the classroom develops into a discourse community: as the alignment of instructor, students, and course content progresses, the group comes to share a set of goals and the genres with which to accomplish them.

In composition studies, the term *discourse community* has a contentious history—scholars debate both the origins and the directions of the term—but it can be usefully applied to classroom communities to highlight the pedagogical and social aspects of successful writing instruction. Swales (1990) defined *discourse community* as a group of individuals who share interests and activities and who use specialized language and genres to achieve their collective goals. Importantly, a discourse community "recruits its members by persuasion, training or relevant qualification" (Swales, 1990, p. 24). Thus, a discourse community actively chooses its members and draws them into what Geertz (1983) has termed "ways of being in the world" (p. 155). Membership in a discourse community is, therefore, not a casual affiliation; membership implies an ideological commitment to a particular worldview. This can, in part, explain why students have such difficulty producing the texts we sometimes expect of them: they are not yet committed to the goals and practices of our disciplinary discourse communities. The alignment model can help us recognize and respond to such difficulties. By making students aware of the enculturation process involved in learning a new discipline (entering a new discourse community), we may help them not only produce better texts but also develop a better understanding of our community expectations.

In this way, the concept of a discourse community can help us understand why the alignment model works for improving student writing in the disciplines. The alignment model asks both expert and novice members of the community to view themselves as part of the shared processes of learning. It asks students to align themselves with the teacher and the subject matter—this process challenges students with new "ways of being in the world." Further, the alignment model asks teachers to align themselves with their students and their subject matter—this involves recognizing students as novice members of the discourse community and therefore creating exercises and strategies that encourage their participation in the activities of the community. Making these community expectations clear to students at the outset of the course—as, for example, the biodemography instructor does by highlighting the four key questions of her field—should help students to see themselves as disciplinary scholars rather than as outsiders. As this process of enculturation continues, students will begin to produce texts that are more recognizably "expert" within the discipline.

Recommendations and Strategies

The following analysis takes each of the biodemography instructor's strategies for aligning content, faculty, and students and offers an explanation for its success in improving student writing.

Using Key Questions to Organize the Course Content

Too often, as composition scholars and writing across the curriculum experts have observed, writing is seen as a separate activity from the *real* learning of the course. As Gottschalk and Hjortshoj (2004) noted,

> when teachers plan courses . . . they usually begin with decisions about the range of topics they will cover, and while they arrange these topics in a logical sequence, their plans do not always extend to ways of moving students through a process of learning. (p. 46)

In the case of the biodemography instructor, this is clear in the initial consultation—the original course plan walks students through major topic areas but does not focus on the important guiding questions that motivate research in this field. Once the consultant and the instructor develop the plan to organize the course around these guiding questions, the course begins to become exciting and new to the instructor herself. In essence, the redesign of the course brings the instructor and the course material into better alignment. Seeing the course in this light, the instructor is then able to develop class activities and writing assignments that focus on developing answers to the guiding questions. As Gottschalk and Hjortshoj (2004) noted, "writing assignments have enormous potential to support directed movement through the learning process" (p. 46). In the biodemography class, the final writing assignment is revised for just this purpose. The new assignment and the daily communication tasks that lead up to it represent the culmination of the students' learning and their entry into the discourse community of biodemography.

Referring to the Key Organizing Questions Throughout the Term (Both Instructor and Students)

In this case study, the development of a discourse community is evidenced by the gradual shift toward student adoption of important communicative practices, like referencing the guiding research questions. Even before the class began, the instructor planned to repeat the key questions that represented her discipline in her classroom activities. Through lectures and class discussions, these questions became guiding principles for students' participation. Eventually, the students began using these questions in their own presentations, demonstrating their affiliation with the goals of the discourse community. This affiliation results in better writing because students are adopting both a stance toward the material and a critical vocabulary with which to present their ideas. Thus, the alignment of the students with the course content—via the guiding questions—enables them to speak recognizably as members of the biodemography community.

Designing Writing Assignments That Build on the Key Organizing Questions

Discourse communities form to accomplish specific activities. In the case of academic discourse communities, these activities often center on advancing knowledge through oral and written genres such as conference presentations and scholarly articles. For students entering the discourse community of biodemography, full participation is contingent upon having something to say that increases knowledge in the community. Revising the writing assignment to address the key research questions—in effect aligning the assignments with the course content—encourages students to contribute to the collective knowledge of the community. Thus, students are invited to use the knowledge they have gained to advance research in the field. As the instructor points out in the response paper assignment, students are welcome to identify "any aspects of the work that [they] feel remain unclear or merit further investigation." This invitation to join the active work of the discipline provides students with motivation and a reason to write that goes beyond simple regurgitation of learned facts. As the instructor discovered, the students' responses are more successful because they address points of interest to the disciplinary discourse community.

Engaging Students in Figuring Out the Material on Their Own and Speaking and Writing About What They Find

In the biodemography course, student presentations offer several opportunities to practice participating in the discourse community. The initial oral presentations, which ask students to relate specific readings to larger course themes, are followed by classroom discussion and a written summary of the presentation. Both oral and written genres form the heart of the biodemography course's advancement of knowledge. These presentations reinforce the membership of students in the community and offer chances to practice communicating with other members of the community. As Gottschalk and Hjortshoj (2004) suggested, learning is enhanced when assignments help guide students through the process. The presentations, the ensuing class discussions, and the resulting summary papers provide a framework for student learning in the biodemography course. Each of these opportunities demonstrates the dynamic process of alignment between the instructor, the students, and the course content. Because they have multiple times to gather feedback on their communicative attempts, the students are able to improve their writing throughout the course.

Using Guidelines to Clarify the Instructor's Expectations and Communicate to Students How They Can Succeed on Assignments

As the classroom's only expert member of the biodemography discourse community, the instructor is in the unique position to demystify the genres of her community. By being explicit about her (and the community's) expectations for the writing assignments, she invites students to write as "near-experts" in the field. These guidelines encourage students to appropriate the communicative practices of the field; they offer students the chance to align themselves with the course content and the instructor's learning goals. In her example response, the instructor models the kinds of questions, information, and conclusions that are expected of community members. Using this information, students are more likely to adhere to the genre conventions of the community (e.g., citation styles, argumentation techniques, appropriate forms and uses of evidence) and to produce better written products.

Brainstorming in Class to Further Clarify the Instructor's Expectations and Give Students Time to Practice and to Ask Questions

The brainstorming activity involves the entire class in both practicing their communicative strategies and providing feedback to each other and to the instructor. Such interactivity is, as Wulff points out in the introduction to this book, intrinsic to the alignment model itself. This interactivity is also characteristic of a healthy discourse community; participants regulate their memberships through negotiations of communicative practices. In classroom communities, more expert members may provide useful advice to less expert members via peer review activities like the biodemography instructor's brainstorming day. Additionally, less expert members draw attention to the tacit assumptions of the community by asking questions and even by making mistakes. Importantly, the brainstorming activity produces better writing because it opens the lines of communication among all community members, bringing to light areas of confusion as well as areas of growing expertise. Such practices encourage flexibility and negotiation, and they lead to better writing.

Conclusion

This case study demonstrates the usefulness of the alignment model for improving student writing. Encouraging a constant negotiation between the instructor, the course content, and the students, the alignment model requires an interactive pedagogy. For writing instructors, this interactivity promotes dialogue about genre and discourse conventions and encourages students to see their writing not as a static product, but as an active engagement in a discourse community. Student writing then becomes not simply a way to demonstrate successful learning of the material covered in a course, but more importantly a way of enacting community membership and producing new knowledge. In the biodemography instructor's own terms, the students have "learned how to learn" as biodemographers.

Note

The authors want to thank Kathleen O'Connor, Assistant Professor of Anthropology at the University of Washington, for her contributions to the case that provides the focus for this chapter.

References

Geertz, C. (1983). *Local knowledge: Further essays in interpretive anthropology.* New York, NY: Basic Books.

Gottschalk, K., & Hjortshoj, K. (2004). *The elements of teaching writing: A resource for instructors in all disciplines.* New York, NY: Bedford/St. Martin's.

Swales, J. M. (1990). *Genre analysis: English in academic and research settings.* Cambridge, England: Cambridge University Press.

13

Aligning Online

Margaret Lawrence, Bonnie O'Dell, & Laurie Stephan

This chapter examines technology and alignment in terms of three techno-logical contexts: threaded discussion boards, hybrid courses[1], and fully online courses. Using data[2] drawn from these contexts and the literature on instructional technology, we suggest that instructors focus on four areas of practice when considering ways to maintain alignment in courses with tech-nological components. Those areas include:

- Addressing obstacles technology might present to alignment

- Aligning expectations for learning

- Aligning expectations for communication

- Using a course web site as a foundation for alignment

Addressing Obstacles to Alignment

Using technology adds another layer of complexity to the alignment process because it complicates the instructional context. When used well, technology can facilitate alignment; but when used poorly, it can obstruct communica-tion, reduce motivation, and lead to misalignment. Instructors must orient themselves and students to the technology, and the choice of technology must fit with course content goals for the alignment of students, content, and instructor to occur. The following strategies can help ensure that technology does not present obstacles to the alignment of instructors and students with course goals and with each other.

Start Small

It is easy to underestimate the amount of time and effort that using a new technology may take. The technology should accommodate your own time and experience constraints. Key guidelines advise beginning with a modest application that can have a relatively broad impact on the course and can be used throughout it (Brown, 2000). For example, having a basic web site or a discussion board is a relatively simple technology with great potential for student learning during the course.

Recognize That You Don't Have to Be a Pioneer

Even if you decide to start small, exploring technological options and determining the potential uses of various tools can be a daunting task. Faculty often assume they need to undertake this venture on their own, but considering what others have done and making use of training opportunities can greatly simplify the process.

Consider what others have done. Familiarize yourself with the capabilities of your tools by researching how others have used them. Confer with colleagues. Look at other course web sites on your campus and on other campuses. Major search engines offer advanced search capabilities that allow you to limit the domain to "edu" endings—this makes it easier to confine your search to course web sites at other colleges and universities as opposed to including commercial web sites. You can find excellent examples of online learning practices that are relatively easy to implement on the Sloane Consortium web site (http://www.sloan-c.org/effective/index.asp).

Make use of training opportunities. Look for instructional development centers or other sites on campus that offer help with instructional technology. Some schools offer courses just for faculty. Look also for web-based tutorials at your own institution and at other sites. A few helpful web-based sites include the IT Curriculum Development Toolkit (http://www.bcc.ctc.edu/wcit/Toolkit/step6_WhatToInclude_Online.asp) and the Virtual Instructional Designer (http://www.thevid.org), both of which describe good practices for designing online content. While some of the University of Washington's Catalyst site information (http://catalyst.washington.edu) is institution-specific, it also includes information about making effective use of instructional tools like discussion boards as well as stories of successful implementations of technology. The Teaching, Learning, and Technology Group (http://www.tltgroup.org) is another source of information on using instructional technology.

Be Aware of the Complexities of Using the Technology

Planning effectively with technology involves not only learning its uses, but also maintaining awareness of how its use requires different approaches to time and space.

Some activities take more time or require more planning when undertaken in technological contexts. For example, in a traditional course, it may be possible to put off some details of the course or the PowerPoint slides until the last minute; in an online course, however, you need to allow plenty of time to get things prepared and posted so students have timely access to them. Another example is the additional time that it takes both you and students to read online text.

Workspace is also different. Where the web becomes the primary learning space, visual organization and layout become much more crucial than in a conventional classroom; a handout that is poorly organized may not make much difference to the course, but a web site that is hard to navigate can present major obstacles to student learning. Another example of the impact of a virtual classroom is the potential confusion that multiple workspaces with different addresses can engender. More than once, faculty have missed a student's electronic submission because it was submitted to an unexpected location.

Familiarize Students With the Technology

Students as well as instructors should be comfortable with the technology if learning is to proceed smoothly. Although you may not see it as your responsibility to train students in the use of technology, effective planning should include some provision for teaching students how to use course tools. Possibilities include providing web links to tutorials or referring students to appropriate on-campus resources. In some cases, you may want to provide a brief handout on the tool, provide instructions on the course web page, and/or provide a FAQ page on questions about the tool.

Match Technology With Course Content Goals

Choice of technology needs to enhance the alignment of students and course content. Learning goals should motivate your use of technology and not the other way around. For example, if your learning goal is for students to learn how to articulate and defend their ideas, a discussion board can support that goal. If your learning goal is for students to work and think more independently but have access to others when they need it, a course listserv or using the board only for posting questions might be more appropriate. Keep in mind also that you don't need to make use of a technology simply because it's available to you.

In addition to complicating the context for alignment, technology also adds new dimensions to two traditional alignment issues: aligning expectations for learning and aligning expectations for communication. Technology's effects on the learning environment in terms of time, space, and the medium of the communication necessitate rethinking traditional classroom approaches to alignment in these two areas.

Aligning Expectations for Learning

In technological contexts, just as in the traditional classroom, instructors' and students' expectations of what constitutes effective learning and who takes responsibility for learning can vary. These expectations need to be brought into alignment with each other and with the demands of the course content, a process that can be particularly difficult when using technology. For example, online courses tend to require greater student initiative in organizing and exploring content (Knowlton, 2000; Meyer, 2002). Instructors may not anticipate that some students find it more challenging to organize their work as distance students than they do as on-campus students. In addition, instructors might become swamped when the ease of using email leads students to expect more one-on-one help from the instructor than would be expected in a conventional class. In other cases, instructors may expect students to come up with their own new, exciting ways to discuss material on a discussion board while students may find it more difficult to think of anything to say than in a regular classroom discussion. The next section discusses ways to help align student and instructor expectations for learning by preparing students for success and encouraging critical thinking.

Prepare Students With Strategies for Success Online

To help prepare students for success, start by thinking about the unique ways that technology affects alignment, and hence learning, in your class. Are your expectations for learning reasonable given the context? Do you need to shift your expectations? What shifts in expectations might students need to make? Once you have decided on the challenges that characterize your course, you can develop ways to establish realistic expectations for students and to provide clear guidelines in the form of models and assignment criteria.

Establish realistic expectations for students. As in any other course, a first step in alignment may be to ask students what their expectations are for the course or the use of the technological tool. In what ways do they anticipate the technology will help their learning? Are there any ways they anticipate it might hinder learning? How much time do they expect to spend studying and working online? You may need to ask such questions not only at the beginning of class but also periodically throughout the course to check whether effective learning is taking place and to determine whether you or the students need to take more initiative to improve learning.

Instructors can help align student expectations by being clear about such things as amount of work expected and deadlines. It is also helpful to be explicit about such issues as how much help you will offer on assignments or how much you will intervene in online discussions. For example, will you periodically summarize student posts, jump-start the discussion from time to time, or try to engage as a regular participant? Making expectations explicit is particularly important for distance program students who do not have the same informal access to instructors before, during, and after class as on-campus students do. Similarly, they are typically isolated from their classmates who, in on-campus settings, often serve as informal networks of information and socialization.

Particular issues to which you may need to alert distance students are related to differences in time and space. In a conventional course, structure is built into a course in the form of a classroom and a class schedule. The absence of these same structures for online students is a frequent cause of students' dropping out. You can help students succeed by pointing out that they need to create their own structure, a space and time set aside that is conducive to learning. For example, a student's computer may be located in the family room—not necessarily the best place for him or her to be taking an online course. Students also need to know that it takes longer to read online and longer to discuss, since all discussion takes place in writing. Remind students that you expect them to work beyond the time they spend interacting online.

Many colleges have created ways to orient students to the challenges of online learning. For example, the Illinois Virtual Campus (http://www .ivc.illinois.edu/potential/online.html) offers an orientation to online learning that provides information on the technical tools needed, characteristics of successful online learners, student expectations, and links to resources. If you provide an orientation, consider incorporating student testimony regarding online courses. For example, as our data suggest, it can be helpful for students to hear that the biggest lesson their peers learned is that studying online can be more complex and more time-consuming than in a conventional class.

Provide clear guidelines and models for assignments and tasks. In addition to aligning their expectations to student expectations and vice versa, instructors must think about how to align course content to students and students to course content. As students take more responsibility for learning, the balance of responsibilities for alignment with content shifts also. Novice learners may need much help from the instructor to align with content, whereas experienced learners may require very little help. For example, graduate students who use a discussion board to consult with each other on specific course problems may require little instructor involvement. More instructor guidance may be needed, however, when novice students are discussing ideas on a board and have less expertise to share among themselves. In our experience, when instructors simply opened up the threaded discussion board and invited students to use it with no instructor input, many students could not develop an effective approach to using it on their own. As one student commented, "Need more instructor guidance to shape discussion's scope and to shape entry points—without this, community is artificial and thus motivation low."

Providing examples at the beginning of the course of posts or assignments that engage the material effectively can help align students with course expectations. As the course progresses, you can continue to engage in the alignment process by monitoring the quality of student contributions and making decisions about whether students need more or less guidance in order to maximize learning.

Encourage Critical Thinking

In addition to establishing basic guidelines and models for assignments, you can help increase the alignment of students and content by using strategies that encourage students to think critically. Two such strategies are to model in-depth thinking and design strategic assignments.

Model in-depth thinking. Facilitating online discussion can demand a great deal of faculty time, but it offers a unique opportunity to motivate students to think critically and analytically. If you have the time to read and reply to students' responses to specific readings, you can initiate an in-depth discussion that forces students to analyze their responses in a way that is almost impossible to achieve in an ordinary classroom setting. However, this level of attention can be time-consuming. To save time, instead of responding in depth to many students on a regular basis, some instructors periodically choose a specific student's comment in an online discussion, expand on it, and discuss its implications, thus effectively modeling for all students how to take one idea and develop it completely.

Design strategic assignments. When instructors at our institutions designed discussion board assignments that asked students to use higher order thinking skills such as application, synthesis, or evaluation, student response was positive. In their discussions, students applied course content to real world experience, shared information that complemented course content, or evaluated texts or events in light of course concepts. They reported that such assignments "forced" them to think in ways that deepened their appreciation for the content.

Other ways to encourage students to take more responsibility for engaging with the content include requiring independent research and referring to it in student posts. Or, instead of periodically summarizing online discussions yourself, ask students to summarize and encourage them to take some responsibility for helping the entire group align more closely with the content. One instructor puts all readings online with a list of discussion questions and requires students first to answer the questions online. Then he looks over student responses and hones the list down to one or two key questions. This approach enables him to discuss lower-level comprehension questions online, reserving more time for rich, highly focused discussion in class.

Aligning Expectations for Communication

Technological contexts have a considerable effect, not only on expectations for learning, but also on expectations for communication. When technology is used, communication is in writing, requiring different skills than speaking. Communication is also asynchronous, which means that feedback is not immediate. Finally, inflections and visual and kinesthetic clues are lost, creating a greater potential for miscommunication (Weiss, 2000). On the other hand, email can also seem more personal and less threatening than participating in class or approaching an instructor face to face.

What are some ways in which these differences affect the process of alignment? First, instructors must take great care to clarify meaning, intentions, and appropriateness in terms of type and amount of communication. Visual organization, in the design of a web site for example, also becomes a much more important aspect of clarifying expectations. Finally, because feedback is less immediate but opportunity for reflection is greater, the process of aligning students with the content may differ. For example, in a conventional environment, if students express ideas or ask questions that reveal they are out of alignment with an aspect of course content, the instructor can engage in a complex alignment process of probing, restating, checking comprehension, and asking students to apply concepts. Perhaps instructors will repeat these kinds of exchanges with students multiple times in the course of only 20 or 30 minutes. However, since online communication is written and typically asynchronous, the "moves" for this alignment process are attenuated. The resultant increase in time for reflection and opportunity for personal feedback from the instructor can enhance alignment, but the lack of immediate feedback or clarification can cause misunderstanding or extend the time it takes to align. The following strategies of communicating clearly with students and encouraging dialogue online can help align student and instructor expectations for communication.

Communicate Clearly With Your Students

As described in the following sections, you can align yourself more clearly with students' communication expectations by finding out about the students and their needs, defining your communicative role in their learning process, using a variety of modes for communication, and giving timely feedback.

Find out who your students are. Knowing your students is especially important in an online environment that may seem impersonal. Creating a sense of community is essential to learning (Meyer, 2002). When students feel that instructors are interested in them, they usually find it more comfortable to align with instructor expectations and less intimidating to attempt to align with course content. After you have learned more about students, using their names in emails with an occasional reference that shows you know who they are personalizes communication and helps establish rapport. Additionally, knowing more about students helps you align content and expectations more closely with student backgrounds. Helping students get to know each other is also an important way to align them with your expectations for their communication with each other. To get to know your students and to help them get to know each other, you can collect and include the following on the course web site:

- Biographical sketches from all students
- Reasons for being in this course or program
- Experience (if any) they have with technology or distance learning
- Digital photos

Not all students, though, will want personal or contact information on a semi-public web site. Therefore, if you choose to collect and post such information on the site, be sure to let your students know your intentions and give them the opportunity to opt out.

Define your role. Communicating by email can give students the idea that they have unlimited personal access to you. Thus, you need to find an appropriate balance between aligning yourself with students' expectations for helpful information and timely feedback and aligning the students with the limitations of your time and availability.

It is helpful to set up a page in your course web site that states your expectations of students, including the number of hours you expect them to spend corresponding with others on a weekly basis. Inform them of your "office hours," those times when you will be online and available to answer their questions. Let them know that if they ask you questions outside this time, you will not be able to get back to them immediately, and tell them about how long you will need before you can answer questions outside of office hours. Also, on your course web site, let students know what kinds of questions you are prepared to answer, especially technological ones. For questions you cannot answer, tell them where to go to find the answers.

Use a variety of communication modes. Teaching online does not mean that you are limited to communicating by email. Talking to a student by telephone is often more time-efficient than emailing since clarifications are immediate and speaking requires less effort than writing. When teaching an online course, scheduling at least one phone call with distance learners can enhance students' sense of personal communication. The phone is also a useful tool for urgent questions or for times when communication with a student is not going well.

Provide timely feedback. Student comments from our data on the use of discussion boards illustrated the importance of timely input from the instructor: "Delayed responses from professors make it harder to think of (discussion board) as a form of communication." Though timely input is important, you also need to balance student expectations for timeliness with your learning goals for the assignments and the amount of time you can realistically devote to responding to students. Communicating the degree and kind of feedback you will provide and then following through consistently will help align students with your intentions and expectations. As you continue to progress through the course, the amount or type of feedback you give may need to be adjusted in response to student feedback or your own time demands.

Most course management platforms offer tracking mechanisms that faculty and students can use for immediate feedback regarding students' understanding of specific content. If there is time to develop assessments, those assessments can be delivered immediately following students' reading or lab assignments so students can immediately see where they need to reinforce their learning.

Encourage Dialogue, Not Monologue, on Discussion Boards

Because communication via discussion boards is written and asynchronous, students can easily lose their sense of audience. In addition, some types of discussion board tasks may strike them as pointless, and some of the students may feel uncomfortable contributing online. For all of these reasons, it can be difficult to encourage dialogue as opposed to monologue on a message board. However, discussion boards can help align students and content through dialogue if assignments facilitate clear and emotionally comfortable communication. To encourage dialogue, consider participation requirements, encourage students to be courteous to each other, and make it comfortable for students to contribute online.

Consider participation requirements. Requiring students to post messages a specified number of times during the course ensures participation; however, it is important to design meaningful and focused criteria for posts so that students do not regard participation as useless busy work. For example, some instructors require students to respond to each other's online self-introductions; this type of assignment doesn't relate to course content, and many students find it meaningless. If you do require participation, give students clear tasks with clear criteria that relate to the course. As students in our data commented, "Some people write about things that have nothing to do with the course. I think that if there was a question or thought we could respond to each week it would be better for everyone," and "No one actually puts any thought into what they're writing and no one really wants to comment on someone's lame response." Potentially useful types of assignments include: clarifying comments or questions about course content, responding to assignments, commenting on or applying ideas from readings, and introducing relevant material from outside sources.

Encourage courtesy. Courtesy includes consideration not only for the feelings of other people, but also for their time. At the very beginning of class, you might want to share examples of courteous posts: those that respect the audience, include enough extra context cues to communicate tone, and make effective use of emoticons [*e.g.,* :) or ;)]. Requiring students to keep their posts short also preserves everyone's time and patience. Additionally, clear subject headings help students keep track of one another's contributions. Consider providing examples of effective subject headings and of ways the headings might change as students pursue the thread of discussion.

Make contributing comfortable. For some students, posting a message can be more intimidating than making a comment in class. If your class is very large, students may feel intimidated about posting to such a large audience.

Dividing the class into smaller discussion groups of 15 or 20 can provide enough variety of input to keep the interaction stimulating but comfortable for students to post and respond. In some cases, you may also want to give students the option to post with a pseudonym in order to reduce the anxiety. As one student in our data commented, "We get to discuss things anonymously which helps us discuss our thoughts better."

Using a Course Web Site for Alignment

The course web site serves as a central locus for alignment. It can establish expectations, clarify and provide guidance for course content, and facilitate ongoing communication between instructor and students. Unlike a paper syllabus, hypertext facilitates direct access to resources that students need to process course material, submit assignments, communicate with other students, or explore content further. Additionally, a well-organized web site can facilitate alignment at every stage of the course. At the beginning of the course, it orients students to instructor and course expectations. It is also an ongoing resource: students can continue to refer to it throughout the class; instructors can adjust it as they make new discoveries about student difficulties, clarify their own expectations, or find new aspects of content they want to emphasize. As Meyer (2002) noted, "It is fair to conclude that one thing the web does fairly well is give faculty and students the tools to interact, collaborate, and form learning communities" (p. 39). However she also pointed out that "What determines whether that occurs is whether the course is designed to take advantage of the tools woven into the web" (p. 39). Suggestions for designing a web site that effectively presents and integrates course content follow. You might also want to refer to the web sites for web site design cited earlier in this chapter.

Begin With a "Getting Started" Page

In a survey of its distance education students, one institution found that the "Getting Started" page was the factor that rated highest on the satisfaction scale. This Getting Started page should contain everything the students need to know about how to make it through the course. It should, for instance, refer them to the syllabus, to other course policy documents, and to technical support. It should outline a "drumbeat" or rhythm for them to follow on a weekly basis so that they can quickly get into the flow of the course. For instance, they might be directed to access new content on Monday, discuss on Wednesday, and do new research and write a report for Friday.

Include Technical Support Pages

The course should be set up with a unit or two that provides students with instructions on how to access appropriate content and tools to succeed in the course. These technical support units should also contain all the technical requirements and contact information students will need to troubleshoot technical issues they may encounter with software and connectivity. These help pages should be contained in a unit labeled "technical assistance," and students should be referred to the unit throughout the course content whenever necessary.

Develop Effective Content Pages

When designing a course, organize units so that they are sequenced in the order that you expect students to explore the content. For instance, you can label the content units with key phrases that reinforce the major learning outcomes or content foci of the course and with time indicators that reinforce the sequencing of the content. For example, "First Week: Introduction to Design Concepts." It is also helpful to organize the units in the course management platform in the order the students will experience them.

The use of tools should be embedded within the content units themselves. For instance, if students are to comment on specific questions regarding a reading, they should be able to access both the reading and the discussion from the same page. They should not have to leave content areas and look for tools somewhere else within the course to manipulate the content they are learning. The purpose of doing something with the technology should be clearly related to doing something specific with the content.

Some course management platforms make it easier than others to focus on content. Newer content management systems now offer the option of a "learning pathway" development tool whereby faculty can organize an entire set of activities around specific content. Thus, when students log into a content module, they can see a clickable learning path, almost like a navigation menu on the left side of the screen that remains present throughout the course.

Conclusion

To help align expectations for learning in technological contexts, we have addressed obstacles to using instructional technology. We also have suggested ways that instructors can establish realistic expectations for students, provide clear guidelines for assignments, model in-depth thinking, and design strategic assignments. To help align expectations for communication in technological contexts, we have suggested ways that instructors can define their roles clearly, find out who students are, provide feedback, consider participation requirements, encourage courtesy, and make it comfortable to contribute online. We also recommended using a web site as a locus for alignment, and suggested various ways to prevent technology from interfering with alignment.

At the same time, we have tried to emphasize that in determining when, how, and to what degree to use each of these strategies, you will want to reassess the alignment of instructor, student, and content on a regular basis in your class. For example, if you want students to take more initiative in shaping online discussion, you might decide to provide models of effective posts and feedback on the discussion frequently in the beginning of the course and then reduce your input as the course progresses. Or, although it may be beneficial for students if you model in-depth thinking online, you may find it impossible to find the time to do this effectively and may choose other avenues to stimulate student thinking. Because alignment is a recursive process, a focus on specific strategies can become deceptively static. Thus, we have attempted to present the strategies described in this chapter as tools you can use flexibly in the ongoing give and take of the alignment process rather than as fixed solutions.

Endnotes

1) Hybrid courses are courses that are taught partially online and partly in traditional classrooms.

2) Data gathered at Bellevue Community College and University of Washington.

References

Brown, D. G. (2000). *Teaching with technology: Seventy-five professors from eight universities tell their stories.* Bolton, MA: Anker.

Knowlton, D. S. (2000). A theoretical framework for the online classroom: A defense and delineation of a student-centered pedagogy. In R. E. Weiss, D. S. Knowlton, & B. W. Speck (Eds.), *New directions for teaching and learning: No. 84. Principles of effective teaching in the online classroom* (pp. 5–14). San Francisco, CA: Jossey-Bass.

Meyer, K. A. (2002). *Quality in distance education: A focus on online learning* (ASHE-ERIC Higher Education Report, 29[4]). San Francisco, CA: Jossey-Bass.

Weiss, R. E. (2000). Humanizing the online classroom. In R. E. Weiss, D. S. Knowlton, & B. W. Speck (Eds.), *New directions for teaching and learning: No. 84. Principles of effective teaching in the online classroom* (pp. 47–51). San Francisco, CA: Jossey-Bass.

Part IV

ALIGNMENT IN TEACHING AS SCHOLARSHIP

14

Using Alignment in the Scholarship of Teaching and Learning

Wayne H. Jacobson & Deborah H. Hatch

B oyer's (1990) argument for thinking differently about the work of scholars has helped us consider teaching, integration, and application in ways
once reserved only for the scholarship of discovery. The new thinking trig-
gered by this argument has also prompted consideration of an even wider
range of scholarships, such as the scholarship engagement (Boyer, 1996), the
scholarship of assessment (Banta & Associates, 2002), the scholarship of
diversity (Anderson, 2002), the scholarship of academic development (Eggins
& MacDonald, 2003), the scholarship of student affairs (Fried, 2002), the
scholarship of extension (Bushaw, 1996), the scholarship of imagination
(Nicholson, 1998), and the scholarship of practice (Bleich, 2004). The suggestion is that each can be considered a site for scholarly practice: questions
can be purposefully posed and considered in the light of advances made by
others who have examined similar issues; evidence can be collected and systematically examined; conclusions can be brought to a community of scholars
for review and critique and for others to adapt or extend in their own work
(Glassick, Huber, & Maeroff, 1997).

Considering this proliferation of scholarships, we found ourselves asking,
"Is there a scholarship of alignment?" In the alignment model, teaching and
learning can be examined in terms of the alignment of four factors: 1) the
background, preparation, and expectations of an instructor, 2) the nature and
demands of the content for a course, 3) the expectations, abilities, and perceptions of students, and 4) the contexts—disciplinary, institutional, cultural,
and social—in which a course occurs. Alignment is the continual process of
monitoring and responding to these multiple factors with the goal of fostering learning, and it requires the same types of intentional inquiry, examination of evidence, and reflective critique that define scholarship. Though the
alignment model does not by definition require making findings public to a

community of fellow scholars, the continuous assessment, reflection, and intentional decision-making that facilitate alignment could readily be documented and disseminated for review by peers.

Thus, a case could be made for using the framework of scholarship to further the understanding and advancement of alignment. However, at this point, we think it is more helpful to use the alignment framework to foster the understanding and advancement of scholarship—in particular, the scholarship of teaching and learning (SoTL). In this chapter, we propose that alignment offers an orienting framework for advancing SoTL, making it possible for the diverse community of scholars engaged in SoTL to form a distinct SoTL community, within and across disciplines. We will also show that alignment provides a framework for conceptualizing, implementing, and communicating the conclusions of SoTL, and helps transform questions about teaching into questions for scholarly investigation.

A Scholarly Community for Advancing SoTL

Much attention in recent years has focused on defining and clarifying the nature of SoTL. Bender and Gray (1999) distinguished it from other ways of linking scholarship and teaching: "... the scholarship of teaching is not merely teaching our scholarship. Nor is it simply teaching well. . . . *The scholarship of teaching means that we invest in our teaching the intellectual powers we practice in our research*" (emphasis added). Hutchings and Shulman (1999) spelled out some of the implications of examining teaching in this way, emphasizing that SoTL leads to outcomes which are

> public, open to critique and evaluation, and in a form that others can build on . . . in which faculty frame and systematically investigate questions related to student learning—the conditions under which it occurs, what it looks like, how to deepen it, and so forth—and do so with an eye not only to improving their own classroom but to advancing practice beyond it. (p. 13)

These formulations have contributed greatly to the promotion of SoTL as a form of scholarly work. There has been less discussion, however, about how constructive critique and evaluation of SoTL might happen or how SoTL might lead to advances in practice—indeed, identifying something as a form of scholarship is not the same as recognizing contributions of the scholarship.

As Hutchings and Shulman (1999) suggested, advancing SoTL requires making it public in a form that others can critique, evaluate, or build on. Thus, challenges of advancing SoTL can be traced to challenges of making it public: identifying a community to which SoTL is made public and developing shared frameworks for communicating SoTL so that members of the scholarly community can respond meaningfully to one another's work.

Challenges of Identifying a Community for SoTL

Part of the challenge of developing a shared framework for critique and evaluation is that most institutions of higher education are not currently structured in ways that help facilitate SoTL communities (Shulman, 2004). Due to this lack of community, it is not always clear who the best audience is for making this type of work public. Many faculty who have engaged in SoTL have asked how their work will be valued at their institution, in their departments, or by their promotion and tenure committees. They recognize the value of regarding a course as a site for scholarship, and they are examining interesting questions of student learning. However, their scholarly work is often evaluated by peers and colleagues who view their work through the lens of discovery scholarship. On its own terms as SoTL, the work might offer valuable contributions to advancing an understanding of teaching and learning, but SoTL values are not always compatible with the values of discovery scholarship. One can imagine the tables turned: Most would hesitate to require that discovery scholarship be valued in terms of its effect on student learning.

If the scholarly community for SoTL does not necessarily include fellow scholars in the investigator's discipline, is there another audience better situated to provide critique and evaluation? For some SoTL projects, students may provide the best critique of an innovative teaching practice, and students' work may offer important evidence of its effectiveness. However, students would not be expected to make judgments about how this innovative practice might be extended in other contexts, for example, or how it contributes to a better understanding of student learning in the discipline. Students provide evidence, and in some cases, are contributors or even co-investigators (Bulcroft, Werder, & Gilliam, 2002), but that does not qualify them to evaluate what is done as a work of scholarship. Similarly, peers and colleagues who are fellow instructors may be in a position to evaluate for their own purposes or immediate application, but they are not necessarily the ones who can assess the work in a larger scholarly context, unless they are similarly engaged in scholarly work on teaching and learning themselves.

Though each of these potential audiences may have an interest in SoTL, none provides a scholarly community for this particular work. Ideally, SoTL should be evaluated by an audience of fellow scholars who are themselves producers of the same kind of scholarship. In much of higher education, scholars utilize well-developed systems to critique, evaluate, and advance the scholarship of discovery. Though details vary by discipline, there are widely accepted conventions for defining questions, designing programs of inquiry, and disseminating work among fellow scholars. However, the diversity of training and research traditions that people bring to SoTL can make it difficult to collaborate or even learn from one another's work—much less critique and evaluate it.

Challenges of Developing a Shared Framework for SoTL

Huber and Morreale (2002) described SoTL as a "trading zone" where scholars from different fields come together to "trade their wares—insights, ideas, and findings—even though the meanings and methods behind them may vary considerably among producer groups" (p. 3). A trading zone is an exciting place to be, in part because it exists at the leading edge of change. The excitement of the trading zone is double-edged, however, because a trading zone is a place that people visit and leave; it is not usually a place to stay and build a community.

Although scholars from different disciplines may work together on the common goal of advancing SoTL, they often come to the task with different questions and different ideas about what constitutes enquiry: how it can be optimally and intentionally implemented and what constitutes meaningful evidence. For example, at one SoTL discussion, a faculty member from life sciences began comparing notes with a faculty member from humanities. As an experimental scientist, the life scientist's approach to SoTL was to focus on observing change and gathering data from a sample, which could then be generalized to a larger (or future) population of students. The humanist's approach, on the other hand, was based on interrogating the text that emerged through his interactions with two of his students about their writing. Their questions to each other, though friendly, revealed that each saw many limitations in the other's approach: "But how would that help you? What is it that you do when you're doing research? How do you know what your data mean?"

Building a new community where scholars from across disciplinary boundaries can learn from one another's work will require scholars to address the reality that others do not necessarily see data in the same ways that they have been trained to see it. One approach has been to borrow methodologies:

What can a literature professor learn by using surveys or analyzing trends across a population? What can a physiologist learn from textual studies? Some scholars may be able to work across these traditional boundaries, or they may be able to find a "polyglot audience" (Huber & Morreale, 2002, p. 20), but this way of dealing with scholarly boundaries becomes a matter of case-by-case translation rather than a shared basis for bringing together a scholarly community.

The challenge of translation across disciplinary boundaries is compounded by the reality that SoTL is to some extent an epistemological stretch for just about everyone in present-day higher education. Schön (1995) has argued that SoTL is grounded in a framework of knowing-in-action. Knowledge of teaching is often tacit, and problems are often "ill-formed, vague, and messy" (p. 28). Variables can rarely be fully controlled or even predicted, and outcomes are often contingent—on students, instructor, content, and contexts—so that what is learned in one situation is not always readily applicable to another. For example, as one instructor cited in Chapter 4 discovered, strengthening alignment with one group of students weakened it with others. In that case, this was not considered a failure, but an important building block in learning how to increase alignment more uniformly the next time a similar teaching situation was encountered. The "proper test," as Schön put it, is not "'Have I solved this problem?' but 'Do I like the new problems I have created?'" (p. 31). However, those who are looking for generalizeable solutions to common teaching problems might easily miss the value of what was discovered. The good news in this scenario is that most scholars realize that questions with easy answers were probably not very good scholarly questions to begin with; on the other hand, people do not always think about teaching questions in the same way that they think about research questions, and it remains a challenge for scholars to find shared ways of assigning value to the SoTL work that they do.

As scholars move into this relatively unfamiliar epistemological territory, the alignment model provides a framework for what we share as a community of scholars of teaching and learning: a shared objective across courses and disciplines (learning), and shared points of investigation—students, instructor, content, and the contexts in which they come together. These shared points of investigation become a shared set of principles that are readily accessible to scholars from a wide range of backgrounds, providing categories for reflection, analysis, critique, and evaluation of the work that educators do.

An Alignment Perspective on SoTL

What would SoTL based on an alignment model look like? Alignment and SoTL share an emphasis on learning as the definitive indicator of teaching. Both recognize that teaching and learning are multidimensional and shaped by a wide range of factors that the instructor needs to account for and monitor. To organize SoTL based on an alignment model, instructors must first account for each of the components of alignment: context, content, instructor, and students.

Contexts vary greatly across disciplines and courses. SoTL organized on an alignment model would ask instructors to make relevant contextual factors explicit. Features of the context that might be incidental to the investigator because they are part of the landscape of an institution might in fact be vital to interpreting their work. For example, where does a course fit in students' academic programs? Do students tend to take courses as a cohort or are their programs highly individualized? Are students primarily residential or are they commuters? Contextual factors such as these are likely to figure into an instructor's understanding of what is happening in a course, but would not be assumed by a community of scholars unless the instructor makes them explicit.

Content also varies across disciplines and courses but in all cases fundamentally shapes teaching and learning goals, activities, and outcomes. SoTL organized on an alignment model would ask instructors to make explicit their learning goals for the content, identify strategies for learning and assessment in support of these goals, and anticipate the challenges the content typically poses for students (and/or the instructor). Accounting for these decisions about content is central to SoTL design: Given these learning goals, what are appropriate methodologies for helping students learn, documenting learning, and negotiating obstacles to learning?

Similarly, instructors vary greatly in their background, expertise, and approaches to teaching, but instructor involvement is central to any course, and the effect of instructor involvement is part of what is studied. So, for example, what has been an instructor's previous experience with this course or with these types of students? What has been learned from others who have experience with similar courses or students? What gave rise to this question, at this point in time? What should be happening in this course? Questions like these help frame the scholarly work and lead others in the scholarly community to appreciate the decisions that are made and the conclusions that are drawn.

Students vary greatly, too, and their respective backgrounds, identities, and expectations for a course profoundly affect their abilities and efforts to learn. SoTL organized on an alignment model would ask instructors to document how they account for student backgrounds, prior knowledge, and expectations when they make claims about student learning. How do they track student perceptions, participation, and engagement throughout the course? How do they monitor student learning throughout the course and document it at the end to show the basis for justifying their conclusions?

Perhaps the most important dimension of SoTL from an alignment perspective is the representation of balance and interactions among the dimensions of alignment. Teaching is always a matter of accounting for and negotiating these multiple, sometimes competing, interests and variables. SoTL organized on an alignment model would ask instructors to address explicitly what decisions are made to balance these multiple perspectives against one another. For example, when an assignment is changed to create a different type of learning experience, what effect does that change have on the overall course content? What effect does it have on the instructor, who must monitor progress and give feedback about this different type of assignment? As shifting disciplinary contexts motivate changes in course content and design, what effects are there on students who now need a different type of preparation for the course, or on instructors who now must teach differently? As changes become more complex, trade-offs need to be identified and assessed: By adding new features to a course, what former features will be lost? What are the effects for students? What are the effects for instructors?

Using Alignment as a SoTL Framework

Although there is potential for wide variation in each of these dimensions of the alignment model, the dimensions themselves are always present and provide an interdisciplinary framework for SoTL (see Table 14.1). For those who are engaged in SoTL, the issues identified by this framework can guide the design and implementation of their investigation, and help shape the interpretation of evidence and communication of conclusions. How well has each dimension of alignment been accounted for? How well have connections among different dimensions been considered? How have changes in one dimension affected others, and how have these changes and effects been documented?

This framework also provides a set of talking points to help structure dialogue among scholars who work in different disciplines or contexts. It helps scholars to focus on the same issues and provide substantive review

Table 14.1

Using Alignment as a Framework for SoTL

Context

- Where a course fits in students' academic programs and plans
- Department or program requirements that place expectations or limitations on what can happen in a course
- Characteristics of an institution that influence students' experience in a course

Content

- Learning goals
- Challenges typically posed by this course
- Activities for learning
- Strategies for assessment

Instructors

- Previous experience with this course, these types of students
- What has been learned from others with similar courses or students
- What gave rise to this question, at this point in time
- What they would like to see happening in this course

Students

- Student backgrounds, prior knowledge, course expectations
- Student perceptions, participation, engagement throughout the course
- Student learning throughout the course
- Learning gains at the end of the course

Interactions Among Students, Instructor, Content, and Context

- What in each dimension of alignment contributed to learning, obstacles that emerged
- Decisions made as each dimension of alignment was considered in relation to others
- Trade-offs identified and assessed—by adding new features to a course, what former features are lost? What are the effects for students? For instructors?

---

and critique of one another's work, even though they might look at one another's work from different disciplinary perspectives. If scholars ask the same questions and use comparable categories for analysis, it facilitates working together to provide feedback and evaluation, so the quality of work is improved and the lessons earned are extended or advanced in other areas.

Using Alignment to Change Teaching Improvement Questions Into Scholarly Questions

If the alignment model can be used as a framework for SoTL, then one use of this framework can be to identify scholarly questions. Many of the examples cited throughout this book began as broad teaching improvement questions, which (like most broad questions) can be answered only very broadly, at best. When approached from the alignment perspective, however, these broad questions can be focused to guide more systematic inquiry, leading to more focused and useful answers for the instructor in the immediate context, and having potential relevance to a wider scholarly community.

For example, the central teaching question raised by an instructor in Chapter 12 was, "How can I structure my course content to help students learn?" As the instructor began to consider writing as a means for aligning students with course content and learning goals (rather than considering student writing as an end product, in and of itself), she began to design and make use of writing assignments differently in her course. For a SoTL question, she now might ask, "How do writing assignments help students achieve learning goals?" To answer this question, she could examine students' writing in terms of the goals she set for the course, identifying the extent to which conceptual frameworks, approaches, or arguments presented in class are reflected in the thinking that students demonstrate in particular writing assignments. Looking at it from the students' perspective, she might ask them to reflect on and rate the extent to which each of the writing activities helped them engage with the content of the course. Identifying what students have learned or how they perceived their learning would help the instructor plan for future courses and also address a broader scholarly question about teaching and learning.

The technology revolution on campuses has given rise to questions such as "Do students learn better when there is online discussion?" Chapter 13 draws conclusions from several cases where online discussion had widely varying effects. In some cases, online discussion was helpful or even transformative; in other cases, students reported that they considered it little more than busywork. As instructors have observed using online discussion in different contexts and for different learning goals, many have raised questions of how to bring students and themselves into alignment with content through this medium. As they have considered student and instructor experience and expectations for online discussion, their question has become, "What uses of online discussion foster better learning, under what conditions?" To answer this question, instructors could examine student participation in online discussion in relation to variables such as how questions are structured, extent of instructor participation, or ways in which issues raised in online discussion are incorporated into the class. To focus on student learning, instructors might examine ways that themes or issues discussed in class also shape online discussion, and in turn, how content discussed online appears in students' homework, class participation, or tests. Instructors who document their practices, analyze effects of these practices, and present their conclusions to a community of fellow scholars will have much to contribute to the scholarly understanding of how to make best use of this technology to engage students in learning.

Many have looked at historical and demographic patterns in U.S. higher education and asked, "How can we do a better job of eliminating bias and honoring diversity?" Chapters 2 and 11 both explore ways in which teaching and learning are influenced by the complexity of interactions among student and instructor identities and expectations in relation to the content and context for a course. The question for research, from the alignment perspective, becomes, "How do we bring instructor and student expectations into alignment so that they can work together to establish and maintain a fair and equitable climate for learning?" Instructors can begin by implementing specific strategies that have been identified for creating a more welcoming classroom climate; as they monitor and respond to student feedback, in what ways are they observing that students' perceptions are in alignment with the instructor's goals of inclusiveness? In what ways are students who might have experienced marginalization in other contexts participating and learning in this course? By documenting student learning and perceptions in response to specific instructor initiatives to include all students, instructors will be better prepared to foster alignment in their own courses and also to join the larger scholarly conversation about diversity in higher education.

An example of how alignment provides a framework for a study that crosses disciplinary boundaries is documented in Chapter 3. The University of Washington (UW) Department of Mathematics found that addressing student misperceptions about learning math was an important first step in aligning expectations in its introductory calculus sequence. Their "Note to Students" (see Table 3.8 in Chapter 3) now has direct counterparts in UW departments as diverse as physics, geography, and dance. What began as a general teaching question about aligning students with the content for the course—"How can we give students realistic expectations for learning in this class?"—can become a scholarly question with interdisciplinary implications: "How does preemptively addressing student misperceptions affect students' subsequent learning and perceptions in a course?" As a SoTL question, the next step could be to identify ways that students respond to efforts to set expectations: What helps students remember expectations as a course proceeds? How do these expectations affect students' ongoing perceptions and decision-making? How accurate and helpful do students find these efforts to align expectations at the beginning of a course? Though disciplines vary widely and novice learners face distinct challenges in each, the alignment perspective provides these departments with a common point of analysis—addressing student misperceptions—which would allow them to learn from one another's examples and benefit from one another's experiences.

In each of these cases, what begins as a more general question about assessing or improving teaching becomes increasingly focused as it examines learning in terms of interactions among context, content, instructor, and students. These factors then help define the terms of enquiry: In each dimension of alignment, what is being changed? As changes are made in one area, what are direct and indirect effects to other areas? In each dimension of alignment, what contributes to learning and what obstacles emerge? As investigators use these questions to conceptualize, implement, and communicate their work in SoTL, their audience can use these same questions as a framework for determining under what conditions conclusions can be reviewed, what can be learned from them, and how they can be extended or adapted to other settings.

Aligning Scholarship

Much progress has been made in recognizing SoTL as a form of scholarship. We propose that alignment provides a unifying framework for the diverse community of scholars engaged in SoTL—a framework that can help them advance SoTL, and as a community of scholars, advance its standing in the broader academic community. For those who are just beginning to consider SoTL from this perspective, we propose starting with the following steps:

1) Use the components of the alignment model—context, content, instructor, students, learning—to frame a teaching question as a question for scholarly investigation.

2) Devise a plan for addressing the question through your teaching:

- Review what others have done to address similar questions in their teaching.

- Determine what indicators of student learning will be relevant for addressing your question, and how these data will be systematically collected.

- Analyze and interpret the data in terms of each component of the alignment model.

3) Make your conclusions public to a community of fellow scholars, using the framework of the alignment model as outlined earlier in Table 14.1.

- *Context:* Identify relevant contextual factors.

- *Content:* Make explicit your learning goals for the content, strategies for learning and assessment in support of these goals, and challenges the content typically poses for students (and/or the instructor).

- *Instructor:* Account for the effect of your involvement in what you are studying.

- *Student:* Indicate how decisions about teaching reflect consideration of student backgrounds, prior knowledge, and experiences in the course. Document student learning gains and procedures for identifying them.

- *Interactions:* Address explicitly decisions you made to balance effects of context, content, instructor, and students throughout the course.

4) As you make your findings public, seek out critique and evaluation from others who will help reflect on your conclusions, and who will be able to extend or adapt them to other settings.

References

Anderson, J. (2002). *A discussion of diversity and learning communities must incorporate assessment.* Paper presented at the American Association for Higher Education Assessment Conference, Boston, MA.

Banta, T. W., & Associates. (2002). *Building a scholarship of assessment.* San Francisco, CA: Jossey-Bass.

Bender, E., & Gray, D. (1999, April). The scholarship of teaching. *Research & Creative Activity, 22*(1), 3. Retrieved December 13, 2004, from the Indiana University, Office of Research and the University Graduate School web site: http://www.indiana.edu/~rcapub/v22n1/p03.html

Bleich, M. R. (2004). The scholarship of practice within the academic clinical enterprise. *Journal of Nursing Education, 43*(2), 51–52.

Boyer, E. L. (1990). *Scholarship reconsidered: Priorities of the professoriate.* San Francisco, CA: Jossey-Bass.

Boyer, E. L. (1996). The scholarship of engagement. *Journal of Public Outreach, 1*(1),11–20.

Bulcroft, K., Werder, C., & Gilliam, G. (2002). Student voices in the campus conversations. *Inventio, 4*(1). Retrieved December 13, 2004, from http://www.doit.gmu.edu/inventio/past/display_past.asp?pID=spring02&sID=bulcroft

Bushaw, D. W. (1996). The scholarship of extension. *Journal of Extension, 34*(4). Retrieved December 13, 2004, from http://www.joe.org/joe/1996august/comm1.html

Eggins, H., & MacDonald, R. (Eds.). (2003). *The scholarship of academic development.* Buckingham, England: Society for Research in Higher Education and Open University Press.

Fried, J. (2002). The scholarship of student affairs: Integration and application. *NASPA Journal, 39*(2), 120–131.

Glassick, C. E., Huber, M. T., & Maeroff, G. I. (1997). *Scholarship assessed: Evaluation of the professoriate.* San Francisco, CA: Jossey-Bass.

Huber, M. T., & Morreale, S. P. (2002). Situating the scholarship of teaching and learning: A cross-disciplinary conversation. In M. T. Huber & S. P. Morreale (Eds.), *Disciplinary styles in the scholarship of teaching and learning: Exploring common ground* (pp. 1–24). Washington, DC: Carnegie Foundation for the Advancement of Teaching and the American Association for Higher Education.

Hutchings, P., & Shulman, L. S. (1999, September/October). The scholarship of teaching and learning: New elaborations, new developments. *Change, 31*(5), 10–15.

Nicholson, M. (1998). C. S. Lewis and the scholarship of imagination in E. Nesbit and R. Haggard. *Renascence: Essays on Values in Literature, 51*(1), 42–63.

Schön, D. A. (1995, November/December). The new scholarship requires a new epistemology. *Change, 27*(6), 26–34.

Shulman, L. S. (2004). Visions of the possible: Models for campus support of the scholarship of teaching and learning. In W. E. Becker & M. L. Andrews (Eds.), *The scholarship of teaching and learning in higher education: Contributions of research universities* (pp. 9–24). Bloomington, IN: Indiana University Press.

15

Applying Alignment in the Faculty Reward System

Donald H. Wulff, Carla W. Hess, & Debra-L. Sequeira

I struggle every time I start preparing my teaching dossier to document my teaching. I find it impossible to put together something that describes what I actually do to contribute to the students and the institution. In desperation, I usually end up trying to create a complete list of the courses I have taught, supplemented by some student ratings, an indication of the number of students served, and lots of samples of syllabi, exams, and important course materials. I feel that is the best I can do given the constraints of the current system.

—Comment from an instructor

During a recent workshop for new chairs, I heard two suggestions that made a lot of sense: that evaluation of teaching should—and often does— include conversations between the chair and the instructor about teaching and that evaluation should be based, in part, on direct observations of the teaching by the chair. But when I got ready to carry out these activities, I realized I didn't have a clear way of organizing my approach for either suggestion. I ultimately realized that even though I've taught for 20 years myself, I'm still not sure how to think about teaching and learning in ways that help me with my job as chair.

—Comment from a department chair

All of us in academia are a long way from having completed our best thinking about teaching and learning within the reward system. As the preceding comments suggest, on most campuses faculty and administrators still struggle with many legitimate questions about evaluating the teaching part of faculty work.[1]

In this chapter we propose that the alignment model can assist in addressing such ongoing questions and concerns. We know, of course, that it cannot provide all the definitive solutions. Our combined 82 years as teachers and administrators in higher education convince us, however, that the model can make important contributions. Thus, using the perspective that effective instructors strive to align context, content, instructors, and students to achieve learning, we explain how the alignment framework can help instructors and administrators. Specifically, we focus on using alignment to *conceptualize, evaluate,* and *document* teaching effectiveness within an institution's system of rewards.[2] In doing so, we also propose specific recommendations for faculty members and some associated implications for administrators.

Using Alignment to Conceptualize Teaching Effectiveness

Like the instructor and chair quoted at the beginning of this chapter, many faculty and administrators do not have an adequate framework to conceptualize the evaluation of teaching. Without such a framework, it is challenging to determine what information to collect and how to use that information in the reward process. Because we believe that the alignment model can serve within the reward system as a conceptual framework, we offer the following recommendations to assist faculty and administrators in using alignment to *conceptualize* teaching effectiveness.

Use the Alignment Model to Conceptualize in a Variety of Instructional Settings

The alignment model is applicable in various instructional settings; its use is not limited to "classroom" instruction. It is also appropriate for evaluating instruction in settings as varied, for example, as laboratory instruction, one-to-one instruction such as advising or mentoring (see Chapter 8), or online learning (see Chapter 13).

Use the Alignment Model to Conceptualize Areas of Focus for Evaluation

Regardless of the setting, the alignment model, first, identifies key components to consider in evaluating teaching effectiveness: context, content, instructor, students, and learning. More importantly, though, the model depicts the interrelationships among those components, providing productive areas of focus both for promoting student learning and for evaluating teaching effectiveness. We define effectiveness by what happens to promote or detract from learning at the intersections of those key components.

Use the Alignment Model to Conceptualize Appropriate Evaluation Purposes

The literature usually identifies two major purposes for gathering information about teaching effectiveness: formative and summative (Scriven, 1967). The formative information is collected primarily to help instructors look forward and think about how to improve teaching performance and enhance learning in the future. The summative information, often collected at the conclusion of an activity, tends to regard teaching as a static event and provides insights that are primarily useful for looking back at what happened.

Although both purposes are important in evaluating teaching effectiveness, too often approaches to evaluating teaching use only information gathered primarily for summative purposes. The alignment model, however, with its emphasis on teaching as an ever-changing, reflective process, suggests that information gathered for formative purposes also must play a part in evaluating teaching effectiveness. In fact, an underlying assumption of the model is that effective instructors gather formative information on an ongoing basis during the teaching process in order to make the adjustments necessary to promote learning. Granted, instructors use that information to improve teaching in progress and not as evidence for rewards. However, there are ways to incorporate formative efforts in documenting teaching effectiveness, and we address those possibilities more specifically in the documentation section of this chapter.

Use the Alignment Model to Conceptualize Evaluation Questions

Whether we are gathering information for formative or summative purposes, we can use foci of the alignment model to identify important questions to evaluate teaching effectiveness. At the most general level, for example, we might ask what is happening between instructor and students that contributes to effectiveness. Or, what happens at the intersection of students and the laboratory content that contributes to or detracts from the learning of these students? Then, after we identify issues related to effectiveness at the intersections, we can shift our questions to increasingly more specific considerations. For instance, what can the instructor do to create the rapport necessary to increase student use of individualized instruction available during office hours? Or, what adjustments can the instructor make to engage students more fully in the laboratory content?

Use the Alignment Model to Conceptualize Evaluation Methods

Once we have conceptualized questions, it is possible to select methods that will provide information necessary to answer them. Seldin (1998, 1999) identified the most commonly used methods for evaluating teaching effectiveness: student perceptions, including both formal student ratings and informal student opinions; colleague and administrator perceptions, often obtained through observations or review of materials; and self-evaluation focused on the instructor's own perceptions of effectiveness. Individuals such as Seldin (1998, 1999) also have documented the pros and cons of the primary procedures for evaluating teaching, so it is not our purpose here to review the value of those individual procedures.

We do want to emphasize, however, that commonly used teaching evaluation approaches do not always provide the information needed to capture efforts to improve teaching effectiveness using alignment. Such procedures use questions that rarely address the complex interrelationships that alignment involves and, therefore, do not provide feedback about the ongoing adjustments that instructors may make in a course to enhance learning. Therefore, in applying alignment-oriented evaluation of teaching and learning, instructors often have to use combinations of methods and devise approaches and questions relevant to the specific kinds of balance they are trying to achieve in the interrelationships among the key components in the alignment model.

Using Alignment to Evaluate Teaching Effectiveness

In this next section, we present recommendations about how instructors can use the alignment framework to identify what to *evaluate* in the teaching/ learning process. To explain our suggestions, we provide brief examples to illustrate how instructors ask questions about their teaching effectiveness and use multiple methods and results to decide what issues to address in trying to improve alignment. We vary the instructional settings in the examples to reinforce the point that the approach is applicable in a variety of contexts.

In presenting these examples, we demonstrate how the instructors applied the alignment model in the early stages of their evaluation of teaching effectiveness. In each case, we show how their thinking about the results moved the instructors to a subsequent stage with another, more specific, question that illustrates the ongoing process. For these examples, we do not focus on the specific instructional strategies that the instructors decided to use. Our purpose is not to reach resolution in these short cases or to capture all of the complexity of the process. Rather, we want to emphasize initial areas of focus that the alignment perspective provides for evaluation at the intersections of the key instructional components.

Although the recommendations address instructors evaluating their own teaching effectiveness, there also are implications for administrators. When these academic leaders understand this use of alignment for evaluating teaching effectiveness, they are better able to support and reward faculty involved in such efforts to improve teaching and learning. The administrators also can obtain insights about key variables for possible use in their own aggregation of data to represent effectiveness across faculty members at the departmental or school/college levels. For example, a departmental chair might provide the number and percentage of her faculty, by academic rank, who are pursuing increased student learning through strategies designed to enhance alignment at one or more of the intersections of the alignment model.

Evaluate the Alignment of the Students and the Content

Table 15.1 provides an example of a beginning effort to evaluate the alignment between students and content while a course is in progress. The example begins in Stage 1 with a general question about the interrelationship between students and content, then identifies two of the evaluation methods the instructor used. Next, it lists two of the results the instructor used formatively to proceed within an alignment framework. The table then illustrates the instructor's move in Stage 2 to a second more specific teaching effectiveness question that evolved from the initial question. Lastly, the table presents some ways the instructor proceeded to address that question.

Evaluate the Alignment of the Students and the Instructor

Table 15.2 illustrates the use of the alignment model to evaluate how well the relationship between the students and instructor is achieving learning goals. We chose this example because the individual conference setting is one in which many instructors and administrators do not usually gather feedback to evaluate teaching effectiveness. Unlike the previous example, this one begins with summative data from the end of the program. Thus, the instructor will implement any desired modifications in subsequent advising situations with different students.

Evaluate the Alignment of the Instructor and the Content

In Table 15.3, the focus is on the intersection between instructor and content—how effectively the instructor has adapted to the content and how well

Table 15.1

An Abbreviated Example of the Evaluation of the Alignment Between Students and Content

---

In an upper-division child development course in psychology taught for the first time online by a newly appointed instructor

Stage 1 Evaluation

Question	How effective is the alignment between students and content?
Methods	• Student performance. • Informal written student feedback.
Results	• Students performed more poorly than expected on the first exam. • Students reported that the content is "boring" and "too difficult."
Next step	Gather more information to determine what to do to improve alignment.

Stage 2 Evaluation

Question	What can be done to engage students more effectively in the content and improve test performance?
Methods	• Colleague or administrator review of online materials. • Classroom assessment technique.*
Results	• Colleague noted that materials on the web provide lots of information about concepts in the course but lack practical examples of application of the concepts. • Students indicated a need for examples or short cases that illustrate application of the most complex and relevant concepts.
Next steps	• Decide whether to adjust course content, instructional strategies used with the content, student perceptions of the content, or some combination of these factors. • Then implement chosen strategies and gather more data to determine if student-content alignment improves.

---

* Angelo, T. A. & Cross, K. P. (1993). *Classroom assessment techniques* (2nd ed.). San Francisco, CA: Jossey-Bass.

the content has been adapted to the instructor. In contrast to the previous examples, this one illustrates the use of alignment in the more typical classroom setting. Like the second example, it begins with summative data, so any proposed changes would be implemented with a different group of students in a subsequent course.

Table 15.2

An Abbreviated Example of the Evaluation of the Alignment Between Students and Instructor

An experienced instructor conducting conferences with undergraduate students to provide advice on their projects in an honors program in history

Stage 1 Evaluation

Question	How effective was alignment between students and the instructor?
Methods	• Student ratings. • Instructor self-evaluation.
Results	• Students provided ratings of 2.2 on a 5-point scale (1 = lowest; 5 = highest) for "instructor's one-on-one advising during conferences"; in open-ended comments several students used terms such as "unapproachable" and "intimidating." • Instructor noted that during conferences, students had few good questions and did not talk much.
Next steps	• Determine what adjustments the instructor can make in her behavior, in the students' perceptions and behaviors, or in both in order to improve instructor-student alignment with the next group of students. • Gather formative information with the next cohort of students in the program.

Stage 2 Evaluation

Question	What is happening to contribute to alignment or misalignment between students and instructor in this advising setting?
Methods	• Student feedback focused on student-instructor relationship. • Instructor self-evaluation.
Results	• Students indicated a lack of instructor openness to their questions and perceptions. • Instructor determined that she needed to encourage students to be active participants in the conferences.
Next steps	• Determine what adjustments the instructor can make in her behavior, in students' perceptions and behaviors, or in both in order to improve instructor-student alignment. • Then implement chosen strategies and gather more data to determine if student-instructor alignment improves.

Table 15.3

An Abbreviated Example of the Evaluation of the Alignment Between Instructor and Content

In a law course taught for the first time by an experienced instructor

Stage 1 Evaluation

Question	How effective is the alignment between instructor and content?
Methods	• Student ratings.
Results	• Students ranked "instructor knowledge" at 2.1 on a 5-point scale (1 = lowest; 5 = highest).
Next step	• Gather information as instructor teaches the course the second time to help understand the low rating on this item.

Stage 2 Evaluation

Question	What evidence is there to support the misalignment perceived by previous students?
Methods	• Colleague observations and consultation in the subsequent course. • Student midterm assessment of instructor's knowledge.
Results	• Colleague noted the need for more examples that illustrate key concepts. • Student midterm feedback suggested need for real-life examples from instructor's experience in the field.
Next steps	• Decide whether to adjust by using examples from the instructor's own experience, by using other strategies to provide examples, by changing students' perceptions, or by some combination of these factors. • Then implement chosen strategies and gather more data to determine if instructor-content alignment improves.

Evaluate the Alignment of the Context With the Students, Instructor, and Content

The example in Table 15.4 illustrates the importance of evaluating teaching effectiveness within the larger context of a department. At the intersection of the context with the other important components of the instructional process—students, instructor, content, and learning—we are interested in knowing how effectively a course fits into the larger departmental context and how that context affects teaching effectiveness in the course. The specific example of the chemistry course sequence (Chem 101 and 102) illustrates a

Table 15.4

An Abbreviated Example of the Evaluation of the
Alignment Between a Course and the Departmental Context

In a chemistry course sequence (Chem 101 and 102) in which students are expected to retain and recall important concepts from a prerequisite, large lecture course (Chem 101) for application in smaller sections of a subsequent course (Chem 102)

Stage 1 Evaluation

Question	How effective is alignment among the instructor, students, content in Chem 101, and larger context?
Methods	• Student performance on tests in Chem 102.
Results	• Tests in the subsequent course confirm that students cannot apply basic concepts that should have been taught and learned in Chem 101.
Next step	• Gather information to understand where the misalignment between the Chem 101 course and the larger context lies.

Stage 2 Evaluation

Question	Is the problem related to the relationship between the context and the instructor, the context and the students, the context and the content, or between the context and some combination of these components?
Methods	• Instructor self-evaluation. • Course artifacts: syllabus, web site, assignments from Chem 101. • Observation in Chem 101 conducted by colleagues teaching Chem 102.
Results	• Instructor noted he is teaching the concepts that students cannot apply in the subsequent course (Chem 102). • Artifacts confirmed that concepts are being taught in Chem 101. • Observers noted that concepts are being taught quite effectively in Chem 101.
Next steps	• Analyze data across the sources to determine whether the instructor of Chem 101 can make adjustments to help students apply and retain the information, whether instructors in Chem 102 must make adjustments to help students recall and apply information, whether students themselves must make adjustments to recall and apply information, or whether adjustments in some combination of these factors is necessary. • Then implement chosen strategies and gather more data to determine if course-context alignment improves.

setting in which students are expected to retain and recall important concepts from a prerequisite, large lecture course (Chem 101) for application in smaller sections of a subsequent course (Chem 102). This example reflects the unusual collection of summative evaluation data by instructors in the sections of a later course (Chem 102) for future use by the instructor of a prerequisite course (Chem 101). It also involves a set of players—the instructors in the various sections of Chem 102—in addition to the instructor of Chem 101. The Chem 102 instructors have important roles in helping align the earlier course within the larger departmental context of the subsequent course.

It is important to note that these examples identify only areas in which adjustments were necessary. In the actual cases, the evaluation procedures also revealed strengths in the teaching. The instructors used the alignment framework as well, then, to obtain additional data to discover why those strengths had emerged. The instructors learned what specifically contributed to their effectiveness and their students' learning and should, therefore, be retained or maintained.

Using Alignment to Document Teaching Effectiveness

In this section we recommend ways of using the alignment framework to *document* teaching effectiveness. The suggestions must be considered, however, within the context of guidelines and expectations established within individual institutions. Instructors who document teaching effectiveness should provide materials or subject matter that is consistent with policies on their own campuses. Our experience suggests, though, that most guidelines developed by institutions, collective bargaining units, administrators, and/or review committees are flexible enough to accommodate the individuality inherent in evidence-based support of teaching effectiveness.

Again, although we have addressed the suggestions to faculty members who are documenting their work, chairs or deans who are aggregating data across instructors or departments also could easily adapt the recommendations for application in their broader contexts.

Describe General Components of Teaching in the Documentation Process

The first step of documentation is description based on self-reflection that sets the stage for discussing teaching effectiveness. The alignment model provides possible areas to address in this descriptive portion of your dossier/teaching portfolio.

- *Content:* Describe the content of your course. What makes it interesting, distinctive, and/or special? What opportunities and challenges does it present?

- *Instructor:* Describe yourself as a teacher. What do you believe about teaching and learning? What instructional approaches, methods, or strategies do you use? What makes you and your approaches particularly interesting and/or distinctive? What opportunities and challenges do your style, needs, preferences, and beliefs present in your teaching and your students' learning?

- *Students:* Describe your students. What makes them and their needs, goals, or expectations particularly interesting and/or special? What opportunities and challenges do their backgrounds, needs, goals, expectations, or perceptions present in your teaching and their learning?

- *Context:* Describe the context for your teaching. What makes your teaching unique within the department, college, or university? What special forces in the context affect the ways your courses can or should be taught? Which of the forces present particular challenges? Which of the forces provide opportunities for teaching in unique and engaging ways? How do your courses build on students' prior knowledge and prepare them for subsequent courses in your discipline or others? How does your teaching contribute to the larger mission and/or goals of the department, discipline, school/college, institution, and/or society?

- *Learning:* Describe what is most important in what, how, and why your students learn. What are your most important overall learning goals for students? What are your students' learning goals?

Describe Interrelationships in the Documentation Process

To document effectiveness, you should be able to explain what you have done to enhance alignment at the critical intersections of content, instructor, students, and context, and, especially, how the overall degree of alignment contributed to student learning. To begin, you might briefly explain the overall approach taken to evaluate your teaching effectiveness within the alignment framework. Then, you are ready to address specific intersections identified in the alignment model, including the interrelationships between content and instructor; instructor and students; students and content; and context and content, instructor, and students. The questions that follow are the kind that you might ask about each interrelationship. The example focuses on the interrelationship between the instructor and the content, but with minor changes in wording, the questions can be used for any of the other interrelationships as well.

- What strategies did you use to adapt your needs, expectations, perceptions, preferences, and priorities to the content you were teaching?

- What strategies did you use to adapt the content to your needs, expectations, perceptions, preferences, and priorities?

- To what extent did you achieve a balance between content and instructor that contributed to instructor/student satisfaction and, more important, to student learning?

- How do you know? What evidence led to your conclusions? How did you collect it?

- What challenges remain in achieving an appropriate balance between content and instructor?

- How do you know? What evidence led to your conclusions? How was it collected?

- What kinds of goals have you established to address these challenges in ongoing ways?

- How will you collect additional information to address those challenges and determine the impact of changes?

Be Purposeful in Selecting and Synthesizing Information

No matter how successfully data reflect instructional innovation, outcomes, and impacts, documentation does not fulfill its potential if it is not communicated effectively. To be convincing, you must both select pertinent information and synthesize it as fully as possible. Useful synthesis is much more than lists of courses taught, numbers of students served, and documents such as syllabi, exams, and raw data from student ratings and colleague and administrator evaluations. Most reviewers do not have time to sort through such isolated pieces of information to pull together a coherent view of teaching effectiveness. In fact, because some instructors present as many different materials as possible, many institutions now have specific guidelines, not only about what to include, but also about how much information is appropriate.

The use of an alignment framework generates extensive potential information for documenting teaching effectiveness. So it is particularly important to stay focused on the purpose for the documentation as you prepare to select and synthesize materials to represent the alignment perspective. You are providing evidence about what you are doing to improve teaching effectiveness and what you have achieved relative to learning outcomes. Consistent with the increasing use of teaching portfolios (Seldin, 1998), you are also providing some reflective commentary that documents for the reader how you are thinking about and using the process and the results of evaluation.

The literature on development of teaching portfolios provides some suggestions for selecting and synthesizing information (e.g., Edgerton, Hutchings, & Quinlan, 1991; Seldin, 2004; Seldin & Associates, 1993). You also undoubtedly will need tables, figures, and numbered and bulleted lists to summarize both qualitative and quantitative information. In some cases, it may be appropriate to reference documents and artifacts that "will be supplied upon request."

Use Formative Data Appropriately

As suggested throughout this chapter, the alignment model reinforces the importance of using both formative and summative data to document teaching effectiveness. Although faculty and administrators recognize that most procedures for data collection are typically used in the reward system, they are not always as aware that the use of formative evaluation in the reward system raises some important ethical issues. First, formative data are collected for improvement purposes. Often when colleagues, administrators, and, especially students, are providing formative data, they are not expecting someone to use it for summative (i.e., determining or rewarding quality) purposes. In fact, our experience suggests that students will provide different results if they think they are helping an instructor improve instruction rather than helping that individual navigate the reward system.

Therefore, it is important to maintain the distinction between data gathered for the two different purposes. Formative results are most often not appropriate for direct use in documenting teaching effectiveness. However, instructors can use formative evaluation for documentation of their efforts to be effective. They can describe their perspective and the improvement process in which they have engaged. Evidence of such engagement in formative evaluation is an important indicator of an instructor's ongoing efforts to make adjustments necessary to maximize learning for each group of students, and, in and of itself, demonstrates teaching effectiveness.

Be Positive About Challenges

At the intersections of the context, instructor, students, and content there are important issues that instructors must struggle with to enhance learning. Often these challenges seem insurmountable. As a result, instructors sometimes include in their documentation strong rationales bordering on excuses, complaints, and even blame to explain why they could not address certain challenges. For example, an instructor might provide justification for low student ratings related to content by arguing that students today are not interested in the subject matter of the course or are incapable of doing the kind of thinking required. Or, an administrator might contend that the requirement of a standardized national qualifying exam at the end of a professional program makes it impossible to develop the curriculum that the faculty and administrator think is most important for student learning.

Although such arguments may have merit, our experience suggests that documentation can be more successful if it avoids complaints, self-deprecation, or deprecation of the system. That is not to say that challenges should be ignored in the documentation process; rather, they should be addressed in a positive way. Specifically, instructors and administrators gain ground by approaching the challenges as *opportunities* that they attempt to address. In this way, everyone involved can perceive teaching as a work-in-progress in which instructors and administrators are using the opportunities to address key issues associated with the learning needs of each successive cohort of students.

Be Proactive in Presenting Your Story Using a Scholarly Approach

No one can develop your specific case within the reward system for you. You have to be proactive in presenting your work in a form that demonstrates what you have done. Then evaluation becomes something that you do for yourself rather than something that someone does *to* you. At the same time you do take control, however, it is important to understand that some individuals may not recognize the teaching-learning process as an interactive and, therefore, dynamic process. They may also be unaware that teaching effectiveness can be coherently defined, evaluated, and documented.

In our experience, the key to gaining acceptance of your documentation in such settings is to present that evidence as objective, data-based scholarship. Remember, though, that such documentation involves more than just explaining that you experimented with different instructional strategies to improve your teaching. Rather, as the examples in the previous section on evaluation illustrate, the process involves the ongoing gathering of information, thorough interpreting of that information, thoughtful selecting of instructional strategies, monitoring the implementation of those strategies, and, especially, evaluating their impact on student learning. In the same ways that researchers establish tentative hypotheses, gather data, analyze and interpret the data, reach conclusions, and identify the implications of their inquiry, faculty and administrators using an alignment perspective can approach the evaluation of teaching as a scholarly activity (see Chapter 14). Taking a scholarly approach means not only following the basic research steps in your instructional improvement efforts, but also being proactive in capturing the complexity of that process in your documentation of teaching effectiveness.

Using Alignment to Identify Implications for Administrators

As emphasized throughout this chapter, all of the ideas discussed also have implications for administrators thinking about evaluating teaching effectiveness. As chairs and deans attend to and participate in the continuous improvement efforts and successes of their teaching faculty, they develop understandings and identify information for use in their administrative roles as evaluators, decision-makers, resource managers, and guardians of their institution's vision, mission, and goals. When they document their faculty's engagement in formative evaluation and the outcomes of summative evaluation across academic units (e.g., department, college, school, or division), the effective aggregation, analysis, and interpretation of those data create evidence to support their decision-making and accountability. Ultimately, the evidence not only demonstrates effectiveness at the level of the individual instructors and departments and schools/colleges, but it also provides important information in support of institutional effectiveness.

To gain these understandings and document them successfully, however, administrations need appropriate, useful information from their faculty. The mechanisms for gathering this information are likely to be an integral part of an already existing data collection system. For example, most faculty members submit an annual report of their scholarly activities to their departments and/or schools/colleges. However, they may not submit a cohesive and scholarly view of teaching effectiveness as alignment. Such a perspective helps with the conceptualization, evaluation, and documentation across instructional settings—not only in classrooms but also in settings such as laboratories, practica, field experiences, and academic and research advising. Administrators must prepare themselves to encourage and support faculty in working within this more complex and realistic view of the teaching/learning process.

The suggestion that instructors submit evidence of effectiveness based on such dynamic, interactive views of instruction across settings may initially present some challenges. Some faculty, understandably, will not be used to thinking in these ways. It is important to remember, however, that the rewarding of such documentation, and of instructional effectiveness itself, demonstrates a cultural valuing of teaching and learning as a complex and dynamic enterprise. And, as our experience suggests and Lucas (1994) has said so succinctly: "Behavior that is rewarded is the behavior to which faculty will devote their time and effort" (p. 68).

Conclusion

So, what do we gain from implementing an alignment perspective in the reward system? First, we get a cohesive, consistent approach for understanding teaching effectiveness and addressing concerns like those of the instructor and chair quoted at the beginning of this chapter. We also get a framework of which the validity and utility have been tested for two decades. Most important, we get a model for conceptualizing, evaluating, and documenting teaching effectiveness in ways that place the emphasis on the most basic mission of institutions of higher education—student learning.

Endnotes

1) Given that the alignment model emerged from the study of teaching effectiveness, we are limiting our chapter to the discussion of evaluating teaching and are not addressing research and service, the other major dimensions of faculty work.

2) In this chapter we define the reward system broadly to include retention, tenure, promotion, salary increases, merit pay, teaching and teaching scholarship awards, and other forms of recognition.

References

Angelo, T. A., & Cross, K. P. (1993). *Classroom assessment techniques: A handbook for college teachers* (2nd ed.). San Francisco, CA: Jossey-Bass.

Edgerton, R., Hutchings, P., & Quinlan, K. (1991). *The teaching portfolio: Capturing the scholarship in teaching.* Washington, DC: American Association for Higher Education.

Lucas, A. F. (1994). *Strengthening departmental leadership: A team-building guide for chairs in colleges and universities.* San Francisco, CA: Jossey-Bass.

Scriven, M. (1967). The methodology of evaluation. In R. W. Tyler, F. M. Gagne, & M. Scriven (Eds.), *Perspectives of curriculum evaluation* (pp. 39–83). Chicago, IL: Rand McNally.

Seldin, P. (1998). How colleges evaluate teaching: 1988 vs. 1998. *AAHE Bulletin, 50*(7), 3–7.

Seldin, P. (2004). *The teaching portfolio: A practical guide to improved performance and promotion/tenure decisions* (3rd ed.). Bolton, MA: Anker.

Seldin, P., & Associates. (1993). *Successful use of teaching portfolios.* Bolton, MA: Anker.

Seldin, P., & Associates. (1999). *Changing practices in evaluating teaching: A practical guide to improved faculty performance and promotion/tenure decisions.* Bolton, MA: Anker.

Part V

ALIGNMENT:
SYNTHESIS AND CONCLUSIONS

16

Aligning for Learning:
Synthesis and Conclusions

Donald H. Wulff

Throughout this book, we have focused on an alignment model of teaching effectiveness—its conceptualization of the instructional process, various applications of it, and strategies for its use. In this chapter, I provide some concluding synthesis and final thoughts. As a way of synthesizing, I first reinforce some of the important considerations in the alignment process by placing them in the context of faculty comments and concerns. Then, in the latter part of the chapter, I briefly discuss conclusions in three areas related to future thinking about teaching effectiveness.

Considerations in Implementing the Alignment Model

My work with instructors on teaching effectiveness has revealed some persistent issues that they encounter when attempting to implement an alignment perspective in their teaching. Most of these issues focus on the natural tensions in teaching and learning that I discussed briefly in Chapter 1. Five issues that occur consistently are maintaining challenging content, using student perceptions, using strategies selectively, interpreting findings, and managing time.

Maintaining Challenging Content

- "What I worry about in trying to adapt my course to students is sacrificing content. I don't want to feel that I have to 'dumb down' my course just to accommodate students."

In this instructor's comment the tension exists because of the need to maintain course content while simultaneously adapting to the needs, expectations, and abilities of students. From an alignment perspective, there are two key recommendations.

Stay focused on learning. Remember that the ultimate goal is that students learn. It does little good to try to teach content—no matter how much or how challenging—if students are not learning it. It is quite easy to get so focused on "covering" the content that you lose sight of whether students are actually mastering it sufficiently.

Recognize that aligning content and students works both ways. In some cases, getting better alignment may require some adjustment of the content for students. For example, you might adapt the content by finding additional ways to engage the students in it. (Throughout this book there are strategies for such engagement.) Sometimes, though, it may be more important to adjust the students' perceptions and expectations in preparation for the complex content. Thus, you might encourage students to consider what their roles should be in meeting the demands of the content. For example, you might stress that certain aspects of the content will be difficult and that students will have important responsibilities for doing their part—attending class regularly, completing important assignments designed to promote learning, participating in activities intended to engage them in the content, and spending extra time on challenging concepts or problems. At the same time, you can emphasize explicitly that the content is important to them and that their learning is a key consideration in the choices you are making. Explain that you will support them in working toward that end.

Thus, whether you adjust the content to the students or the students to the content, or both, *adaptation* in alignment clearly does not mean that you simply eliminate challenging content. The adjustment may require more selectivity because you cannot teach the same amount of content. It does not mean, however, that the content has to be simple. By focusing on learning and adapting content to students as well as students to content, you move closer to alignment that maintains challenging content in ways that are sensitive to students and that meet your needs as well.

Using Student Perceptions

- "I find it difficult to use student perceptions of my teaching. In some ways I feel that as the expert who understands best what content I want students to learn, I shouldn't have students dictating how I teach my course. It just seems that if I ask for student input, I am then compelled to follow-through on it, thus relinquishing my own commitments and beliefs about how the course should be taught."

The preceding instructor comment is a variation of one I hear often about the extensive use of student perceptions in evaluating teaching and learning. It is further complicated by the fact that student ratings remain the major source of input about teaching effectiveness (Seldin, 1998, 1999). Such an emphasis on student ratings makes some instructors cautious about the way student input is incorporated in any evaluation of teaching effectiveness.

At the same time, however, students can be an important source of information about teaching and learning. As demonstrated throughout this book, students can provide useful formative data to help instructors decide when and how to make changes. Students also can contribute summative information about how successful any changes were in supporting their learning. So, how can you begin to reconcile this tension between using student input—both as ongoing feedback during the course and as a source of insight at the end of course—and not allowing it to dictate the entire instructional process?

Think about what function student input can serve. First, it is helpful to realize that students can more appropriately provide feedback in some areas than others. For example, students are not the best judges of whether content is up-to-date, appropriately linked to emerging ideas in the field, or appropriately sequenced in the curriculum. But, they can tell you how they are experiencing the teaching and learning. For example, they can let you know whether they understand the content or whether they are able to apply it.

Second, during a course, student input can help you link your improvement efforts to summative evaluation at the end of the course. If you are using student ratings as the primary measure of how well you conducted the course, it is a good idea to be responding to student perceptions as the course progresses. If you make improvements in a course based on what you or your colleagues think without considering students' perceptions, you could find that students have completely different perceptions that are expressed in feedback at the end of the term. Although it is certainly important to rely on your own expertise and experience in making instructional decisions, you undoubtedly will achieve the best alignment as measured by student ratings if you also include some student perceptions in determining what adjustments to make throughout the course.

Recognize that seeking student input does not mean simply doing what students suggest. In deciding how to use student feedback, you always have choices based on the needs, expectations, and perceptions of the students, on the content, and on your own needs, expectations, and preferences. You can make suggested changes if you believe the changes are appropriate; you can decide you don't want to make the changes suggested but instead offer alternative strategies that can accomplish both your goals and those of the students; or, you can choose not to make changes in strategies but rather in students' perceptions. In the case of the final option, you might provide rationale that explains to students, in terms of learning, why you have chosen to use certain instructional methods and what students can do to help you in implementing those methods.

Know that students are attaching meaning to your behaviors. Students are constantly attaching their own interpretations to what you do when you are teaching. Often, these perceptions about what you are trying to do and why can be inaccurate. For this reason, you should stay in touch with students to be aware of what perceptions they may be attaching to your behaviors. Then you are able to correct misperceptions and misunderstandings that might affect learning.

Follow through on student feedback. Regardless of the extent to which you rely on feedback, you should follow through if you request it. Our experience indicates that students do not want to spend a lot of time listening to details of how you are evaluating teaching effectiveness in a course or how you are working to improve your teaching effectiveness. But, briefly explaining to students what option you chose based on the feedback and why you chose it maintains student-instructor alignment, not only by demonstrating respect for the students and their perspectives, but also by providing an important opportunity to reinforce your choices in terms of your commitment to specific course goals and students' learning.

Thus, gathering feedback does not necessarily mean that you are letting students dictate what you do in your courses. Instead, it means that you, as the expert and more experienced learner, are seeking information that can help you determine what adjustments you are willing to—and can—make to promote learning in your courses.

Using Strategies Selectively

- "In a discussion among faculty, I heard one instructor talk about how he uses group projects. As one who is always looking for straightforward approaches, I decided such projects would be a good way to engage my students more fully in the content of my course. But, when I changed my approach to use the projects, many of the students were upset with me because they hated working in groups on the projects."

This instructor's comments reflect some interesting complexities about the teaching process. The tension emerges because the instructor clearly is thinking about how to improve her teaching. When she tries to make adjustments to engage the students more fully in the content, however, another area loses some of its alignment. Thus, she is pulled in two directions as she tries both to implement a new strategy and to have it support the instructor-student relationship that was previously fairly well-balanced.

This dilemma reminds us that the alignment model does not provide simple, straightforward strategies that are easily applied to teaching. In fact, it can be quite difficult to adopt simple prescriptions that suggest strategies or teaching behaviors without fully considering the key components of instruction in a particular situation. Although there are some broad categories of communication behaviors that apply across courses, specific strategies that work in one context with a particular body of content, instructor(s), and students may not work in the same way in another course. Thus, when you seek specific strategies to help you with your teaching, doing the following will help you to stay consistent with the alignment model.

Look for strategies drawn from situations most like yours. You can study situations where the context, students, and content are most like your teaching situation. Then you can determine how you might adapt the selected strategies for your needs. The important point is that if you are going to borrow ideas, you should recognize that some adjustments may need to be made to adapt the ideas for your specific situation.

Recognize that there is a big step between selecting a strategy and implementing it successfully. Adopting a strategy does not necessarily mean that you know how to *implement* it. For the instructor who tried to use group projects, the overall approach may well be helpful. However, she may need help to adjust the way she and/or students use them. To do so, she could seek input from the students to determine why the projects are not helping in their learning and whether she should address those issues or help her students to do so. In addition, she also might enlist the help of colleagues. Others who have used group projects or other professionals such as instructional development specialists can help her think about how to implement group projects in ways that can make them successful in her situation.

Know that changes in one area can affect balance in other areas. The statement about using group projects also illustrates that, because instructional components are all interrelated, any change in one area has the potential to affect, either positively or negatively, any of the others. These interrelationships demonstrate why striving for alignment is a process that requires ongoing monitoring.

Continue to assess as you implement new changes. As has been strongly emphasized throughout this book, keeping components aligned requires ongoing assessment. In the previous example, merely implementing the group project strategy and proceeding as if it were working would be a mistake. The instructor must determine whether an implemented adjustment actually establishes better rapport with students and, especially, whether it promotes better student learning.

Interpreting Findings

• "I do try to stay in touch with how my students are doing. I talk to them about how the course is going for them; I listen carefully during office hours to the kinds of challenges they are having with the content; and I conduct some informal checks periodically at the end of class. Despite my ongoing efforts, I am not always good at figuring out why students are having trouble. So, it is not easy to pick a helpful strategy and make it work."

This instructor has identified an important issue that has been only indirectly addressed in this book. The issue is this: As you implement the alignment model, there is an interpretation stage that should not be overlooked. In previous chapters, we have suggested that you need to "monitor" alignment, find ways to determine how well strategies are working, and constantly make adjustments. All of these suggestions stress gathering information about what is happening, analyzing that information, and determining next steps. However, when you use a research perspective to enhance teaching and learning, there is an interpretation stage between analysis and decision-making that is too often glossed over (Nyquist & Wulff, 2001).

Interpretation, important in any research process, provides the insights to determine what you do next to improve teaching and learning. It is the stage after data analysis when you ask: What do these findings mean? What is happening here? Or, what would explain these findings? It is a time when you engage in the reflection that is essential to making informed decisions about how to proceed. The tension arises because, although you may know you need to make changes, it may not be as clear how you should proceed. Although the initial procedures used for evaluating teaching can identify problem areas and strengths, they do not as readily help you understand *why* certain areas emerge as effective or ineffective or what you can do to make productive changes. So, what can you do to interpret findings as you strive to improve your teaching effectiveness?

Look to your own perceptions and experiences. First, you can review what you know about what has happened in a course to see if your perceptions or experiences can help you interpret feedback. Is there something you know you are doing that would help explain the feedback? For example, you might think to yourself, "Oh, I know why students are saying there is too much repetition. The synthesis I have been trying to provide after each major point is somehow coming across as repetitious." Or, drawing on your experience, you might think, "Oh, I had that same difficulty the last time I taught this course; maybe the same thing is happening again."

Enlist the help of colleagues. Colleagues who have had similar teaching experiences provide another source of insight. They may be able to offer perspectives about similar feedback they have received and about ways they have learned to make sense of conflicting results. In the same way you use your own perceptions and experiences, then, you may be able to use colleagues' understanding to help you interpret feedback you receive.

Use the literature and research on teaching. An important source of insight for interpreting your findings exists in teaching literature and research results or frameworks. For example, you might develop understandings based on research that explains general tenets about adult learning or the freshman experience that will help you in interpretation. However, unless you have previously consulted that literature, you might not understand what it advocates or how you might best implement it. For these reasons, it is important to seek the assistance of colleagues with expertise in the literature and the research. Instructional development resources are especially helpful, and many campuses now have such resources. Because instructional consultants are familiar with literature on teaching and with some of the relevant research, they can help to provide you with the insights that you need to interpret your findings. With their assistance, you do not have to be familiar with all the literature or the specific theories that are most applicable. In fact, for the cases in many chapters of this volume, there is an instructional consultant working with an instructor or instructors—sometimes in very prominent roles, sometimes providing support in the background. Chapter 12 on aligning through writing demonstrates the kind of insights that experts can provide.

Be prepared to collect additional data. When you are unable to interpret findings from your efforts to improve teaching effectiveness, you may need to collect additional data. For example, in a recent course that I was assisting, there was concern about the amount of reading. Some students said there was too much reading; others thought that all reading was relevant and important. It wasn't until I collected more information for the instructor that he and I identified an intervening variable—the time required for students' internships—that was affecting the students' perceptions. For the most part, the students who were heavily involved in internships were among those who were most concerned about excessive reading. Thus, the instructor was able to interpret what students were saying and determine next steps. In consideration of both student concerns and his own goals for the course, he chose not to decrease the amount of reading. He did, however, talk to students about what they could do to read more efficiently, and previewed readings as they were assigned to emphasize goals for the reading and to highlight key insights and ideas that students should be looking for in the reading.

Allow time for reflection. The interpretation stage of teaching improvement is a time to think about what you are hearing and seeing in feedback and how you should proceed. Reflection is vital because teaching is such a dynamic decision-making process. It is also important because going through such a reflective process prepares you to discuss your teaching effectiveness with others, particularly as you prepare dossiers or teaching portfolios to capture the ways you are enhancing your teaching and student learning.

Managing Time

- "While I think such an ongoing reflective approach to learning is certainly important, the reality is it requires a lot of my time. Sometimes, I can barely keep up with what it takes to keep my classes going from day-to-day without worrying about keeping everything aligned."

The concern expressed by this faculty member is certainly legitimate. The fact remains, however, that good teaching is complex. As demonstrated in this volume, success dealing with that complexity requires not only a range of strategies, but also time to gather data and thoughtfully reflect on what those data mean for making adjustments in courses. To address the tensions that are a natural part of the dynamics of the teaching/learning process, you have to spend some additional time.

Although, unfortunately, there are no straightforward strategies to make extra time in your days, some strategies can be time-savers. We identified some of those in the preceding chapters, and the most important ones are summarized here.

Take advantage of available resources that can assist. One important time-saver is to use the instructional development resources located in your campus center for teaching and learning. Instructional development specialists or consultants at such centers are available during the design and planning stages of a course. These specialists can save you time because they know what to do to help you focus your approach to instructional change. As they assist with the alignment in a course, they also can save you time at various stages of the process. They can help you determine what evaluation questions to ask and what methods to use to gather data. In some settings, these consultants may also assist in gathering, analyzing, and interpreting data and, ultimately, in making choices about what strategies to consider in response to the data. Thus, although you ultimately determine the process and own any resulting data, the specialists are able to serve as resources in ways that can save you valuable time.

Talk to colleagues. Again, talking to colleagues who have taught in similar class formats or with similar content and/or students can also provide useful insights. Such interactions are always helpful but are particularly useful when instructional development resources are not available. Colleagues can provide ideas for course designs, syllabi, or approaches that can be adapted for use in other situations. When you are not starting from scratch in the development of materials or strategies, you can also save time.

Be preemptive. You also can save time by taking preemptive approaches. Whatever is done during the design stages of a course to anticipate and avoid potential areas of difficulty will be helpful in saving time in the long run (see Chapter 3 on course design). Chapter 10 on aligning in the foreign languages stresses the importance of being preemptive not only in planning but also in early sessions of a course. The major issue that I have observed for instructors and students who are unhappy with the way a course is progressing is lack of aligned expectations. Thus, in my efforts to assist instructors, I stress the importance of using the first day of class to work on aligning expectations. If, on the first day of class, you review the syllabus briefly and then move right into the content of the course, you miss an important preemptive opportunity to align expectations and resolve important questions. This alignment of expectations can save you valuable time later on in the term. In my own teaching, I like to discuss with students on the first day of class a list of issues designed to make a preemptive approach a reality in my courses. Table 3.2 in Chapter 3 lists some of the issues I emphasize in that process.

Final Thoughts: Looking to the Future

As I reflect on the development of the alignment model, think about its many different applications as discussed in this book, and review where it has taken us, I have some final thoughts about the future and my vision of what is needed to address issues of teaching and learning in the 21st century. These issues help to place the idea of teaching effectiveness in the larger context of future thinking, ongoing practice, and communication. First, I briefly discuss future development of our thinking about the complexity of the teaching and learning process and then proceed to two other issues—the use of reflective practice in our approach to teaching effectiveness and the way we communicate to promote a comprehensive view of teaching effectiveness.

Development of a More Complex Conception of Teaching and Learning

The progression in our understanding of teaching and learning during the last 30 years suggests we are moving in directions that can provide new insights and perhaps take us to even more comprehensive conceptions of the complexity of teaching and learning. Since my original work in this area, the focus on quality in teaching has moved from terms like *teacher* behaviors and *teacher* effectiveness to *teaching* effectiveness and, more recently, teaching and *learning.* Such terminology suggests increasing emphasis on instruction as a complex and ever changing *process* and on the variety of factors beyond straightforward teacher behaviors that define that process. Concurrently, we have placed the appropriately important emphasis on the idea of *learning.* Barr and Tagg (1995) and Tagg (2003) reinforced this significance when they discussed the role of instructor as facilitator of learning. Others have extended the learning-centered approaches. For example, the Carnegie Foundation for the Advancement of Teaching increasingly has stressed the focus on learning as part of teaching as a scholarly activity (Hutchings & Shulman, 1999).

In our work at the Center for Instructional Development and Research, with our focus on improving teaching effectiveness within individual courses, in departments, and across the university, we have witnessed increasing complexity that goes beyond that which I identified in my original research. For example, as teaching has moved into areas such as experiential and service learning, team teaching, and interdisciplinary teaching and learning, the opportunities to extend the complexity of the alignment model have already been evident. As some of the chapters in this book indicate, it is now common to talk about more than one instructor teaching a course and the need to align multiple instructors as well as multiple bodies of content, increasingly diverse students, and rapidly changing contexts. As we move forward, all of us in academia must keep abreast of that emerging complexity in the teaching and learning process.

Thus, it is my hope that a broad cadre of academics will join in efforts to think in much more complex ways about the integration of key instructional components into comprehensive models of teaching effectiveness.

Engagement in Ongoing Reflective Practice

Faculty and administrators are increasingly recognizing the complexity of teaching effectiveness. More and more, they are applying the alignment model and approaching teaching and learning as reflective practice. At the same time, there is still much to be done to implement these approaches effectively.

At the level of individual courses, reflection means that instructors must advance their work in systematic and scholarly ways. Further, they must increasingly experiment in designing courses in new and innovative ways, trying alternative methods and encouraging students to participate in learning in ways they may not have done before. Most important, instructors must monitor these efforts, use the best methods possible to determine impacts, and, when appropriate, share results so others can learn from their experiences.

For administrators, such ongoing reflective practice means recognizing that instructors are involved in these processes and finding ways to support such instructional improvement efforts. On many campuses, administrators have adjusted the reward systems in the form of grants, and sometimes teaching awards, to encourage such reflective practice on the part of faculty. Continuing, even expanding, such support is essential so that instructors have opportunities to convene, reflect on their practice, and share the results of their efforts with their colleagues and administrators.

Thus, it is my hope that faculty and academic administrators will engage in ongoing reflective practice based on models like alignment to embrace the complexity in the teaching/learning process, strive to capture that complexity in their work, and continue to find ways to improve teaching effectiveness on their campuses.

Use of Communication to Promote Teaching Effectiveness

We have already stressed the importance of communication in the alignment process in specific instructional settings. For effective teaching, communication is essential between instructors and students and in some special cases, such as team teaching, among two or more instructors and groups of students. At this point, though, I want to think more broadly about the importance of communication for understanding and promoting teaching beyond individual instructors and their students.

Such communication is important at several levels. It is essential that instructors talk with others about their teaching—how they think about it, what they are doing to improve it, and the results they are achieving. At another level, though, communication is essential between instructors and administrators—both chairs and deans. On many campuses, instructors already have conferences with their administrators as part of the faculty evaluation process. Those conversations need to happen frequently enough so that faculty and administrators can share their perceptions about teaching and learning and about ways the more complex views of teaching and learning contribute to the work of individual instructors and to departments, schools, or colleges. At another level, conversations among chairs, deans, and administrators at even higher levels of an institution can promote thinking about how the aggregated work of individual instructors contributes to overall institutional effectiveness. I know these conversations happen informally, but I would like to see them incorporated as part of a systematic, ongoing, and comprehensive approach to communicating about teaching and learning.

As these important conversations occur within institutions, it is also essential to find ways to communicate with constituents beyond academia about the ways instructors and institutional leaders are fostering teaching effectiveness. In recent years, we have made progress in this area by clarifying strategic directions and emphasizing goals for teaching and learning in courses, mission statements, and published documents. We also have moved in this direction through our discussions of the relationships between faculty work and the broader community. At the same time, we must find ways to convey our work in the area of teaching effectiveness. Such communication involves finding the language that works best for describing teaching and learning efforts to others outside academia and for helping them see how the efforts of individual instructors contribute at all levels of institutions and society.

Thus, it is my hope that as we seek ways to address the complexity of teaching and learning, all of us in higher education will communicate more purposefully to disseminate and promote a comprehensive view of teaching effectiveness through all levels of our institutions and beyond.

Conclusion

I am optimistic that with the previous possibilities for progress, we can move in increasingly positive directions in our pursuit of teaching effectiveness. Furthermore, it is my belief that the alignment model provides an important framework for contributing to those efforts. But, there is still much to be done.

If we really want to create a culture of teaching effectiveness on our campuses, as I do, we must continue to think in more complex ways about teaching and learning, acknowledge that complexity in our practice, and communicate at all levels about the impact of our efforts. A systematic and systemic approach is the best way to build coherent perspectives and sustain efforts to disseminate those perspectives. Ultimately, it is the *only* way to promote the culture that is needed to understand, value, and reward teaching effectiveness consistently throughout the academy.

Acknowledgment

The author wishes to express appreciation to Dr. Carla W. Hess, Chester Fritz Professor Emerita of Communication Sciences and Disorders, University of North Dakota, Grand Forks, for her feedback on earlier drafts of this chapter.

References

Barr, R. B., & Tagg, J. (1995). From teaching to learning—a new paradigm for undergraduate education. *Change, 17*(6), 13–25.

Hutchings, P., & Shulman, L. S. (1999). The scholarship of teaching and learning: New elaborations, new developments. *Change, 31*(5), 10–15.

Nyquist, J. D., & Wulff, D. H. (2001). Consultation using a research perspective. In K. G. Lewis & J. T. Povlacs Lunde (Eds.), *Face to face: A sourcebook of individual consultation techniques for faculty/instructional developers* (pp. 45–62). Stillwater, OK: New Forums Press.

Seldin, P. (1998). How colleges evaluate teaching: 1988 vs. 1998. *AAHE Bulletin, 50*(7), 3–7.

Seldin, P., & Associates. (1999). *Changing practices in evaluating teaching: A practical guide to improved faculty performance and promotion/tenure decisions.* Bolton, MA: Anker.

Tagg, J. (2003). *The learning paradigm college.* Bolton, MA: Anker.

Index

Successful studying in the
discipline, 23
Using strategies selectively,
227–229
Structure
Adjustments in, 10
Effective instructors' use of, 8,
9–10
In alignment model, 4
In socially transformative
courses, 155–156
In the mentoring relationship,
114
Supporting student success,
23–24
Student feedback, 226–227
Gathering feedback in large
classes, 90–91
In foreign language instruction,
139
Student learning
Challenges to learning, 46–49
Helping students learn, 44–46
In alignment model, 4, 6, 12, 13
Online, 9
Perceptions of what is required
for, 22–24
Staying focused on, 13, 225
Student participation, 24–28
Asking students to speak as
representatives of groups, 28
Dealing with negative com-
ments, 28
Fostering equitable participa-
tion, 26–28
Honoring diversity in, 27
Perceptions of, 24–28
Planning ahead for, 25, 26
Providing feedback on, 26

Responding to discriminatory
remarks, 28
Seeking feedback, 26
Setting expectations for, 26
Setting the stage for sensitive
material, 27
Using cases and examples in, 27
Student perceptions, 225–226
In math, science, and
engineering courses, 120, 128
Of instructors, 20–22
Using student perceptions,
225–227
Student ratings, 71–75, 226
Meaning for content, 74–75
Meaning in context, 75
Meaning to instructors, 71–72
Meaning to students, 72–74
Norming groups, 74–75
Research on, 71, 75
Student success, 23–24
Student-centered learning
Foreign language instruction,
140
Students
As a consideration in design,
37–39
As knowledge producers, 148
Attaching meaning to instructor
behaviors, 227
Becoming successful learners in
the discipline, 23
Challenges in learning, 46–49
In alignment model, 4, 6, 12
Knowing students as a class,
82–83
Knowledge, 149
Monitoring progress of, 88–89
Note to Students, 48